The Politics of Iran

Groups, Classes, and Modernization

James Alban Bill
Associate Professor,
Government and Middle Eastern Studies
The University of Texas at Austin

Charles E. Merrill Publishing Co.
A Bell & Howell Co.
Columbus, Ohio

Merrill Political Science Series

Under the editorship of

John C. Wahlke

Department of Political Science
SUNY at Stony Brook

The author and publisher gratefully acknowledge The Dial Press for permission to reprint excerpts from *Three Who Made a Revolution* by Bertram D. Wolfe. Copyright © 1948, 1964 by Bertram D. Wolfe.

Published by
Charles E. Merrill Publishing Co.
A Bell & Howell Company
Columbus, Ohio 43216

ISBN: 0-675-09102-0

Library of Congress Catalog Card Number: 73-187714

3 4 5 6 7—77

Printed in the United States of America

For Ann

Contents

Preface

This is a study of the processes of social change and political modernization analyzed in terms of group and class relations. Iran stands as the case study through which the challenge of modernization is perceived and examined. The dynamics of personal, group, and class relations that compose the traditional Irano-Islamic system are first analyzed in some depth. The manner in which these relations have weathered the change of dynasty, elite, monarch, and invader is compared to the manner in which these relations are now being influenced by fundamentally different challenges. Particular emphasis is placed upon the appearance of a new professional middle class. Basic analysis centers upon the relationship of this class to other classes in the society, to group configurations, and to the processes of social change and political modernization.

An understanding of the interaction between class structure and the political system through time provides important insights into the dynamics of a changing society. From such a study, general hypotheses will be generated that provide analysis not only of class and change, but of a particular type of traditional system as well.

This study was completed only because of the support and strength provided by my wife Ann. Her spirit and fortitude invariably repelled the climate of uncertainty and discouragement that many times threatened to engulf us. Combining nursing skills with boundless enthusiasm, she enabled me to survive and to survive well in the years we spent in the field.

A fellowship granted by the Foreign Area Fellowship Program made it possible for me to spend October 1965-June 1967 in the fascinating country of Iran. The cooperation provided by the administrators of this fellowship program was extraordinary. I also received a Fulbright-Hays Faculty Research-Study Grant which enabled me to spend six more months in Iran during the latter half of 1970.

I will remember each of the hundreds of Iranians who extended to me their hospitality and assistance. I am particularly grateful to a student, a teacher, a banker, a statesman, an economist, a bureaucrat, a retired military officer, and an oil man. Special thanks go to an Iranian who has spent his life fighting to transform in order to preserve what he terms *insāniyat* (humanity) in social relationships. I remain deeply appreciative to Her Imperial Majesty Farah Dībā Pahlavī, Empress of Iran, who granted me two extended private interviews in October and November 1970. The sensitive and intelligent manner in which the Empress discussed the social and political issues confronting her country both inspired this scholar and epitomized the magnificent strengths that inhere in Iran. Finally, I thank Walter and Louise Kaiser who flatter America by their presence abroad.

My first interest in non-Western political systems was developed while studying with Georges L. Bissonnette of Assumption College, while my interest in Iran and class analysis was stimulated by Vernon V. Aspaturian of Pennsylvania State University. At Princeton, Martin Dickson offered numerous insights into Iranian history and culture, while T. Cuyler Young's great knowledge of and love for modern Iran provided this study with its "Iranian inspiration." Especially perceptive comments and criticisms of an earlier draft of this book were suggested by Nikki Keddie, Amin Banani, and Marvin Weinbaum. Ali Jazayery of The University of Texas at Austin graciously assisted with the difficult task of transliteration, while Charles T. Field, also of The University of Texas at Austin, helped design the cover of the book.

I am deeply grateful to Manfred Halpern who over a period of five years helped this project develop and mature. This study was born and raised along with Halpern's important theoretical investigations concerning the fundamental problems of political development and modernization. This analysis, therefore, is an implicit adaptation and operationalization of the Halpernian theoretical framework. Thus, whatever contributions or insights might be contained herein have been profoundly inspired by Halpern's provocative theoretical approach.

I gratefully acknowledge the permission of *The Journal of Politics* to incorporate sections from my article "Modernization and Reform from

Above: The Case of Iran" which appeared in the February 1970 issue of that journal. I am also grateful to *Iranian Studies* for granting me permission to use substantial portions of my article "The Politics of Student Alienation: The Case of Iran" which appeared in the Winter 1969 edition of that journal.

The system of transliteration adopted in this study is the one approved by the American Library Association and the Library of Congress. I have introduced, however, the following slight modifications. Anglicized Persian words and well-known geographic names have not been transliterated (e.g., Iran, Tehran, Shah, Pahlavi, Koran, Islam). I have not transliterated the names of Persian authors of English books (e.g., Rouhollah K. Ramazani), nor have I retransliterated the titles of translated Persian books (e.g., *Tadhkirat al-Mulūk*). The roots of Persian words with anglicized endings will be transliterated (e.g., Sāsānian, Tīmūrid). Persian terms will be italicized except in the case of a few words that continually reappear and/or merit more general usage (e.g., khān, dawrah, ṣadr, mujtahid, imām jum'ah, pārtī, bakhshdār).

J. A. B.
The University of Texas
Austin, Texas

chapter one

The Irano–Islamic Social Structure

Political modernization is analyzed in this study in terms of the patterns of change that mark group and class relations over time.[1] These relations dramatically reflect the shifting nature of power and authority configurations in society. In this chapter, Iranian class relations will be presented as they have developed and persisted through the centuries. Personal and group power patterns will be studied explicitly in relation to the class

1. In spite of all the recent literature treating development, modernization, revolution, and change, there has been distressingly little done in regard to distinguishing the fundamental kinds and intensities of change. The analyses that go the furthest in this regard are Manfred Halpern's theoretical contributions which define modernization in terms of an enduring capacity to generate and absorb persistent transformation. According to Halpern, *transformation* is that kind of alteration of a system which results in the exclusion or entrance of sufficient types of elements or linkages to be recognized, at a given level of abstraction and for the sake of the problem to be analyzed, as a new system. Transforming change then means systemic change or a metamorphosis of former relationships. *Modifying change,* on the other hand, is an alteration of ongoing relations between individuals, groups, or classes that involves a change in the relative balance of power between them without, however, witnessing either the destruction of the existing power pattern or the formation of a new pattern. The concept *preservation* refers to a policy that seeks to protect and reinforce the existing relationship in order that it remain as is. For these key distinctions and definitions, see Manfred Halpern, "The Dialectics of Modernization in National and International Society: A Working Paper," Princeton University, Center of International Studies, October 1967. For Halpern's entire theoretical schema, see *The Dialectics of Transformation in Politics, Personality, and Society* (forthcoming).

structure. The challenge of modernization will be analyzed against the overall network of personal, group, and class relations.

Scholars and observers of Iranian society have tended to fall into two groups: those who play down the role and place of class in Iranian society and those who overemphasize the class phenomenon by either explaining everything in these kinds of terms or by viewing it as a rigid, feudal structure. The former group has been the prevalent one, especially in the West. Here it has become commonplace to state that the presence of mobility and/or the absence of feudalism demonstrate that the study of class structure is meaningless. The basic hypothesis of our study is that Iranian society has been marked and profoundly influenced by a structure of interrelated classes. With the coming of Islam, this system underwent a fundamental transformation and a new pattern was established. This system of class relationships has exhibited a flexibility and resiliency that has enabled it to persist for nearly 1,400 years. Today this pattern is confronted with profoundly new challenges as relationships at the class level have begun to shatter for the first time since the fall of the Sāsānian Empire. In order to understand this situation, it is first necessary to analyze briefly the transformation that Islam carried to the class system as it existed during Sāsānian times.

The Sāsānian Class Structure and the Entrance of Islam

The Sāsānian dynasty ruled Iran from A.D. 224–641 and during its peak it represented an uncommonly powerful and extensive empire. The social structure was an extremely rigid one and class relations were marked by a one-sided flow of power that kept the lower classes in a position of subjection. The society was divided into four basic classes: the clerics, the warriors, the bureaucrats, and the peasant masses. Each of these classes was further divided into separate and fixed groupings and the result was a complex and intricate hierarchical social structure. There was little movement between classes. In presenting an idealized picture of the Sāsānian Empire, Arthur Christensen describes the rigid lines and interminable distances that separated the classes from one another:

> . . . social grades existed within all classes. Each had his own rank and fixed place in society and it was a firm principle in Sasanian politics that no person could aspire to a rank higher than that to which he was destined by birth.[2]

2. Arthur Christensen, *L'Iran sous les Sassanides* (Copenhague: Ejnar Munksguard, 1944), pp. 316-17.

The purity of blood of the upper class was prescribed and protected by law and the members of each class were taught to view only the class below their own and never to look at the class immediately above. Within the framework of such a class structure, lower classes could seldom exert power over the higher classes.

Relations of subjection marked other linkages also. On an intraclass level, there were at least four groups within the upper-class nobility that were linked in a chain of subjection. These included the king and ruling family, the seven privileged families, the nobles and high bureaucrats, and the "free people" or inferior nobility. These four groups related hierarchically and the power flow was fundamentally unidirectional. Personal relations exhibited the same pattern and the Zoroastrian religious hierarchy, for example, represented a network of subjection. One was not only born into the cleric class but was also born into a particular rank in that class. The highest cleric (*mubadān mubad*) was not recruited from below but took office on the basis of heredity. Although rigid class hierarchy was the basic pattern, one can document linkages of a more balanced nature. These, however, were usually in evidence on intraclass levels and involved tensions between groups such as the nobility and the clergy. It is interesting to note that this type of intraclass tension became most severe toward the end of the Sāsānian period just before the pronounced but fragile class patterns disintegrated.

The rigidity and harshness of the Sāsānian class system was so extreme that it could reasonably be challenged only through violence. This is what happened when several uprisings took on the appearance of class revolution as the masses turned to violence in order to escape the servitude and oppression. In a system of such subjection, it is not surprising that the lower classes rose violently to challenge the system. The members of these classes continually sought more reciprocally rewarding forms of tension-management. The prime example was the Mazdakian revolt which nearly destroyed the Sāsānian social system. This movement was communistic in the sense that it advocated a leveling of wealth and an extreme sharing of goods. Such a doctrine obviously had extraordinary appeal and the lower-class masses embraced it in huge numbers. Christensen writes: "Communist ideas had begun to germinate among the masses who had suffered for centuries under the oppression of the privileged classes."[3]

By the middle of the seventh century, the class structure had become so brittle that the tiny armies of Arab invaders cracked and conquered the huge empire. The masses would not fight to save a system in which they

---

3. *Ibid.,* p. 357. For an informative account of the Mazdakian revolution, see Nizam ul-Molk's *Siyasat-nama or Siyar al-Muluk* [The Book of Government or Rules for Kings], translated from the Persian by Hubert Drake (London: Routledge and Kegan Paul, 1960), pp. 195-211.

were little more than slaves and in which they were sentenced to eternal servitude. An important part of the answer to the puzzling question of how a few small Arab armies could overthrow the mighty Persian Empire is found here. Accounts of the war reveal that the Persian forces outnumbered those of the Arabs five and ten to one. During two of the final crucial battles, the Persians outnumbered the Arabs 100,000 to 12,000 and 150,000 to 30,000 and in both instances they suffered complete defeat.[4] There is little doubt that the invaders who entered Iran under the banner of a religion which stressed equality struck a responsive chord among the masses of people who made up the lower echelons of an extremely inflexible class system. The end of the Sāsānian system was the beginning of an extended period of chaos and upheaval. When the upper-class guardians of that system were themselves subjected through the campaign of an external force, the dominant power relationship was destroyed.

When Islam appeared, it was in many cases greeted as a saving force and was not unwelcome to the exploited Iranian classes. Islam stressed equality and brotherhood and one of the foundations of Islamic law is the just distribution of wealth. The Koran is replete with passages that stress equality and almsgiving and the Prophet himself is quoted as saying: "The one who sleeps at night and has a needy neighbor is not a Muslim." A man was to be judged not by his wealth or land or power but rather by his behavior and position before the Almighty. Wider distribution in regard to land ownership was observed at least in principle as inheritance laws changed drastically with the coming of Islam. In the Sāsānian Period, the system was one of primogeniture and over the years large landholdings remained intact. Islamic law divided the land among the offspring in varying proportions and thus, although extended families came to control huge holdings, the nuclear family theoretically controlled comparatively little.

The first two centuries after the Arab conquest of Iran were understandably periods of great upheaval and chaos. The lower classes converted to Islam which offered them opportunities for a better future. The upper-class Iranians often became Muslim also in the hope of being better accepted by the Arab governors and in this way to preserve their former privileged positions. The old Zoroastrian clergy worked secretly to turn the people against the Arabs and the new religion. The result was a period of local uprisings and revolts as the newly awakened masses turned on their former ruling classes and on the local Arab governors as well. In Ṭabaristān

4. George Rawlinson, *The Seventh Great Oriental Monarchy or the Geography, History, and Antiquities of the Sassanian or New Persian Empire* (New York: Dodd, Mead and Company, 1882), pp. 212-34.

(today's Māzandarān), the Māzyār rebellion in the middle of the ninth century was a full-scale revolution of the peasant class against the Iranian large landowners and the Arab governors of the area. The lower and middle classes throughout Iran continually revolted and the Caliphs were compelled to dispatch large armies to Iran to quell these uprisings. Some of the rebellions, such as the Khurramdīnān movement, were directly related to the Mazdak revolution of Sāsānian times, while others, such as those led by Bihāfarīd, Sunbād, Ishāq, and Muqanna', were primarily religious in nature although they all had social overtones.[5]

Class upheaval was only one part of an omnipresent ferment that also witnessed a changing and kaleidoscopic array of dynasties that appeared and disappeared with amazing rapidity. Names like Bāwandids, Musāfirids, Shaddādids, Ziyārids, Būyids, Kākūyids, Tabarids, Sāmānids, and Ṣaffārids represent some of the earliest Iranian Islamic dynasties. These dynasties generally lived violent and short lives, yet it was in these systems that the new class relationships of Islamic Iran were being formed. One can perhaps trace the chronological development of the new patterns through detailed study of such dynasties. Surely the more persistent and extensive systems such as the 'Abbāsids, Būyids, and Sāmānids exhibited the new class relations in embryonic form. Yet even these dynasties were torn by constant strife and warfare. It is difficult to analyze new patterns between the eleventh and fifteenth centuries as the inexorable forces of Seljuq, Mongol, and Tīmūrid invaded and devastated. The foreign attacks began just as Iranian dynasties were reestablishing and strengthening their rule and V. Minorsky describes the shattering result as follows:

> Therefore, throughout Persia and along its periphery, Iranian elements were regaining courage and learning again to govern themselves. But soon Turkish and Mongol invasions were to destroy the Iranian governments and to substitute their own new organizations of military fiefdoms.[6]

The well-known Iranian historian Yaḥyā Qazvīnī described this same period when he wrote: "The affairs of the world lost order and organiza-

5. There are three excellent studies of this period of incoherence: Nizam ul-Molk, *Siyasat-nama,* pp. 212-45; 'Abd al-Ḥusayn Zarrīnkūb, *Du Qarn-i Sukūt* [Two Centuries of Silence] (Tehran, 1344/1965); and Gholam Husayn Sadighi, *Les Movements Religieux au 11e and au 111e Siecle de l'Hegire* (Paris: Les Presses Modernes, 1938).

6. V. Minorsky, *La Domination des Dailamites* (Paris: Librairie Ernest Leroux, 1932), p. 17.

tion."[7] Perhaps due to such turmoil we find it difficult to analyze pre-Ṣafavī sociopolitical processes in Islamic Iran. With the advent of the Ṣafavī dynasty in 1501, however, the new patterns become quite evident. The following analysis of Irano-Islamic group and class relations rests upon empirical evidence referring back through the Ṣafavī period. This is also the period of the establishment of Shī'ism as the dominant and official religion of Iran.

The Irano-Islamic Class Structure

> Oh, Son of Ḥārās, know that in no country can the people be alike since the principle of classes is everywhere firm and fixed. . . .
>
> There is a group of soldiers and corpsmen, an elite and a number of princes, a group of jurists and a class of merchants and artisans. Lowest of all are the afflicted and the poor who are the unfortunate and the suffering. They are always the broken-hearted and the weary.
>
> When you look at these different classes, also look for a moment at the members of your own body. While the hand is other than the foot and the eye is separate from the ear, at the same time they carry out their responsibilities of life through mutual cooperation and assistance. . . .
>
> The Compassionate Lord in the great Koran ordained limits and regulations for all of these classes and benefited all with the blessings of law and equality.
>
> —Imām 'Alī (*ca.* A.D. 600–660), *Farmān* to Mālik[8]

As the words of 'Alī indicate, the Islamic influence in Iran did not obliterate classes, but they persisted in interaction with one another, although in quite a different manner than during Sāsānian times. By the turn of the twentieth century, class was officially recognized as the basis of newly established election procedures. Article XIV of the Majlis Election Law of 1907 stated that elections would be overseen by twenty-four persons from six classes *(ṭabaqāt).* The classes then enumerated were the clerics, nobles, landlords,

7. Yaḥyā ibn 'Abd al-Laṭīf, *Lubb al-Tavārīkh* (Tehran, 1932), p. 240, quoted in Michel M. Mazzaoui, "Shī'ism and the Rise of the Ṣafavids" (unpublished Ph.D. dissertation, Department of Oriental Studies, Princeton University, 1965), p. 217.

8. 'Alī, "Farmān to Mālik-i Ashtar, Governor of Egypt," in *Sukhanān-i 'Alī* [The Words of 'Alī], translated into Persian from the Arabic by Javād Fāẓil (Tehran, 1345/1966), p. 242. This volume contains a fascinating collection of sociopolitical statements attributed to 'Alī.

businessmen, tradesmen, and farmers.[9] With the advent of intense Marxian influence in Iran in the 1940s, the word class *(ṭabaqah)* became a standard term for analyzing and describing the social scene. Since that time, Iranian scholars have produced studies in which they have relied heavily upon class analysis.[10]

Before analyzing the patterns of class relationships that have marked Islamic Iran, it is necessary to present a brief description of the class structure as it has existed through the Ṣafavī, Afshārī, Zand, Qājār, and Pahlavi periods. The most vital groups that have been part of these classes will also be presented, for the interaction of group and class relationships has shaped the Iranian social and political system.

The traditional social structure has consisted of seven classes: the ruling class, the bureaucratic middle class, the bourgeois middle class, the cleric middle class, the traditional working class, the peasant class, and the nomadic class. The twentieth century has witnessed the appearance of two new classes which today are also part of the system—the industrial working class and the professional middle class. Figure 1 presents a graphic representation of the Iranian class structure according to power position. This diagram is an adaptation of a scheme introduced by Gerhard Lenski and is a great improvement upon the usual pyramidal views of society. It portrays the power distribution while at the same time does away with the impression that classes are nothing more than layers stacked one upon the other. It indicates that there is overlapping. Lenski writes that this type of diagram shows "that there is a continuum of power and privilege, not a

---

9. In this study, *class* is defined as the largest aggregate of individuals united by similar modes of employment and possessing similar power positions to preserve, modify, or transform relationships among such aggregates. The concept *group* is herein defined as an aggregate of individuals other than class who interact in varying degrees in pursuance of a common interest. For the detailed theoretical discussion and development of these definitions and others central to this conceptual scheme, see the author's "Class Analysis and the Dialectics of Modernization in the Middle East," *International Journal of Middle East Studies* 3 (1972).

10. There have been various approaches. The most common has been a straight Marxist view and a typical example is provided by a series carried in the famous newspaper of the 1940s *Dāryā.* The five-article series translated into English was entitled "The Class Struggle in Iran," and appeared between 28 Khurdād and 1 Tīr 1323/1944. The Marxist and socialist newspapers and journals such as *Mardum, Rahbar,* and *'Ilm va Zindigī* also obviously took such an approach.

A more recent approach has been taken by sociologist Aḥmad Fattāhīpūr in his article "Characteristics of Social Classes in Iran," *Masā'il-i Īrān* [Problems of Iran], 2nd yr., No. 11 (Ābān, 1342–43/1963–64): 498-505. Fattāhīpūr has been educated in the American school of community sociology and he simply lifts that framework and applies it to Iran. He ends with the descriptive six-category "upper-upper class" to "lower-lower class" breakdown.

Relevant articles are periodically printed in more popular journals and magazines as well. An interesting case in point is Muḥīt Ṭabāṭabā'ī, "Ṭabaqah-bandī-yi Ijtimā'ī" [Social Classification], *Khvāndanīhā,* 26th yr., No. 99 (1 Shahrīvar 1345/23 August 1966): 14-15.

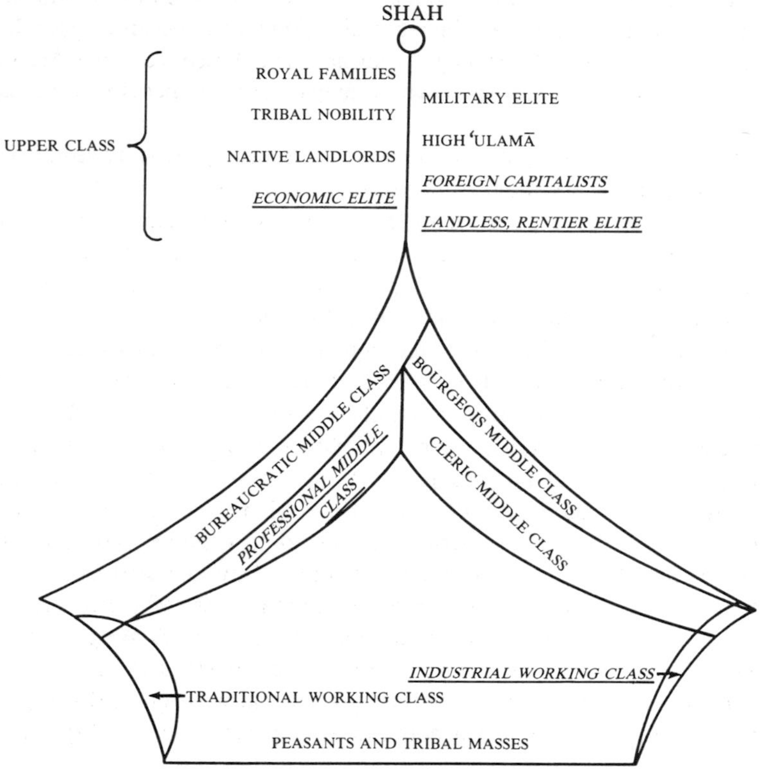

(The new groups and classes are italicized)

FIGURE 1

A Descriptive View of the Iranian Class Structure

series of separate and distinct strata in the geological sense of that term."[11] This kind of figure also better illustrates the great gap that separates the upper and lower classes. It should be cautioned, however, that figure 1 is still primarily descriptive in nature and requires further diagrammatic adjustments. This is done in figure 2 in the following section which commences fundamental analysis.[12]

11. Lenski, *Power and Privilege: A Theory of Social Stratification* (New York: McGraw-Hill, 1966), p. 285.

12. Two studies exist which break the Iranian class structure down and attempt to ascertain the size of the various classes. Both present analyses of the structure as it existed in the 1950s. See James A. Bill, "The Social and Economic Foundations of Power in Contemporary Iran," *Middle East Journal* 17 (Autumn 1963): 400-418; and Muṣṭafā Fātiḥ, *Panjāh Sāl Naft-i Īrān* [Fifty Years of Persian Oil] (Tehran, 1335/1956), especially p. 24.

The Ruling Class

Iranians use various terms to refer to this concept of upper or ruling class. Among these are *ṭabaqah-yi ḥākimah, ṭabaqah-yi mumtāzah, hay'at-i ḥākimah, a'yān, ashrāf, buzurgān, zamāmdārān,* and *aristukrāsī.* These terms generally refer either to a concept of nobility/aristocracy or to the idea of a ruling power group.[13] The traditional ruling class can be analytically broken down into six major components: (1) Shah; (2) families of the reigning dynasty; (3) tribal nobility; (4) native landlords; (5) system-supporting high *'ulamā* (clerics); and (6) military elite. These six groups have composed the ruling class for centuries and their character is quite clearly described by their titles. However, the Shah has always been somewhat detached from the rest of the ruling class because of the special power position that he has held (see figure 1).

Through the years, there have been certain families that have maintained a constant, if at times shaky, presence in the upper-class ranks. These families have come to be called the "thousand families," a term that is both meaningful and misleading. The idea of the existence of a small group of powerful and interrelated families is a correct one; however, the choice of a number is highly inaccurate. The Iranians themselves use this expression which was coined by foreigners, but investigation has shown that the so-called "thousand families" have at no time totaled more than one to two hundred.[14] Many of these families can trace their upper-class presence back to early Qājār, pre-Qājār, and even Ṣafavī days. The most important of these have been the families of the *khān*s of the important tribes such as the Bakhtiyārīs, Qashqā'īs, and Qājārs themselves. Leading Qājār families such as the Farmānfarmāiyāns and Dawlatshāhīs continue to hold vital places in Iranian upper-class ranks. During the Qājār period, the system absorbed important local tribal-clans and as a result the Afshārs of Riẓā'iyah, the Muqaddams of Marāghah, the Qarāguzlūs of Hamadān, and the Zanganahs of Kirmānshāh joined the Iranian ruling class. All of these families predate the Qājārs and today wield important influence in the system. Other important families that are part of the ruling class of the day include the names 'Alam, Pīrniyā, Hidāyat, Nafīsī, Ḥikmat, A'lam, Qavām, Akbar, Samī'ī,

13. These terms are difficult to translate into English in a way that will connote their exact Persian meaning. Iranians often use them interchangeably. The closest English approximations follow. They are presented in the order that they appear in the text: ruling class, privileged class, ruling group or elite, nobles/aristocrats *(a'yān* and *ashrāf),* notables, rein-holders, and aristocracy.

14. For documentation, see Abulfaẓl Qāsimī, *Tārīkh-i Siyāh yā Ḥukumat-i Khānivādah-hā dar Īrān* [The Black History or the Rule of Families in Iran] (Tehran, n.d.), pp. 45-46. My research into Iranian family history and genealogy indicates that there are forty families of national political influence in Iran. Besides this, there are approximately 150 provincial elite families, i.e., families that exert periodic influence at the national level but who persistently hold great power in particular towns, cities, or provinces. The families subsequently listed in the text are all national elite families.

Manṣūr, Amīnī, Mahdavī, Dībā, and 'Adl. Several studies have been made in Persian which expose the roots of these families and examine their bases of power, interconnections, and activities. Such studies leave little doubt that these families compose an interrelated aristocracy that possesses roots of surprising depth.[15]

As figure 1 indicates, the following groups have become part of the upper class relatively recently: foreign industrialists and businessmen, an indigenous economic aristocracy, and a landless, rentier elite. With the advent of British and Russian influence in Iran in the early nineteenth century, foreign business and economic interests gradually gained a foothold. These interests pursued their own goals and in order to further them they exerted great influence over the indigenous ruling class and allied themselves with it. The first real indications of the strength of this alliance occurred in the late nineteenth century when various concession agreements were concluded between the Iranian upper class and English interests. With the discovery of oil and the appearance of the Anglo-Iranian Oil Company, foreign industrialists became a firm and influential partner of the Iranian ruling class. The violent reaction of the other classes in the society as they sporadically attempted to sever this alliance can be seen in revolutionary uprisings that have stretched from the Tobacco Rebellion in 1891–92 to the Muṣaddiq Movement of 1951–53.[16] In contemporary Iran, the foreign economic interests include not only the powerful oil interests but also contractors and even public relations firms that paint and protect the ruling class's and dynastic family's image abroad.

Besides this foreign element which has been symbiotically combined with the other upper-class groups and which reinforces and supports the indigenous ruling class, there are other groups that have relatively recently joined the upper class. A network of large and wealthy merchants, bankers, contractors, financiers, and industrialists has appeared largely since World War II. Several of the most economically powerful men in Iran have come from the ranks of the lower and bourgeois middle class and include names like S̱ābit and Nimāzī. Others have been former landlords who have adjusted to the land reform program by transferring their wealth and interests to industry and commerce. This trend has been so strong that social critics have been producing articles against what they term "industrial, bourgeois feudalism," which many feel is worse than the rural feudalism that has been shaken by the land reform program.[17] This economic aristocracy is closely related to the other upper-class groups and especially to the royal family

15. See, for example, *Ṭabaqah-yi Hākimah-yi Īrān-rā Bishnāsīd* [Know the Ruling Class of Iran] (Tehran, 1321/1944).

16. For the two best works in English on these movements, see Nikki R. Keddie, *Religion and Rebellion in Iran: The Iranian Tobacco Protest of 1891–1892* (London: Frank Cass and Company, 1966); and Richard W. Cottam, *Nationalism in Iran* (Pittsburgh: University of Pittsburgh Press, 1964).

17. See, for example, *Khvāndanīhā,* 12 Mihr 1345/4 October 1966, pp. 9, 50.

which itself controls and deals in the biggest of Iranian businesses. The largest and most influential contractors, for example, are either members of the royal family or they are closely related to it. Most of the industrial elite are members of the Tehran Chamber of Commerce or the Iranian Chamber of Mines and Industry. The intricate intertwining of interest can be best seen in the persons of men like Ja'far Sharīf-Imāmī who not only are involved in most big business but also are inner members of the political elite and active in scores of other projects and organizations.[18]

One final group that is a part of the upper class can be termed the landless, rentier elite. These are the wealthy who have lost most of their land and have at the same time refused to become part of the industrial elite. They have sent much of their capital abroad and live in semiretirement preferring travel and gambling to business in Iran. Most of these new forces that have been absorbed into the upper class have developed as a result of the rapidly changing times. Major accelerating forces have been the growth of industry occasioned by two world wars, oil funds, and an influx of foreign investment.

The Traditional Middle Classes

The traditional middle classes have included the bureaucratic, bourgeois, and clerical classes. Three classes are presented here because there are indeed three similar modes of occupation involved. These classes are together termed "middle" on the basis of the variable "power" for they all possess relatively similar power positions. The traditional middle classes have existed for centuries and have been the elements that have controlled and benefited from the traditional educational system. This education centered about the *maktab*s and *madrasah*s and stressed religion, memory, and the basic skills of reading, writing, and mathematics.

The bureaucratic middle class is what the Iranians refer to as *ṭabaqah-yi kārmandān* (civil servant class) which has traditionally consisted of those individuals who have staffed the state apparatus.[19] The highest ranking government officials have usually been attached to the royal court or household and have been either part of the royal family or of other groups in the upper classes. The *kārmandān* have been the mass of government employees who have formed the bulk of the administration. One of the basic characteristics of this class was the fact that its members usually possessed

18. In 1968, this influential personality was Deputy-Trustee of the Pahlavi Foundation, President of the Senate, President of the Chamber of Mines and Industries, President of the Engineer's Association, President of Lions of Iran, and Chairman of the Board of the Industrial and Mining Development Bank of Iran.

19. The best study of the development of this class in Iran is Taqī Mudarrisī, *"Nākāmī-yi Khānivādah-yi Kārmandān"* [The Frustration of the Bureaucratic Family], *Ṣadaf,* Nos. 9-10 (Murdād-Shahrīvar, 1337/1958): 692-94, 788-92, 899-903.

a minimum of the traditional education and could carry out the important tasks of recording and accounting. One authority on Qājār history has written that during these years the members of the bureaucracy "held a clearly inferior position in society to the tribal leaders and landowning classes, who regarded them with slight contempt. They were often men of education and polish."[20]

As figure 1 indicates, the *kārmandān* class overlaps more with the ruling class than any of the other middle classes. It has always been the heart of the government apparatus which has been directed and controlled by the ruling class. In this sense, the bureaucratic middle class has been more the servant of the upper class than the representative of the lower classes. This is reflected in the age-old conflict between government officials and the Iranian masses. The bureaucracy became a mobility channel to the upper class while maintaining an important power of its own.

The bourgeois middle class in Iran has been composed of merchants, traders, and businessmen. Its symbol and center of activity has been the bāzār. This class has been able to preserve its interests through the years and has struck at the upper class whenever the latter's policies have seriously endangered the interest of business. At such times, the bourgeoisie has converted the bāzār into a dangerous center of opposition for the political elite. In contrast to Europe where important segments of the bourgeoisie became an early part of the ruling class, in traditional Iran few members of the bourgeoisie ever moved into upper-class ranks. In terms of power position, the bourgeois middle class has stood approximately between the bureaucratic and cleric middle classes.[21]

The clerical middle class was composed of *ākhūnd*s (clerics) and *ṭalabah*s (student clerics). The members of this class were related to the bureaucratic middle class due to the fact that the *ākhūnd*s controlled the educational system. Also, many of the bureaucrats were *sayyid*s (descendants of the Prophet) and not infrequently the *ākhūnd* and *ṭalabah* would become directly involved in the government apparatus, especially in the area of justice and law. However, while the bureaucratic class tended to serve the interests of the upper class, the clerics generally represented the masses. They lived and worked with the lower classes and although they were often notorious for pursuing their own interests at the expense of the people, they always identified more with the latter than with the ruling class. The clerics were often convinced that the members of the ruling class were not really concerned with Shī'ī doctrine and this also contributed to the tension.

---

20. Ann Lambton, "Persian Society Under the Qajars," *Royal Central Asian Journal* 48 (April 1961): 133.

21. For a fine analysis of the bourgeoisie as a class in Islamic society, see S. D. Goitein, *Studies in Islamic History and Institutions* (Leiden: E. J. Brill, 1966), pp. 217-41.

These traditional middle classes have been born and brought up in similar environments and have held comparable educations and values. They have tended to be very conservative, but have always risen to challenge and change when their own interests were considered to be threatened. The famous constitutional movement, for example, was dominated by the activity of merchants and clerics who felt their economic and religious interests were being damaged. This is one reason why the movement never became a revolution and ground to a surprisingly abrupt halt. The traditional middle classes fled the scene once they saw their goals satisfied and their upper class detractors shackled.[22]

With the rise of the Pahlavi dynasty and the accession of Riẕā Shāh to the throne, the groundwork for the appearance of a profoundly different middle class was established. This was accomplished when that Shah directly attacked the traditional bureaucracy and educational system and thus confronted the old bureaucrats and clerics. The new middle class was the unintended answer to the demand created by Riẕā Shāh when he roughly and forcefully provided the impetus for modern education and government administration in Iran. This class which is the subject of this study and is herein termed the professional-bureaucratic intelligentsia has recently become a new addition to the traditional social structure. It is related to the old middle classes in the sense that many of its members are the offspring of families of these classes. Its appearance, however, has not destroyed the traditional middle classes, although it has slowly weakened and undercut the position of both the old bureaucrats and the clerics.

The Lower Classes

The traditional system consisted largely of masses of workers, peasants, and nomads who made up the lower classes. In terms of size, the peasant and nomadic classes have dwarfed the working class since Iran has been predominantly an agricultural society. Agriculture still accounts for between forty to fifty percent of the gross national product. The 1966 census revealed that approximately one-half of the employed population were peasants directly engaged in farming occupations.[23] There has been a comparatively large mass of literature in English, Russian, and Persian that has

22. For the real goals of the clerics in the constitutional movement, see Firaydūn Ādamiyat, *Fikr-i Āzādī va Muqaddamah-yi Nihẕhat-i Mashrūṭiyat-i Īrān* [The Freedom of Thought and the Beginnings of the Constitutional Movement of Iran] (Tehran, 1340/1961), especially pp. 245-47.

23. Plan Organization, Iranian Statistical Center, *National Census of Population and Housing: November 1966—Demographic, Social and Economic Characteristics of the Population—Advance Sample Data for Total Country Urban and Rural,* Bulletin No. 3, May 1967, p. 35. Hereafter cited as *National Census: November 1966—Advanced Sample.*

described the peasant class and has analyzed landlord-peasant relations. Through all of this literature it is possible to discover common threads and, in general terms, these stress the poverty, dependence, disease, and ignorance that has prevailed among the peasant masses. The peasant class traditionally suffered at the hands of the other classes in the society and in terms of the individual peasant this usually meant the landlord, merchant, and government official. The situation of the tribal masses was much the same although they enjoyed a certain amount of natural freedom.

The working class has included such groups as servants and manual laborers, on the one hand, to craftsmen and artisans, on the other. These groups have tended to be slightly better off than the peasants although their situation has grown steadily worse through time. The lack of modern industry meant that the working class was as much a rural phenomenon as urban. This class was one of the most active in brotherhood and guild activity and thus enjoyed some organizational protection. In a moving speech before the Majlis in 1947, a renowned Iranian statesman referred to the working and peasant classes as "the people's classes" and "the condemned classes." He described the centuries of suffering that these classes had undergone and accused "the ruling class" of creating and supporting this situation.[24]

The development of industry and the process of urbanization have resulted in the appearance and growth of a new urban industrial working class. By 1970, there were more than one million employed members of this class. Between 1956 and 1966 alone, employment in the mechanized manufacturing industry increased by nearly 165 percent.[25] This new section of the lower classes is still in its embryonic stage, but its strategic location in the large cities and its social awareness make it a force quite different from the traditional working classes. The Tūdah Party realized this in the 1940s and expended much energy in organizing these workers whose number was then very small. In the 1960s, the political elite recognized the same thing and the Shah directed one of the original six points in his "White Revolution" to this new and burgeoning segment of the working class.

With the implementation of the land reform program, the intraclass relationships of the peasantry have undergone various modifications. One of the most dramatic has been the widening gap that has separated those peasants who have had the right to work a particular piece of land and those who have had no such right. The land reform has been directed only to the former and the resulting situation has seen the wealthier peasants become

24. Sayyid Ḥasan Taqīzādah, *"Muzākirāt-i Majlis"* [Majlis Proceedings], 15th Majlis, 30th Session, 21 Ābān 1326/1947, quoted in Fātiḥ, *Panjāh Sāl,* pp. 23-24.

25. For these figures and others that document the impressive growth of the industrial working class in Iran, see William H. Bartsch, *Problems of Employment Creation in Iran* (Geneva: International Labour Office, 1970).

wealthier and the poorer peasants, poorer. By 1970, it had become evident that tensions were building up between these two groups and that the peasants who had not benefited from the reform were becoming increasingly restless.[26]

Group Relations and the Class Structure

> Above all else, we must observe the sacred principle of equality. . . . So it is that Islam does not know ugliness and beauty and does not respect imaginary classes of nobility.
>
> —Imām 'Alī, *Farmān* to Ibn Bakr[27]

Viewed in terms of pre-Islamic Iran, this statement by Imām 'Alī carries a revolutionary impact. Indeed, it described the setting for the establishment of a new pattern of power relationships. The Islamic class structure in Iran has been knit together in constant movement because of the existence of what is herein termed "the web-system." The web-system is composed of networks of power relationships which possess profound plasticity due to the balancing nature of these tensions. Everpresent characteristics of power reciprocity, informality, personalism, secrecy, and insecurity have interacted in a manner that has served to build persisting safety valves into the system.[28] These factors have served to distribute and fracture concentrations of threatening power. They have permitted a great deal of controlled change and movement as personalities and groups are always provided with a certain opportunity to advance and circulate. In such a system, a premium is placed upon one's ability to maneuver and manipulate as the construction of connections and the bargaining for influence are the proven means of preservation and advancement. A concerted effort is constantly made to form new personal connections, to join new groups, and to improve class standing. Thus, personal antagonisms and group conflicts feed into one another and are supported and maintained throughout the society. Individual, group, and class conflict interlock and overlap in a

26. Iranian sociologist Ahmad Ashraf was among the first to notice this unintended consequence of land reform. He analyzed its implications during a December 1966 academic conference in Tehran. See Ashraf, "An Evaluation on Land Reform," in N. Afshar Naderi, ed., *Seminar on Evaluation of Directed Social Change* (Tehran University: Institute for Social Studies and Research, 1967), pp. 143-69. For further analysis of this problem, see chapter 6.

27. *Sukhanān-i 'Alī,* pp. 221, 222.

28. For a detailed analysis of these characteristics, see James A. Bill, "The Plasticity of Informal Politics: The Case of Iran," in Amin Banani, ed., *State and Society in Islamic Iran,* forthcoming.

manner resembling a gigantic web composed of continually fluctuating networks of strands of power transactions.[29]

The Patterns of Class Interaction

Class relationships in Islamic Iran have been characterized by reciprocal but permanently imbalanced power patterns. Figure 2 provides a graphic characterization of the class system diagrammed in these terms. It reveals how power flows between all classes in uneven reciprocity.

In this kind of system, the class relationships represent a general hierarchy and the class *qua* class remains firmly in place. Thus, although individuals and groups belonging to classes may move in and out of the concentric power circles illustrated in figure 2, the classes themselves remain in general hierarchy. This means that the power flow is always much heavier from upper to lower classes and that the lower class is consistently in a disadvantageous power position. The members of a lower class possessed power handles that were smaller and weaker than those which belonged to classes higher than their own. They owned but a varying fraction of the education, wealth, and representation that marked the classes above and were the perennial victims of taxation and conscription imposed upon them by the ruling class. One of the more recent dramatic instances of the ruling class exercising direct power over the peasant class occurred during the Riẕā Shāh Period when a crushing tax was imposed on the sale of tea and sugar in order to finance the construction of the railroad. This tax hurt most the millions of peasants who could now obtain two of the basic items of their diet only with the greatest difficulty and sacrifice. This example calls attention to the ever-present tendency of this relationship to slide toward a rigid, caste-like pattern of subjection. At this point, it is relevant to examine the weaker but persistent relationship that enabled the class situated in the more subservient position to exert pressures on those above.

The middle classes moved in lively conflict with one another. The cleric class through its privileged religious position and control of the traditional educational system was not without resources of its own. The bourgeois middle class always had certain economic and financial tools to bargain with, while the bureaucratic class enjoyed a political-administrative position. There was a constant checking confrontation between these classes which enjoyed relatively similar power positions. The merchant would pay

29. Manfred Halpern was the first to point to the special flexibility based upon balanced tension that infused Islamic society. He discusses the matter in depth in his unpublished manuscript entitled "The Dialectics of Traditional Society: Continuity and Change, Collaboration and Conflict in Pre-Modern Islam." The writer first explored these ideas in relation to Ṣafavī Iran in a manuscript written in 1965 and entitled "The Ṣafavī Administrative System: An Analysis."

Only the basic vertical power flows are shown

FIGURE 2

An Analytic View of The Iranian Class Structure

off the bureaucrat to obtain permits and licenses; the cleric would educate the *bāzārī*'s son in exchange for certain goods and business concessions; the bureaucrat would assist the *ākhūnd* in acquiring nominal employment in the government in return for gratuitous religious services for his family and relatives.

The three traditional middle classes used these same tools to check ruling class activity against them. Sir John Malcolm explains how this worked in terms of the bourgeois middle class:

> The merchants are a numerous and wealthy class; and no part of the community has enjoyed through all the distractions that kingdom has

> been afflicted with, and under the worst princes, more security, both in their persons and property. The reason is obvious; their traffic is essential to the revenue; oppression cannot be partially exercised upon them, for the plunder of one would alarm all; confidence would be banished, and trade cease.[30]

Classes with less power have been able to check classes with more power throughout the history of Shīʿī Islam. Both the Tobacco Rebellion and the Constitutional Movement at the turn of the twentieth century are examples of serious traditional middle-class pressure being effectively applied to the ruling class.[31] The Tūdah Party organized the working class in the 1940s in a manner that enabled this lower class to gain concessions from the ruling class. Even the Muṣaddiq movement was essentially a class upheaval as old and new middle classes joined to challenge seriously the ruling class. It here becomes evident that in connecting many groups and classes with networks of power, the web-system reinforces itself by allowing the occupants of weaker positions to coalesce against the more powerful. This often deterred and thwarted concentrated drives for subjection. Thus, Raphael Patai writes concerning Islamic society: "In spite of this great inequality in standard of living between the few rich and the many poor, and in spite of the spatial proximity of the two groups, there was a certain balance between the two. . . ."[32]

The most difficult linkage to explain in terms of power reciprocity is the one which relates the classes at the extremes of the social structure, i.e., the ruling class and the peasant class.[33] By nature of the wide power gap, it was this relationship that was least flexible and that existed in the greatest imbalance. Nonetheless, the peasants were not left without leverage against the upper classes. In the past, they have often belonged to brotherhoods and guilds which have provided them with organization and protection.[34] More recently, the Shah and ruling class have attempted to gain the support of the peasants and in so doing they have been forced to make many conces-

---

30. Sir John Malcolm, *The History of Persia from the Early Period to the Present Time,* 2d ed. (London: John Murray, 1829), 2: 304.

31. For an interesting indication of the role of the traditional middle classes (especially the clerics) in the constitutional movement, see three pictures in Edward G. Browne, *The Persian Revolution of 1905–1909* (Cambridge: University Press, 1910), pp. 124, 252, 304.

32. Patai, *Golden River to Golden Road: Society, Culture, and Change in the Middle East* (Philadelphia: University of Pennsylvania Press, 1962), pp. 278-79.

33. Fredrik Barth explains in some detail how this reciprocity and balanced power invested master-servant relations in a closely related Islamic setting. See Barth, *Political Leadership Among Swat Pathans* (London: Athelone Press, 1959), esp. pp. 48-50.

34. For an excellent study of peasant guilds in Iran, see I. P. Petrushevsky, *Kishāvarẓī va Munāsibāt-i Arẓī dar Īrān: ʻAsr-i Mughul: Qarnhā-yi 13 va 14* [Agriculture and Land Relationships in Iran: Mongol Period: 13th and 14th Centuries], translated into Persian from the Russian by Karīm Kishāvarz, 2 vols. (Tehran: Tehran University Press, 1344/1966), 2: 128-54.

sions. Today, therefore, the peasant class is gaining more and more access to power handles that will enable it to improve its position vis-à-vis the other classes.

Through the centuries, the traditional upper class-peasant class relationships can be understood in terms of landlord-peasant relations. Although the peasant held a subservient position, he could exert a checking power on the landlord in various ways. In the first place, the landlord was expected to keep the peasants alive and this meant food, clothing, shelter, and medicine. During periods of famine, earthquake, pestilence, and war, the peasant expected and received help from the landlord. The peasant could achieve certain aims by playing off the landlord's representatives against one another as well as against the landlord. The peasant came to expect the protection of the landlord and his representatives against government agents and policies. The landlord often intervened to help the peasant escape crushing tax exactions and to rescue the peasant's sons from military conscription.[35] Paul Vieille describes this interaction as follows:

> Without the protection which the name of the landlord was able to provide the peasants, they would be rapidly plundered by government agents who instead of providing assistance and cooperation stood as threats to the villagers. The village head is accustomed to handling these relations. He knows the expediencies, the bargains, and the costs. He knows the low-level government agents and their superiors from whom he is able to get recourse. Invested with the authority of the landlord and his administrative influence, he is able to soften the demands of the government agents in the affairs of the peasantry.[36]

The peasants have used every shred of their native intelligence to protect themselves and to improve their position. They have taken advantage of any force that they could use against the landlord or government agent. This is interestingly documented in the reports and papers of foreign advisory missions that have worked in the Iranian countryside.[37] The papers of Colonel Melvin Hall, a member of the 1922–27 Millspaugh mission, contain

35. This is no longer the case. One landlord friend who purchased a servant's son's freedom from conscription in 1962 could not do the same for his own son in 1966.

36. Vieille, "Un groupement Féodal en Iran," *Revue Française de Sociologie* 6 (April-June 1965): 185. This study provides an excellent and detailed analysis of how these relationships operated at the village level. It is based on research done in the tea and rice-growing regions of the Caspian provinces in northern Iran.

37. See, for example, F. A. C. Forbes-Leith, *Checkmate: Fighting Tradition in Central Persia* (New York: Robert M. McBride and Company, 1927). Forbes-Leith was a retired British military officer who supervised the extensive properties of an Iranian landowner. He was in the direct employ of the landlord who preferred to live in Tehran. Forbes-Leith's first-hand account of village politics includes examples of how the peasants sought his assistance against their traditional enemies.

numerous fascinating petitions and pleas of the peasants of southern Iran against their various exploiters.[38] Colonel Hall, who was Administrator of the Finances of Fārs and the Southern Ports at the time, used his office to support and protect the peasants.

When the peasant, however, had no cards with which to bargain, he would drop out of what Vieille terms "the game." No longer able to relate in the web-system the peasant would flee the village. This would snap the relevant power relationships. The last card that the peasant would often play before deserting the village was the threat to flee. In 1926, for example, seventy-three peasants from the village of Ardakān petitioned the Administrator of Provincial Finance in Shīrāz to deliver them from the oppression of a local official. They threatened to desert the village if they were not assisted. This particular petition is one of dozens that exist in the Melvin Hall papers and the following is a relevant excerpt as translated by Hall's staff.

> We all beg of you on the name of God and all his prophets not to put us, a number of poor men, under Shokrollah Khans supramacy [*sic*] and oppressions, otherwise having no power to bear his oppressions we will carry away our families to some other place and desert our village.[39]

Despite these meager devices which too often rested upon what the landlord considered of most utility to himself, the relative position of the peasant class has been appallingly low. There was also, however, a system of personal and group relationships which was more fluid and which blurred class lines and assisted the lower classes to survive and improve their position.

The Patterns of Group Interaction

Shī'ī Iran is a society where groups are bound together in relationships, in contrast to class relationships, in which either group can become the more powerful one. Through time, tension may build to the advantage of either

---

38. The Millspaugh mission of 1922–27 involved an American financial team under contract with the Iranian government. The members of this team had offices in the various provincial capitals where they were in charge of taxation and revenue collection. Colonel Hall was first assigned to Khurāsān and later to Fārs Province. He was an active administrator and keen observer who collected data incessantly. The Colonel Melvin Hall Papers are deposited and available at the Princeton University Library. For A. C. Millspaugh's own account of his missions in Iran, see his two books: *The American Task in Persia* (New York and London: Century Company, 1925) and *Americans in Persia* (Washington, D.C.: Brookings Institution, 1946).

39. See the Colonel Melvin Hall Papers, Princeton University Library.

side as groups relate in constant balancing movement. There is a freedom for all groups to interact with each other. Interclass as well as intraclass groups are involved as the merchants compete with the economic aristocracy and the landed peasant moves in conflict with the landless peasant. The following is an analysis of this general process as it has operated in the case of two key groups during the last five centuries.

During the Ṣafavī Period, lines of tension were drawn between two groups in the religious system who were represented by the *ṣadr* and the *mullābāshī* (chief *mujtahid*). The ṣadr was the leading member of the group of spiritual leaders that included the "sayyid, 'ulamā, mudarris, shaykh al-Islām, pīsh-namāz, qāḍī, mutavalli, hafiz."[40] He was the chief religious figure bound within the administration and he wielded important power in the area of secular law and endowments. The mujtahids, on the other hand, were theoretically the most important group in Shī'ī society in the sense that they had the right to interpret the *sharī'at.* They were considered by all believers to be the closest to the hidden Imām.[41]

The chronic friction that existed between these two groups has survived to the present day, although the title ṣadr has given way to *imām jum'ah.* The latter is today approximately what the ṣadr was in Ṣafavī days. This particular group relation was inextricably intertwined with other vital relations such as the political elite-religious elite competition centering about secular-religious tensions. The ṣadr-group was an integral part of the administrative machinery and they were the direct appointees of the Shah. The mujtahids stood outside the secular organization and rested their power on a foundation of spiritual and sacred authority. They had advanced to this rank because of their knowledge and acceptance by the Shī'ī masses.

During most of the Ṣafavī Period, the reciprocal power flow was quite evenly balanced as both poles constantly and effectively checked one another (see figure 3, diagram A). The inbuilt legal-economic-administrative advantages of the ṣadr were offset by the mujtahid's influence with the people and the Shah. During the reign of the first Ṣafavī monarch, Shāh Ismā'īl, the ṣadr was one of the King's top four advisors.[42] In this period

---

40. V. Minorsky, *Tadhkirat al-Mulūk,* E. J. W. Gibb New Series (London: Luzac and Company, 1943) 16: 42. This is a Ṣafavī administrative manual available in translation and with notes by Minorsky. Hereafter, the manual will be cited as TM, while Minorsky's notes and commentary will be referred to as Minorsky, TM.

41. For a clear, concise, and accurate statement of the position and role of the 'ulamā in Shī'ī Islam, see Leonard Binder, "The Proofs of Islam: Religion and Politics in Islam" in George Makdisi, ed., *Arabic and Islamic Studies in Honor of Hamilton A. C. Gibb* (Cambridge: Harvard University Press, 1965), pp. 118-40. The classic study of the various clerical positions especially during Ṣafavī times is Ann K. S. Lambton, "Quis Custodiet Custodes," *Studia Islamica* 5-6 (1956): 125-46.

42. Ghulam Sarwar, *History of Shāh Ismā'īl Ṣafawī* (Aligarh: Muslim University, 1939), p. 102. The other three were the *Vakīl* (Counselor), *Amīr al-Umarā* (Prime Minister), and *Vazīr* (Minister).

of the construction and consolidation of a new dynasty, the ṣadr was more advantageously situated than the mujtahid. In the historic battle of Chaldirān (1513), two ṣadrs lost their lives while fighting at the side of the Shah.[43] The balance shifted slightly in the other direction during the rule of Shāh Ṭahmāsb and the tension is well-documented in the chronicle, *Aḥsan al-Tavārīkh.* It is recorded that in 1534 the influential ṣadr, Amīr Ni'matullāh Ḥillī, died.[44] According to the chronicle, this *amīr*'s life was dominated by a feud with Shaykh 'Alī bin 'Abd al-'Alī Mujtahid. The latter was an extremely powerful mujtahid who was referred to as *Khātam al-Mujtahidīn* (Seal of the Mujtahids).[45] This man had also been engaged in a tense power struggle with a previous ṣadr. The *Aḥsan al-Tavārīkh* describes the charges and counter-charges that marked this dispute between the mujtahid and the ṣadr, Amīr Ghiyāṣ al-Dīn Manṣūr.[46] In both of these disputes, the mujtahid prevailed and succeeded in bringing about the dismissal of the ṣadrs.[47]

By the end of the Ṣafavī Period, the mujtahids had improved their positions greatly at the expense of the ṣadr organization (see figure 3, diagram B). Mujtahids such as Muḥammad Bāqir-i Majlisī and Mīr Muḥammad Ḥusayn wielded enormous influence not only at this level but in the political system and society as well. Shāh Sulṭān Ḥusayn, for example, was under the direct influence and control of the great mujtahids of his day who took the opportunity to debilitate all their rivals.

Between the fall of the Ṣafavids and the rise of the Qājārs (1736–79), Nādir Shāh temporarily destroyed this relationship by attacking the groups at both competing positions (figure 3, diagram C). He confiscated all the *awqāf* (endowment) properties and in the process destroyed the office of ṣadr. The mujtahids did not fare much better as Nādir undercut their great influence through violence and periodic support for Sunnism. In 1736, the Chief Mujtahid, Mīrzā 'Abd al-Ḥasan, was strangled and in 1743 another leading mujtahid was forced to defer to Sunnī doctrines.[48] Within the context of the political-religious pattern of tension, these policies reflected a dramatic shift in favor of the secular political authorities who had been the weaker pole in late Ṣafavī times.

---

43. *Ibid.*, p. 79.

44. Ḥasan-i Rūmlū, *Aḥsan al-Tavārīkh* (Baroda: Oriental Institute, 1931), 1: 254.

45. *Ibid.*

46. *Ibid.*, pp. 303-4.

47. For references to the appointment and dismissal of Amīr Ghiyaṣ al-Dīn Manṣūr as ṣadr, see *ibid.*, pp. 234, 244.

48. Viewed in terms of group, class, and power, the much-debated point of whether Nādir Shāh favored Sunnism or Shī'ism seems to miss the point entirely. Nādir was primarily a politician who used Sunnī support to help weaken a Shī'ī religious organization that had come to control Iranian politics. For reference to the two mujtahids concerned, see L. Lockhart, *Nader Shah: A Critical Study Based Mainly upon Contemporary Sources* (London: Luzac and Company, 1938), pp. 99, 233.

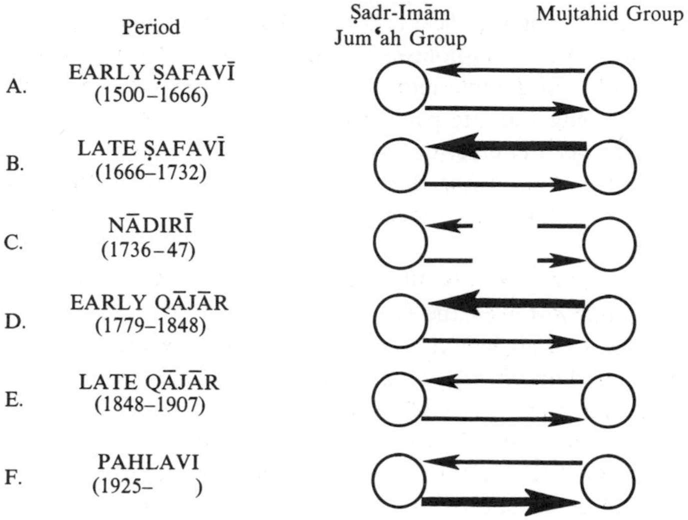

FIGURE 3

Ṣadr—Mujtahid Group Tensions, 1500–1960

With the rise of the Qājārs, the mujtahid power point reasserted itself. Many mujtahids who had retired to the Najaf-Karbalā area during the Afghānī and Nādirī periods returned to Iran and acquired important influence. The ṣadr group was represented primarily by the *shaykh al-islām*s who were appointed and paid by the monarch himself. They were located in all the major cities where they served as chief jurists and their existence assured these cleric-jurists of some bargaining power (figure 3, diagram D). The ṣadr, however, no longer existed as an office and in 1800 Sir John Malcolm recalls having met the principal descendant of the last family of ṣadrs.[49] The balance of power now flowed once again in favor of the mujtahids and this became especially evident during the reign of Fatḥ 'Alī Shāh. This was the period of influence of the famous Mīrzā Qumī who exercised great power in the system as well as over the Shah.

During the long reign of Nāṣir al-Dīn Shāh, the tension once again acquired more balance (figure 3, diagram E). The major event in this development was the Shah's appointment of an imām jum'ah who became an important force balanced against the mujtahids. The imām jum'ahs were in charge of the Friday mosques in the large cities and the head imām jum'ah exhibited characteristics strikingly similar to those of the ṣadr of

49. Malcolm, *The History of Persia,* 2: 313.

Ṣafavī days. He took control of some *awqāf* and was the direct appointee of the Shah.[50] It is significant to note that the first politically influential imām jum'ah was a son-in-law of Nāṣir al-Dīn Shāh and quickly assumed a position of considerable importance. The rivalry between the two poles tightened during the late part of the nineteenth century and broke into obvious and open conflict during the reign of Muẓaffir al-Dīn Shāh. It is often forgotten that during the constitutional movement there was an important clerical force that sided with the monarch. The imām jum'ah led this group.[51]

The imām jum'ah forces survived the fall of the Qājārs just as the mujtahid forces had survived the fall of the Ṣafavids. Although the mujtahids were on the winning side in the constitutional movement, in the long run they have fared poorly in relation to the imām jum'ah group. Under the two Pahlavi Shahs, the balance of tension has tilted sharply against the mujtahids (figure 3, diagram F). An imbalance of this degree has not existed since the last years of the Ṣafavī Dynasty. In the contemporary situation, however, the more secular-oriented forces have the advantage. Part of the reason lies in the drive for industrialization and westernization and it was in the name of these gods that Riẕa Shāh chopped at the mujtahid pole, destroying many of the forces located there. The imbalance has continued to exist under the monarchy of Riẕa Shāh's son who has consistently supported the imām jum'ah forces against the mujtahids. In 1967, an Iranian religious leader and scholar summed up the present situation as follows:

> The people accept this struggle as inevitable—as *dunyā* versus *dīn* (the secular versus the religious). What becomes unacceptable to them is when one side tries to destroy the other side. This is what happened during the Riẕā Shāh period. The secular did not even go through the motions of appealing to the religious. This is in a way what has happened again in Iran during the last several years. In the land reform, for example, the mujtahids were not even consulted nor was the Islamic method even considered. Thus, the opposition of mujtahids like Khumaynī was not to the idea of land reform, but rather to the manner in which it was implemented.[52]

---

50. The contemporary Imām Jum'ah of Tehran controls the huge Shah Mosque and all its properties. This particular man, Sayyid Ḥasan Imāmī Imām Jum'ah, although a relative of Muṣaddiq, stood by the Shah during the Muṣaddiq-Pahlavi confrontation in the early 1950s. During the three days when Aḥmad Qavām replaced Muṣaddiq as Prime Minister in July 1952, this Imām Jum'ah held the post of Speaker of the Majlis. According to the Imām Jum'ah himself, there are approximately thirty-five Imām Jum'ahs situated throughout Iran today. Personal interview, November 25, 1970.

51. See E. G. Browne, *The Persian Revolution,* p. 113.

52. Personal interview, January 10, 1967. See also, Leonard Binder's sensitive discussion relating Shī'ī Islam to processes of change in Makdisi, ed., *Arabic and Islamic Studies,* pp. 118-40.

The analysis of the particular groups above immediately begins to explain relationships between other groups that relate directly to the two under investigation. Since the group represented by the ṣadr and imām jum'ah was an overlapping part of the political authority and the mujtahids represented the heart of the religious establishment, one can see the particular tension analyzed here in terms of a larger and perhaps more significant linkage. In this relationship, the two religious-cleric forces would represent one competing pole and the political authority would occupy the other. At this level, one could hypothesize that in the Nādirī period the political power point became so overwhelming that it snapped the reciprocal relationship subjecting *both* religious groups. The Pahlavi period has witnessed reciprocity but heavily in favor of the political pole because of the latter's support for the ṣadr-imām jum'ah group in the more constricted relationship. At the same time, one could suggest that in the late Ṣafavī and early Qājār periods, the religious system was more powerful since the ṣadr-mujtahid tension flowed heavily in favor of the latter.

From this example also, one discovers that in such systems forces tend to relate to one another in an interlocking and overlapping manner. The lines are always blurred. During the constitutional movement, therefore, certain mujtahids (e.g., Shaykh Faẕlullāh Nūrī) sided with the government. Also, during the contemporary Pahlavi period, a number of mujtahids (e.g., Āyatullāh Mar'ashī) have also become instruments of the political authority.[53] This intertwining characteristic enables one to gain helpful insights into important power relationships other than the one under examination. It also calls attention to constellations of relationships and stimulates hypotheses that might link these relationships to other areas and issues. Figure 3 not only presents information about certain group interaction but it can also be used to relate types of power flows to dynastic changes for example.

While both class and group relationships reflect uneven and reciprocal power patterns, the group linkage represents a balancing fluidity and flexibility. Class relationships, on the other hand, are marked by a fixed hierarchy and a more limited flexibility. Both patterns, however, have existed together and the relationship between the two is vital.

The Group Pattern and Class Relations

In class relationships, one class possesses a consistent power advantage over the other. This would seem to indicate that the class relationships might be extremely fragile relationships. The hypothesis here, however, is that this

53. In so doing, these religious leaders risk losing their followings. In June 1966, the former leading mujtahid of a large Āẕarbayjān city told me during an extended discussion that ever since he had begun supporting the government and seeing the Shah, the number of people who prayed behind him had steadily dwindled.

kind of class interaction is extraordinarily resilient. Much of the reason lies in the fact that when classes interact with one another, they subsume groups and individuals who are themselves bound together in highly elastic relationships. These group linkages, for example, pervade the class relationships into which they are woven.

One effect of this related group-class tension is the blurring of class lines. This is best understood in terms of two principles: (1) the overlapping membership that characterizes interclass groups; and (2) the high rate of personal mobility that occurs between classes. These two characteristics are interrelated since overlapping membership facilitates mobility and vice versa. It can be generally stated that group and class memberships continually change, but group and class power points always remain. This occurs partly because of natural cycles such as life-death and health-disease, but it is also reflected in overlapping membership and mobility.

Although there is a great deal of overlapping membership between intraclass groups, it is the interclass group that is most relevant here. Throughout Iranian history, many groups have been composed of individuals who represent two or more classes. This can be seen best in family, tribal, ethnic, and religious groups. Figure 2 indicates that the tribal elite is one of the key ruling-class groups, while the nomadic masses are a vital lower-class component. In cases where tribal khāns have felt special responsibility to their tribe, this alone could serve to mellow the class situation of the common tribesmen. When viewed through time and in terms of all the tribes, the situation of the tribal nobility itself takes on interesting significance. Much, of course, has always depended upon the particular tribe, monarch, and dynasty. During the period under review, the tribal-upper-class relationship has been very intimate and the Ṣafavī, Nādirī, Zand, and Qājār periods have risen from tribal movements. Although tribal khāns have always been present in upper-class ranks, there has been constant fluctuation in terms of *what* khāns from *which* tribes have been those involved. There has been a kind of rotating membership through time as particular khāns from particular tribes move in and out of the ruling class. This very special type of overlapping membership has permitted wide tribal representation in the upper class and has helped obscure class lines. It has also intensified a system of deep tribal rivalries that have pitted the various tribal elites (and tribesmen) against one another. The violent Rūmlū-Takkalū-Ustājlū conflicts during the rule of Ṣafavī Shāh Ṭahmāsb revealed all these characteristics in a telescoped period of time as tribal groups competed for upper-class positions.[54] All such groups witnessed alternate success and failure. In more

54. For the details of this conflict, see Rūmlū, *Aḥsan al-Tavārīkh.* See also, R. M. Savory, "The Principal Offices of the Ṣafawid State During the Reign of Ṭahmāsp I (930-84/1524/76)," *Bulletin of the School of Oriental and African Studies* 24 (1961): 65-85.

recent years, Bakhtiyārī and Qashqā'ī khāns have both led and helped put down rebellions. Riẓā Shāh Pahlavī put to death nearly a dozen Bakhtiyārī khāns including the influential Sardār As'ad, while his son married a Bakhtiyārī princess who became a powerful queen. This alternating membership of tribal khāns in the ruling class has tended to soften class lines for most tribal groups since their leaders have moved in and out of the ruling class through the years.

One of the most basic groups that has witnessed overlapping membership of class is the family. Due to mobility (see below), individuals have moved into classes other than the one represented by their families. A system of families divided in class membership results. Class conflict is usually mellowed in such cases as the members in the higher class assist relatives in a less advantageous position. When class lines are spanned in this manner, there is greater mobility and less hostility between classes. Some of the most powerful upper-class Iranian families have been split in this way as a minority of the members adopt political views that demand deep change in the ongoing system. In so doing, the latter often forego their upper-class positions. Names like Ṣālaḥ, Hidāyat, Amīnī, and Amīr-Sulaymānī are well-known contemporary families in this position. During the Muṣaddiq Period, families that carried such a division were in better shape than those who did not since they automatically had a representative in the new political elite. More than one Iranian has voiced the opinion that the more prescient families maintain membership of various political color and class so that in times of sudden political or class change the family will not necessarily lose its power position. Although this may be an exaggeration, it is a fine example of the way group membership can mellow and dull class confrontation.

This characteristic of overlap along with the reciprocal and balancing nature of group interaction is closely related to the mobility factor. As groups have alternated, with those in the weaker position sporadically moving to the stronger, individual members of these groups have consistently been able to take advantage of the change in fortune to move ahead in the class structure. They gain leverage and impetus by riding the incoming group tide and by the time the tide ebbs again they have managed to move to higher ground. Not all groups, however, facilitate mobility. Islam brought only four major class mobility channels to Iran and these have been the following groups: the Family of the Prophet, the Shī'ī religious group, and the bureaucratic and military occupational groups. None of these existed as such in the pre-Islamic Iranian empires where social class circulation was virtually unknown.

The Family of the Prophet. The members of the Prophet's family represent the only innate aristocracy in Islam for they have automatically always possessed a special power and respect. If, for example, they have suffered some misfortune, the community has always taken special pains to assist them. The members of this family have often had a charismatic power and thus almost all of the violent political movements that have arisen in Islamic areas have occurred in the name and under the leadership of a person claiming direct descent from the Prophet. The kings of Ṣafavī times expended a great deal of energy tracing their origins directly to the Prophet through the saintly Shaykh Ṣafī al-Dīn. Even in contemporary Iran, the term *sayyid* carries with it special respect and Muḥammad Riẓā Shāh, if not a direct descendant of the Prophet, nonetheless still claims direct communication with 'Alī and 'Abbās.[55] This channel broadened through time as it became a vehicle of advantage not only to those who were in fact descendants of the Prophet but also to all who *claimed* this relationship.

The Religious Channel. Throughout history any Muslim could endeavor to become a member of the *'ulamā* regardless of his class origins. The major qualifications centered upon knowledge and morals and young people who aspired to become *ākhūnd*s and *mullā*s were seldom rejected because of their class backgrounds. The mujtahids still distribute the money for the necessary education and religious training, while the community itself provides the resources. Iranians of lower-class background have moved into the middle class in large numbers over the years as they have benefited from the traditional education and have then moved into society as religious leaders. Many have moved up through this channel even into the ruling class. It is a little-known fact that women as well as men have moved into higher classes in this manner and Iran has a colorful history of female mujtahids.[56] The body of clerics in Islamic Iran provides a profound contrast to their counterparts in Sāsānian Iran where even mobility within the *mubad* class was unusual and difficult.

The Bureaucratic Channel. The government administration has been a means through which many individuals have been able to move out of their own class and into higher classes. Qājār history is replete with dramatic examples of this. None of the Qājār *ṣadr-i a'ẓam*s (prime ministers), with the exception of 'Ayn al-Dawlah, were of royal blood and most were of lower-class origin. They have moved into positions of great influence through their association with the bureaucratic machinery. Key examples include such figures as Mustawfī al-Mamālik, Mīrzā Taqī Khān, Āqā Khān

55. The Shah himself vividly explains such experiences in his book *Mission for My Country* (London: Hutchinson and Company, 1960), pp. 54-55.

56. A record of the lives and deeds of some of the great female mujtahids exists in the three volume work by I'timād al Salṭanah, *Khayrāt-i Ḥisān,* published in 1304/1925.

Nūrī, and Ḥājjī Ibrāhīm. An important tributary of this channel has been the court and royal household out of which gardeners, water carriers, stable boys, and cobblers have moved to positions of tremendous power. An instructive case here involved the son of a court cobbler who became a water carrier *(ābdārbāshī)* for Nāṣir al-Dīn Shāh. While accompanying the King on a hunting trip, he moved at the critical moment to assist the Monarch down a dangerous mountainside. From that moment on, the waterboy never looked back as he rose to great influence and his son became one of the most important figures in Qājār history, the powerful Amīn al-Sulṭān.[57]

The Military Channel. In direct contrast to the Sāsānian Period, the Islamic Period in Iran presented any clever and brave soldier with the opportunity to move up through the military ranks and into the ruling class. This channel of mobility has been of particular importance because of its immediate control over the means of coercion in the society. Frequently, those who have risen by these means have not only gained a place in the ruling class but also have been able to become kings and found dynasties. Key examples in Iranian history stretch from the founders of the ninth- and tenth-century Ziyārid and Ṣaffārid Dynasties to the twentieth-century founder of the Pahlavi Dynasty. The Ziyārid and Pahlavi founders were of lower-class background and moved to the top from low-ranking military positions. The Ṣaffārid head was a coppersmith who came to rule an empire the center of which was in Sīstān and which covered almost all of present day Iran. Less spectacular examples include the many military leaders and general officers who have through the years become an integral part of the ruling class because of their loyalty and military aptitude and despite their lower-class origin.

These classic mobility channels have fluctuated in importance through the centuries as the two that are directly religious-oriented have lost much of their effectiveness to the others. In contemporary times, the growth of industry, liquid wealth, and modern education have served to provide new tools with which more and more individuals have been able to etch their own channels. The greatest change has been the establishment and expansion of modern education which has opened many new possibilities. Yet, even with significant new educational opportunities, those of lower-class

57. *Downward mobility* has been just as common since Persian history is replete with examples of the dramatic plunges of individuals and families who apparently held unassailable positions. Some of the greatest books on politics have been written by those who have sought to advise the most powerful of Muslim monarchs and princes on how to keep from joining the downward exodus. In the case of Iran, these include Nizam ul-Molk's *Siyasat-nama* and Kai Ka'us Ibn Iskandar's *Qabus-nama.* Both are available in English. See *Siyasat-nama;* and *The Qabus-nama* [A Mirror for Princes], translated from the Persian by Reuben Levy (London: Cresset Press, 1951).

origin continue to move into higher classes through the bureaucratic and military-security channels. One further trend that is immediately related to the others has been the increasing importance of planned or controlled mobility. With the slow drying up of the religious channel and the greater control of the political elite over the bureaucratic-military systems, contemporary mobility, especially into the ranks of the ruling class, has been directed from above. The two Pahlavi monarchs have been extremely active in this matter and thus there has seldom been a lower- or middle-class individual who has risen to high political position without the direct intervention or approval of the political elite in general and the Shah in particular. A dramatic example of this involved a semiliterate worker who was selected to the Twenty-first Majlis (Parliament) and who stated in 1966:

> I am not a human being. I am a worker *(man ādam nīstam. kārgar hastam).* . . . His Imperial Majesty the Shāhanshāh for years knew about my loyalty and devotion and commanded that I be elected to the Majlis. Now I am proud to be the servant and soldier *(khidmatguzār va sarbāz)* of His Majesty.[58]

The Iran Novin Party and the Secret Police became especially significant in the 1960s as bureaucratic mobility channels through which numerous lower- to middle-class individuals were pulled to positions in the ruling class and political elite.

Thus, entry into the ruling class has been primarily a process of conquest and co-optation. Movement through conquest changed elites and personalities, but the class structure remained basically unaltered. Mobility through co-optation only reinforced the ongoing structure. These are a few examples of the trends and modifications that have marked mobility relationships through time.

The dynamics of mobility and overlapping membership tend to blur class lines which is the crucial effect that group interaction has on class relationships. There have been other noticeable trends that indicate the important role that groups play in the preservation of class relationships. Certain group interests have been periodically sacrificed in this regard. This has usually been the result of a deliberate policy taken by the political elite to protect their own position at times when class relationships have been severely strained. In some instances, this has meant the creation of an entirely new group such as Shāh 'Abbās I's formation of the Shāhsavan

58. Personal interview, September 27, 1966. There were eleven other workers chosen as representatives to the Twenty-first Majlis.

tribe. The latter became an appendage of the upper class and served to buttress the existing class structure.[59] Three and a half centuries later, Muḥammad Riẓā Shāh undercut the power position of the landlord group within his own ruling class. This was done to preserve the existing class patterns which were being threatened by persistent middle-class demands. Another significant trend has been the accelerative growth in the number of groups which has resulted in new strands of tension. This has occurred through the splintering of groups and classes, whose members then enter new bargaining relationships. The institution of the land reform program in 1962, for example, has already resulted in the unintended appearance of new rivalries both in upper- and lower-class ranks. A vital case in point is the peasant division explained above. Further examples of this proliferation of conflicting confrontation through the breakup of groups and classes will be provided in the pages that follow.

In conclusion, although the patterns whereby groups interact together in balanced fluidity have buttressed and strengthened class relationships, there have been still other forces involved. These center upon vital personal relationships.

Personal Relations and the Class Structure

Interpersonal interaction has had a profound impact upon both group and class relationships in Iran. The interpersonal power patterns have served a function very similar to group linkages in that they buttress class relations which are the focus of this study. The empirical investigation of this hypothesis follows below.

---

59. Malcolm tells us how Shāh 'Abbās checked the forces of powerful nobles and tribes "by forming a tribe of his own, which he styled *Shah Sevund* [Shāhsavan], or 'the king's friends'; and he invited men of all tribes to enroll themselves in a clan devoted to his family, and therefore distinguished by his particular favour and protection. Volunteers could not be wanting at such a call; and we have one instance of ten thousand men being registered by the name of Shah Sevund in one day. This tribe, which became remarkable for its attachment to the Suffavean [Ṣafavī] dynasty, still exists, though with diminished numbers. It could once boast of more than a hundred families." *The History of Persia,* 1: 369. V. Minorsky questions Malcolm's account but points out that Shah 'Abbās "continued vigorously and successfully the policy of regrouping the great tribes." See "Shah-sewan," in *Encyclopedia of Islam,* 1924 ed., 4: 267. For recent evidence that the Shāhsavan tribe was originally composed of various peoples gathered through the efforts of the early Ṣafavī monarchs, see R. Tapper, "Black Sheep, White Sheep and Red-Heads," *Iran* 4 (1966): 62-67. For an analysis of how tribes were artificially formed in Africa see Crawford Young, *Politics in the Congo: Decolonization and Independence* (Princeton: Princeton University Press, 1965), pp. 232-72. The cases cited by Young occurred more spontaneously than the deliberate invention of the Shāhsavan in Iran.

The 17th-Century Ṣafavī Network of Politics

The powerful Ṣafavī dynasty ruled Iran from the beginning of the sixteenth to the middle of the eighteenth century. There are a number of chronicles and manuals in existence that provide a detailed picture of the Ṣafavī administrative system and an examination of these reveals the network of vital relationships that marked the system.[60] The interpersonal relationships that marked Ṣafavī politics are congruent with the group patterns analyzed in a general context above. They were characterized by strongly reciprocal and continually shifting power exchanges. The major modification in personal interaction concerns the existence of certain individuals who maintain especially crucial and powerful positions in the system. These individuals, represented, for example, by *shaykh*s, *imām*s, *pīr*s, and *shah*s played a highly disproportionate role in controlling and influencing the outcome of various conflicting relationships. They often came to treat others as extensions of their own will and consciously reinforced the rivalry and division that dominated the relations among their subordinates.[61]

Tension, conflict, fluidity, flexibility, and uncertainty were built into the Ṣafavī administrative system in such a way as to render it dynamically stable. A fissured unity and a cohesive disunity characterized it at all points. This system was split and divided both vertically and horizontally with administrative officers and influential individuals exerting persistent pressure on each other at all times.

The Ṣafavī Web-System in Focus. Figure 4 presents a diagram of the Ṣafavī administrative system as it existed in the late years of that dynasty. The Shah stands at the heart of the system and the twenty-six members of the political elite surround him.[62] These personalities moved around the mon-

60. The most valuable source is the *Tadhkirat al-Mulūk.* Rumlu's *Aḥsan al-Tavārīkh* is an important chronicle, while the best firsthand account by a traveler is J. Chardin, *Voyages,* 10 vols. (Paris: Le Normant, 1811).

61. Manfred Halpern's theoretical schema presents this kind of relationship as the "Polarity of Emanation." Halpern points out that this is an especially critical relationship in Shīʿī Muslim societies. For intellectual support of this hypothesis, see W. Montgomery Watt, *Muslim Intellectual: A Study of Al-Ghazali* (Edinburgh: University Press, 1963), pp. 38-43, 74-82.

62. This diagram is based on an analysis of the administrative manual, *Tadhkirat al-Mulūk,* as well as the reading of Ṣafavī history. It is quite possible that someone else might arrange these offices slightly differently depending upon the sources consulted and the period considered within Ṣafavī history. The basic structure and relationship, however, should stand as presented. This figure does not include important provincial officials. There is also some confusion on just who were the fourteen great *amīr*s as the *Tadhkirat al-Mulūk* omits the name of the *Mustawfī-yi Khāṣṣah* and includes instead the Grand Vazir. In figure 4, we have included both and have placed the *Khalīfat al-Khulafā* (a kind of spiritual leader for Ṣūfī affairs) in the third circle of influence. For the Persian titles of the twenty-six offices, see *Tadhkirat al-Mulūk.*

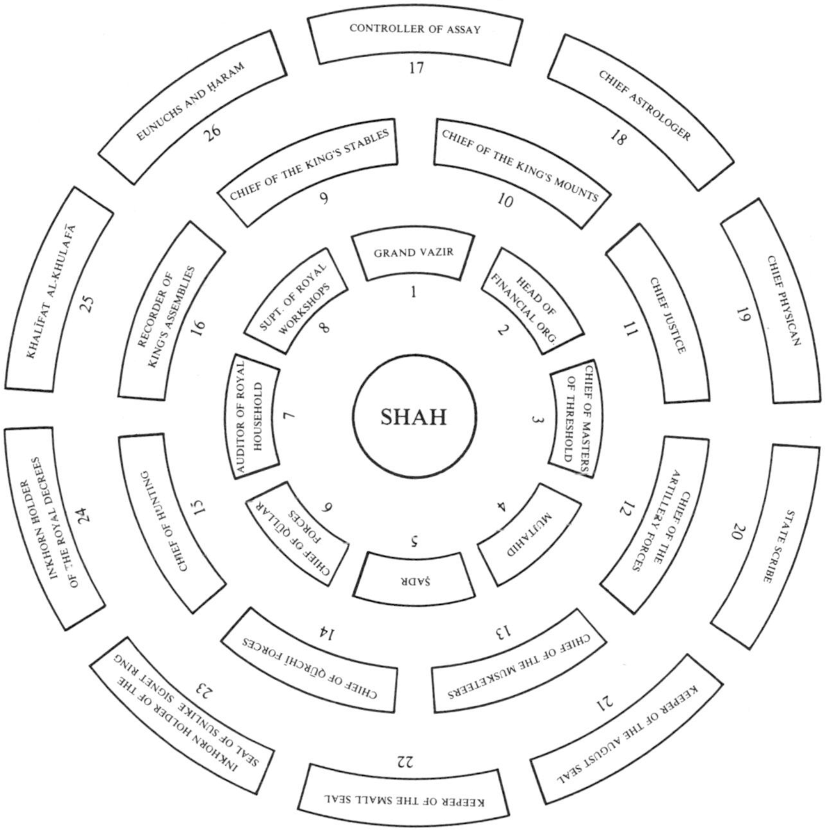

FIGURE 4

The Ṣafavī Political Elite

arch in constant tension with one another. The first concentric circle represents those closest to the Shah and they consistently wielded the most influence in his name. The first two concentric circles together include thirteen of the fourteen great *amīrs*, the Grand Vazir, and the two important religious officials, the ṣadr and the chief mujtahid. The great *amīrs* carried the special title *'ālī-jāh* and held the highest administrative posts in Ṣafavī Iran. The third circle is dominated by those officials who were especially closely associated with the person of the Shah.

This network of relationships was highly dependent upon the monarch who moved the personalities back and forth from position to position and circle to circle. At times, they lost their place in the elite and at other times they lost their lives. Any member of this elite could exert power over any other member as permanent lines of tension were built into the elite by virtue of institutionalized administrative rivalry (see sections below). In the eleventh century, the Ziyārid Prince, Kai Ka'us Ibn Iskandar, wrote his son a guidebook on how to survive in such a system. The following paragraph reveals how members of the political elite were related to one another in persistent rivalry while at the same time being bound to the monarch in a more deferential pattern.

> Should he at any time pretend to you that you are completely secure with him, begin from that moment to feel insecure; if you are being fattened by someone, you may expect very quickly to be slaughtered by him. However greatly you may be held in honour, never cease to be aware of your position nor speak any word that is not to the king's taste. Do not persist when in argument with him; there is a proverb that he who argues with a king dies before his alloted time.[63]

The last Ṣafavī Shahs lost their superior power position and charisma and the system of personal relationships built around them quickly disintegrated. Shāh Sulaymān (1666–94) and Shāh Ṣultān Ḥusayn (1694–1722) fell under the visible influence and control of the mujtahids and ḥaram (figure 4, points 4, 21).

Tensions between the Khāṣṣah and Dīvān. In his valuable study, *Turkestan Down to the Mongol Invasion,* V. V. Barthold writes: "Throughout the whole system of the Eastern Muslim political organization there runs like a red thread the division of all the organs of administration into two main categories, the dargah (palace) and diwan (chancery)."[64] In Ṣafavī times, this division *(khāṣṣah* and *dīvān)* was an integral part of the administration and it played a major role in both the rise and decline of the system. These two forces were in constant tension with one another and in the end this tension snapped as the *khāṣṣah* absorbed and digested the functions and power of the *dīvān.* It was at this time that the Ṣafavī system crumbled.

The *khāṣṣah* was the royal household or court while the *dīvān* was a kind of state administration.[65] The latter was headed by the Grand Vazir while

63. *The Qabus-nama,* p. 191.

64. See Barthold, *Turkestan Down to the Mongol Invasion,* 2d ed. (London: Oxford University Press, 1928), p. 227.

65. *Dīvān* here must not be confused with the general meaning of the term usually referring to an administrative bureau or in the Ottoman system to the high council of ministers. We have followed Minorsky who consistently uses *dīvān* to refer to the non-*khāṣṣah* branch of administration which is closer to the state bureaucracy proper. See, for example, Minorsky, TM, pp. 25-26, 44-45, 116.

the former was the special preserve of the Crown. Both had corresponding officials and officers. The financial affairs of the *dīvān,* for example, were directed by the *Mustawfī al-Mamālik* while the *khāṣṣah* finances were supervised by the *Mustawfī-yi Khāṣṣah.*

In the Ottoman system, this division is described as having existed between the "Imperial Household" and the "Central Administration." The entire Central Administration was under the aegis of the Grand Vazir who had no direct authority over the Imperial Household. As the Grand Vazir's power increased in later Ottoman times, however, there is little doubt that he exerted a great deal of control even in the Imperial Household.[66]

Although many of the developments and changes that marked the fortune of the Ṣafavī system can be explained by the tension that characterized the *khāṣṣah-dīvān* division, this separation must not be viewed as being sharp and complete. Actually many threads bound the branches together helping unify that which paradoxically enough remained divided. Thus, the Grand Vazir who was essentially bound up with the *dīvān* also exerted influence in the *khāṣṣah.* The *Mustawfī al-Mamālik* had certain powers over the *Mustawfī-yi Khāṣṣah* despite the fact that the latter gained in influence in later Ṣafavī times. On the other hand, the *Nāẓir-i Buyūtāt* (Superintendent of the Royal Workshops), who after the monarch headed the *khāṣṣah,* "looked into some affairs of the *dīvān* administration."[67] Thus, several key officials who were a part of one branch of administration were often deeply involved in the affairs of the other branch.

As time passed, the balance of tensions that marked *khāṣṣah-dīvān* relations was gradually upset. The *ūymāq* (tribes) were gradually eliminated as the base of the Ṣafavī power structure[68] as Shāh 'Abbās I and others began relying more and more on the qūllars who were the special troops of the royal household. As this occurred, the *khāṣṣah* constantly gained in influence at the expense of the *dīvān.* According to Minorsky, this burgeoning of *khāṣṣah* influence was one of the chief reasons for the fall of the Ṣafavīds.[69]

Besides this major division which represented perhaps the most crucial line of tension in the entire system, there were other major forces that competed with both the *khāṣṣah* and *dīvān.* These were the military and

66. H. A. R. Gibb and Harold Bowen, *Islamic Society and the West—1,* Part 1 (London: Oxford University Press, 1950), pp. 71-88, 107-37. It is important to note that the Grand Vazir assumed more and more power during later times of both the Ottoman and Ṣafavī dynasties.

67. Minorsky, TM, pp. 118-19.

68. Martin B. Dickson, "Shāh Ṭahmāsb and the Ūzbeks—The Duel for Khurāsān with 'Ubayd Khān: 930-946/1524–1540" (unpublished Ph.D. dissertation, Department of Oriental Studies, Princeton University, 1958), p. 9.

69. Minorsky, TM, pp. 23, 26, 123.

religious-justice hierarchies which possessed special independence and pursued certain goals of their own. All four power points were bound together within the total system in the form of an interlocking web, the strands of which were knit together in stabilizing conflict.

Four Key Ṣafavī Officials: Balanced Tension. In the Ṣafavī political system there were certain officials who wielded an extraordinary amount of power and influence. Among these, the following four have been selected for closer examination.

1. *Grand Vazir:* Head of the *dīvān* and formally second to the Shah in the system
2. *Nāẓir-i Buyūtāt:* Superintendent of the Royal Workshops and the Shah's deputy in charge of the *khāṣṣah*
3. *Mustawfī al-Mamālik:* Head of the Financial Organization
4. *Nāẓir-i Daftar-khānah-yi Humāyūn:* Superintendent of the Royal Secretariat

By examining the authority channeled to these posts, one can gain another insight into the intricate system of checks and balances that marked Ṣafavī politics.

Next to the Shah himself, the Grand Vazir was generally the most powerful man in the Ṣafavī system. Entitled *I'timād al-Dawlah* (The Trust of the State), he headed the state apparatus and enjoyed wide powers of appointment and finance. In later Ṣafavī times, the Grand Vazirs became so powerful that they sometimes controlled even the Shah.[70] Despite this formidable position, the Grand Vazir was in fact checked from at least four directions (see figure 5).

From above, the Shah usually exerted great influence upon the Grand Vazir, while from below the *Nāẓir-i Daftar-khānah,* the *Mustawfī* and the *Nāẓir-i Buyūtāt* penetrated his authority at various points. The *Nāẓir-i Daftar* was a kind of secretary-general who checked and endorsed the orders of the Grand Vazir. He was appointed directly by the Shah and Chardin describes him as "surveillant" of the Grand Vazir.[71] Although the Grand Vazir was the chief minister of finance, he did not act in these affairs "without the confirmation *(taṣdīq)* of the *Mustawfī al-Mamālik.*"[72] He was

70. For examples of the great strength of the Grand Vazir, see Chardin, *Voyages,* 5: 337-40.
71. *Ibid.,* p. 341.
72. TM, p. 54.

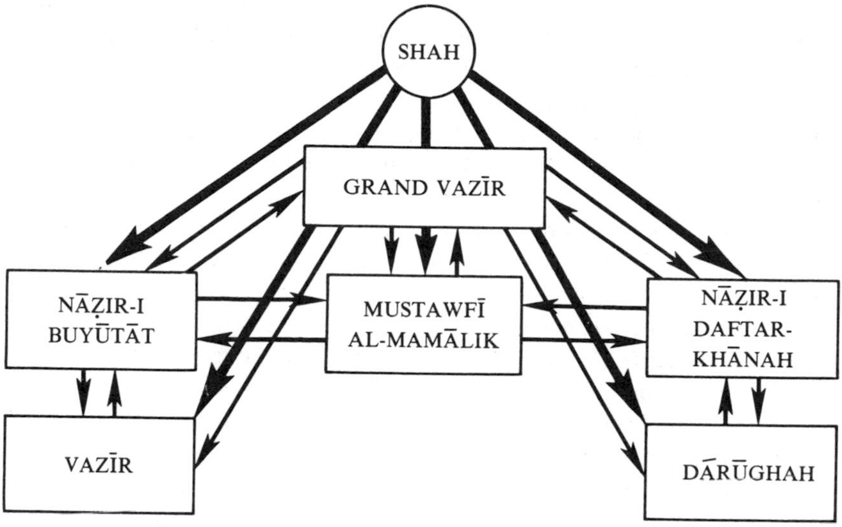

FIGURE 5

Ṣafavī Administration: Balanced Tension Among Key Officials

also checked in some degree by the *Nāẓir-i Buyūtāt* who administered the *khāṣṣah* section. The latter check was built into the Ṣafavī system by virtue of the important *khāṣṣah-dīvān* division described above.

All three officials who exerted influence upon the Grand Vazir from below do not escape the same type of pressure themselves (see figure 5). The *Nāẓir-i Buyūtāt* was obviously checked and controlled from above by both the Shah and the Grand Vazir. At the same time, he was closely watched by his own chief assistant, the *Vazīr-i Buyūtāt.* In this connection the *Vazīr* was directly appointed by the Shah.

The *Mustawfī al-Mamālīk* was also subject to control by the Shah and the Grand Vazir. From below his power was to some degree circumscribed by both the *Mustawfī-yi Khāṣṣah* (not shown in figure 5) and the *Nāẓir-i Daftar.* The *Mustawfī-yi Khāṣṣah* was of less import than the *Mustawfī-yi Mamālīk,* however he did exert control over certain revenues of the *khāṣṣah.* The *Nāẓir-i Daftar* who headed the secretariat wielded the same kind of influence vis-à-vis the *Mustawfī* as he did in relation to the Grand Vazir. It must also be noted that relations between the *Mustawfī* and the *Nāẓir-i Buyūtāt* were characterized by that same intrinsic tension that marked Grand Vazir-*Nāẓir* relations and which was partly founded on the *khāṣṣah-dīvān* fissure.

Finally, the *Nāẓir-i Daftar-khānah* was also checked by forces above and below him. He was considered subordinate to the Shah, the Grand Vazir, and the *Mustawfī al-Mamālik.* Besides the influence that these officials exerted upon him, this *Nāẓir* was also subject to observation from within his own office. The *Dārūghah-i Daftar-khānah* settled disputes and maintained order in the secretariat thus sharing key authority there with the *Nāẓir.*

The above analysis reveals certain significant facts about the intricate workings of the Ṣafavī system of checks and balances. First of all, tension and checks were evident at virtually all points. The pressure was usually a two-way proposition moving in opposite directions within the same major channels (see figure 5). Thus, the Grand Vazir exerted great influence upon the *Mustawfī* and the two *Nāẓirs*; however, none of these three was without some kind of tool specifically designed to check some activity of the Grand Vazir. It is obvious that power was unevenly distributed, yet it is of prime importance to note that "those with least" often were systematically able to check "those with most." It is also clear that figure 5 represents more than an exposition of checks and balances between certain key offices. As was explained in two instances above, also implicitly present were the tensions between the *khāṣṣah* and *dīvān.* All of these checks and counterchecks were inextricably intertwined and lay at the heart of Ṣafavī politics.

Class and the Ṣafavī Web-System. The Ṣafavī administration was one example of the web-system as it bound and contained integrating conflict. It helped hold the class structure together through the mechanism of relationships analyzed above. Much to their own chagrin, the Grand Vazirs were often controlled by lower and middle bureaucrats who were average members of the middle class. The tensions and reciprocal power relations were ever present to seal and heal gaps and differences before they reached explosive proportions. Men of religious profession and mental ability constantly moved out of lower-class ranks by understanding and following the right lines of tension. They sometimes became an integral part of the upper class and political elite where they held great—but not too great—power. Once they joined the upper class as ṣadr or mujtahid, they found themselves surrounded by institutionalized enemies. In the realm of religion and justice, the ṣadr was always confronted by the mujtahid and vice versa. Whenever any upper-class official became so powerful that he threatened to widen the gap indefinitely between himself and the other power points or between his class and the other classes, he was quickly shorn of all power. This happened continually in Ṣafavī Iran in a multitude of different ways. The ṣadr who held not only religious-judicial power but great economic power as well is a case much in point. Those ṣadrs who managed to gather such influence that they threatened to upset the balance of the web-system were checked by measures ranging from the establishment of a two-ṣadr system to the outright dismissal of the particular threatening official.[73]

In terms of the central locus of the political system, i.e., the Shah, there was a concerted effort to keep the entire system functioning in terms of divided and dividing tension. Yet, there was constant pressure even on the Shah as influential individuals sporadically stirred from unquestioned monarchical allegiance to plot and bargain against the King. The latter was thus also bound tightly within this fluctuating network of personal power patterns.

The 20th-Century Pahlavi Network of Politics

The above analysis of selected areas of Ṣafavī politics has concentrated on the systemic relationships that marked the period. It is hypothesized here that these same relationships have carried over to the Pahlavi political system. A study of the latter complements the Ṣafavī analysis and completes the examination of the dynamics of the web-system which buttresses and vivifies the class structure.

The Pahlavi Web-System in Focus. In analyzing the Pahlavi web-system, it has been decided to select as the empirical focal point the national political elite as it existed in Iran between 1965–67. In this study, the political elite refers to the Shah and the thirty Iranians who are closest to him in terms of political influence. The members of this elite have been selected through interviews, observation, and on-the-spot study which included close relationships with many of those near the monarch. This study will not stand or fall on whether any particular individual is or is not a member of the elite since faces and personalities change with the wind. The point is, however, that there has always been an elite and the systemic relationships that have characterized it explain a great deal about the web-

73. Early Ṣafavī rulers appointed two men to the post of ṣadr in order to dilute the influence of one man. Early and obvious examples of this occurred at the beginning of the reign of Shāh Ṭahmāsb in the years 1524, 1529, and 1530. Significantly, Amīr Jalāl al-Dīn Muḥammad served as ṣadr under Shāh Ismāʿīl, but was forced to serve as joint-ṣadr at the beginning of the reign of Shāh Ṭahmāsb. See, Rūmlū, *Aḥsan al-Tavārīkh,* pp. 185, 224, 235. This division later became institutionalized when Shāh Sulaymān brought into being a *Ṣadr-i Khāṣṣah* and a *Ṣadr-i ʿĀmmah.* For an instance of the dismissal of an influential ṣadr following a bitter power struggle with the mujtahid of the day, see *ibid.,* p. 224.

system and class structure. The elite is, of course, nurtured in a class and springs from it.

Figure 6 provides a diagram view of the elite network as it surrounds the Shah who represents the heart of the system. Roughly the same diagram could be drawn to represent any Irano-Islamic political elite at any time (see, for example, figure 4).[74] In figure 6 which is nonhierarchical and therefore circular, names have been replaced by titles and occupational descriptions. The center of the diagram represents the Shah who is the vital power point in the system. The first concentric circle represents the heads of the various security and military organizations who have been located here because of the fact that they have organizations behind them. The second concentric circle represents the King's closest confidants and the third encompasses the close collaborators and ministers with direct periodic access. The personalities move back and forth from circle to circle (as well as in and out of the ring of circles) while the circles themselves move in and out pinwheel fashion. The solid lines represent conflicting tension that has been personally documented and power moves both ways along these indicated lines. More detailed analysis is required.

Systemic Conflict Examined. As figure 6 implies, there is existent two-way tension between virtually every power point. The more severe conflict is indicated and it is clear that this has involved personalities at every level. The figure introduces a division between "economic and political confidants" which simply means that the relationships between these individuals and the Shah are primarily economically or politically oriented. It is impossible to draw sharp lines between the two as the former often wield political influence and the latter economic influence. The "economic confidants" deal principally in contracting, banking, industry, and business and are represented by points 2, 15, 16, and 19 on figure 6. There has been extraordinary tension here and this has been reflected in struggles between the Tehran Chamber of Commerce and the Iranian Chamber of Mines and Industries on the one hand and the Distributors Cooperative Organization and High Council of Guilds on the other. This in turn represents a further tension between the bourgeois middle class and the industrial upper class although both sides are headed by two conflicting members of the political elite. The entire conflict stems from the struggle of the individuals con-

---

74. This can be easily done and documented, for example, in the case of the Qājār kings. Excellent sources are available in Persian. Two of the best are I'timād al-Salṭanah, *Rūznāmah-yi Khātirāt-i I'timād al-Salṭanah* [Daily Memoirs of I'timād al-Salṭanah] (Tehran, 1345/1966); and 'Abdullāh Mustawfī, *Sharḥ-i Zindigānī-yi Man yā Tārīkh-i Ijtimā'ī va Idārī-yi Dawrah-yi Qājārīyah* [The Story of My Life or the Social and Administrative History of the Qājār Period], 4 vols. (Tehran, 1324–26/1945–47). For a discussion that explicitly exposes these elite patterns in Qājār times, see James A. Bill, "Modernization and Reform from Above: The Case of Iran," *Journal of Politics* 32 (February 1970): 21-25. See also Colin Meredith, "The Development of the Early Qājār Bureaucracy," *Iranian Studies* 4 (1972).

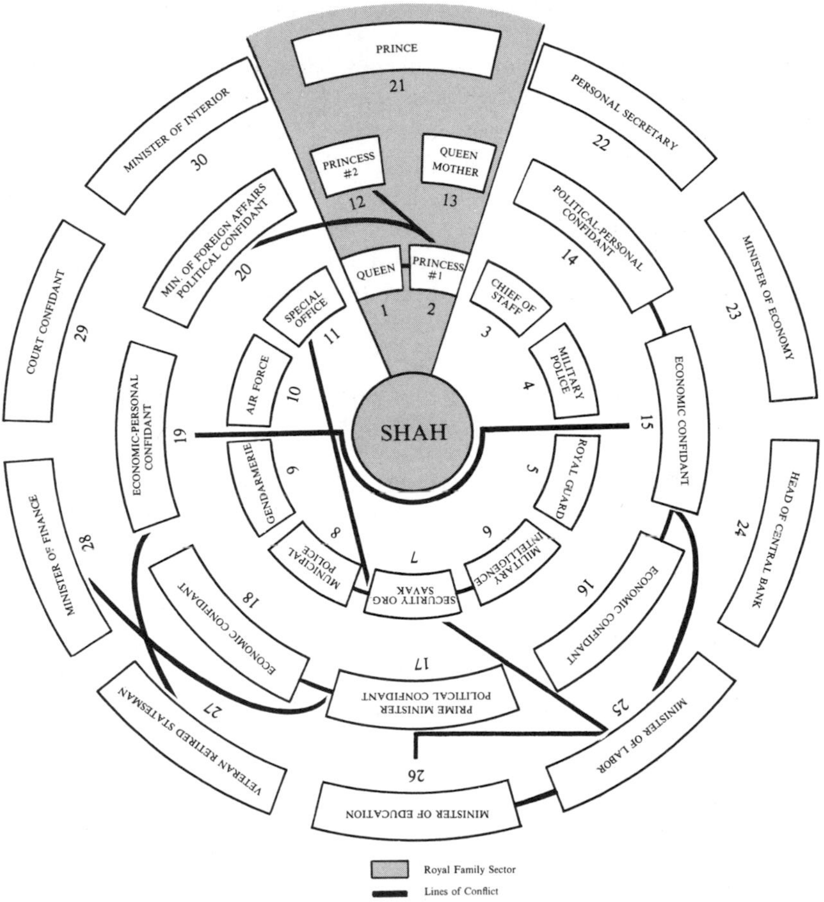

FIGURE 6

The Pahlavi Political Elite

cerned to gain greater favor with the Shah and at the same time to capture more control in the Iranian economic arena. Neither side has been able to gain supremacy over the other and victories are only temporary.

In the area of formal politics, a tight web of conflict centered around numbers 17, 25, 26, and 28 has been highlighted by basic tension between the Prime Minister and the Minister of Education. The latter faced the implacable opposition not only of the Prime Minister but also of the entire Iran Novin Party, as these forces tried to uproot him and destroy his influence. With the Shah's support, however, he managed for an incredibly long time to exert great power and to remain in the system as a balancing force.[75]

The royal family has itself been an apt microcosm of the web-system maintained through the most severe tensions. Examples of this are revealed in the segment of figure 6 reserved for the royal family and especially power points 1, 2, and 12 which represent two of the Shah's sisters and his wife. With the 1967 announcement of the Regency Plan in which the Queen was declared Regent, the relevant lines of tension drawn in figure 6 tightened considerably. The pressures of the continuous tensions involved, especially with regard to the same two sisters but a different wife, are described by the latter, the forceful Soraya.

> I also began to study psychology. I wanted to arrive at a closer understanding of the people about me. Since they were almost all acting a part, I was anxious to get behind their masks and to uncover the real motives for their behavior. I read many textbooks and for a time I even had a tutor who came to the house. He was one of the few trained psychologists in Persia, and he introduced me to the works of Charcot, Freud and Jung.[76]

The present Shah himself is more intimately bound in this web than in the national one where he has more control and influence. It is no secret that he has been checked and controlled to a surprising extent by the most powerful of his sisters.

The military-security web is one of the most complex and crucial networks and in figure 6 it is generally represented by numbers 3-11. Actually, there are at least ten power points involved here and they include the heads of the following organizations: (1) Security Organization *(Sāzmān-i Amniyat);* (2) Military Intelligence *(Rukn-i Du);* (3) Military Police *(Dizhbān);* (4) Imperial Guard; (5) Town and City Police *(Shahrbānī);* (6)

75. This conflict was well known in Tehran in the mid-1960s and the Persian press occasionally hinted at it. See, for example, the special political edition of *Irādah-yi Āẕarbāyjān,* 27 Isfand-5 Tīr, 1345–46/March 1967, esp. p. 5. By 1970, this particular line of tension had been broken as the Ministry of Education was divided into two ministries and the Minister described was removed from his position. The new lines of tension that formed in the wake of this disruption existed between the two educational ministries at one level and then between these ministries and the Ministry of Court and Tehran University at another level.

76. *The Autobiography of H. I. H. Princess Soraya,* translated from the German by Constantine Fitzgibbon (London: Arthur Barker, 1963), especially pp. 82-83. This book provides an extraordinary view of a vital web-system at work. See pp. 44-49, 53, 70-83. For a sophisticated analysis by a contemporary Iranian scholar of the persistent rivalry that pervades interpersonal relations in Iran, see Dr. N. Ṣāḥib al-Zamānī, *Rāz-i Kirishmah-hā* [The Play of the Mind] (Tehran, 1341/1962), esp. pp. 62-68, 281-89.

Gendarmerie or Rural Police; (7) Minister of War; (8) Chief of Staff; (9) Commander of the Air Force; and (10) Special Office *(Daftar-i Vīzhah).* These positions are held by senior officers of various grade, all of whom have proven their loyalty to the Shah over a period of many years.[77] It is here that the system of checking tensions can be seen at its best as all ten of these particular power points are knit together in common rivalry. Each individual reports *immediately* to the monarch not only with regard to routine business but with regard to the activities of the other nine personalities as well. This checking and cross-checking provides the central point with a prismatic view of the overall military-security activity and situation.

The checking system is intricate. The perennial struggle between the heads of the Security Organization and Military Intelligence is well known and the presence of other persistently threatening power points builds and at the same time lessens and distributes the tension. The Deputy Head of the Security Organization has been at the same time the Head of the "Special Office" which is the Shah's own private capsule-reporting security office. This particular individual has been a classmate and lifetime friend of the Monarch and one of the quieter and less known powers in Iran for years. He is, however, only *assistant* to the director of the Security Organization and as such takes orders from him. There have been great tension and rivalry between these men with both reporting the other's activities to the King. There is little doubt that in the end the Security Organization chief runs his establishment and has not allowed the other man to take over in any way despite his closeness to the Shah. The latter presides over and permits this tension to balance itself, apparently well aware that neither side will become a threatening power in such circumstances. This example is one which indicates the manner in which tension and conflict exist among power points. The pattern is strikingly similar to the Ṣafavī story.

A further example of rivalry as it exists within a particular power point concerns the Chief of Staff. The situation has been such that there were *two* four-star generals (*artishbuds*) in Iran. One was *slightly* more influential for he was titled Chief of Staff. For a number of years those involved were Generals Ariyānā and Ḥijāzī, the latter being Chief of Staff. In 1966, Ḥijāzī was considered a little too powerful and threatening in other ways and as a result he was suddenly retired. Ariyānā immediately took his place and another was promptly promoted to the position vacated by Ariyānā. In this way, the individual who threatened to disrupt the balance of rivalry was

77. A relevant example is four-star General Air Force Commander Muḥammad Khātamī. In 1953 when the Shah was forced to flee the country, *Major* Khātamī was the pilot who flew the escape craft. Khātamī later improved his connections when he married the Shah's sister Fāṭimah.

quickly cut out of the system and the tension was immediately reestablished.[78]

The military-security web is itself tightly intertwined with the entire political elite web and an excellent case in point concerned a bitter conflict that took place between the same Security Organization head referred to above and the Minister of Labor of the time. The Minister of Labor was also Secretary-General of the Iran Novin Party and had three brothers with high positions in the Gendarmerie, the Military Court of Justice, and the Ministry of Foreign Affairs. The struggle became intense and the tension severe as both sides had numerous connections through the system. Not only were the Security Organization and the Ministry of Labor involved but also the Iran Novin and Mardum Parties, the Gendarmerie, the Court of Military Justice, and the Police. Both sides were able to generate enough power and influence to hold the rivalry in balancing existence and thus the tension continued unabated.

This particular web points up several other interesting propositions including the fact that all of these power points are manned by individuals who are profoundly insecure. They have all come to realize that loyalty, competence, and service do not necessarily insure them of their position, but that becoming too popular or too unpopular or too powerful or too weak are also vital variables. The most trusted and loyal (and powerful) of generals such as Vus̱ūq, Hidāyat, and Ḥijāzī have been suddenly retired and pushed aside. Otherwise puzzling relationships immediately become explainable in terms of such a web-system. Former friends and close associates upon gaining important influence in the political elite abruptly become fierce rivals (figure 6—rivalry between 17-18). Even the incredibly powerful work overtime not only to build their own networks of influence domestically but also to build international ties and support (figure 6—particularly points 15, 20, 30).

The Dawrah: Confluence of Personal and Group Relations

The dynamics of individual and group relationships as they have been presented above intertwine in an instructive manner in what the Iranians term the *dawrah.* A brief analysis of this phenomenon can help in general

78. The prevalence of this pattern has been documented twice since the 1966 incident. In May 1969, Ariyānā lost his position and was replaced by the popular and capable Firaydūn Jam. As Chief of Staff, Jam became too influential and he in turn lost his position in July 1971. The demotion of Jam and his subsequent appointment as Ambassador to Spain stunned and surprised close observers of Iran. Within our theoretical perspective, however, it was entirely predictable. This balancing rivalry at the highest echelons of the Iranian military organization necessitates the periodic retirement of Chiefs of Staff. The stronger and more capable the particular individual is, the shorter will be his term in office. Jam, therefore, survived only two years in the position.

to clarify power relationships and in particular the effect of individual and group patterns upon class linkages.

The exercise of power in Iran has been marked by the fact that it has been largely done informally[79] and very personally and the lines of tension that have been termed the web-system move in this manner. Figures 4, 5, and 6 support this hypothesis as each power point, formal office, or title has been represented by a particular personality or group of personalities. Committees, commissions, associations, and formal organizations have never been prevalent and where they existed they have not operated as such. They have been characterized by fissures, arguments, inactivity, personalism, and, in general, by organizational chaos. Even professional organizations such as the Iranian Medical and Bar Associations have been little more than gatherings characterized by strife and factionalism.[80] The more subtle, intricate, and complex facets of tension and rivalry do not thrive in a formal setting where votes are counted and minutes recorded. In such organizations, one must take stands, submit to chairmen, presidents, and moderators, cooperate with others one does not really trust, open oneself to much unnecessary criticism, and bind oneself to time schedules, rules, and procedures.

Informality prevails and this is best seen by the huge network of cliques here termed the dawrah system. A dawrah is an informal group of people who *always* meet periodically *usually* rotating the meeting place among the membership.[81] In fact, there is a great divergence among dawrahs and the looseness of the dawrah system can only be matched by that of each individual dawrah. There are professional dawrahs, gambling dawrahs,[82] religious dawrahs, student dawrahs, family dawrahs, political dawrahs, intellectual dawrahs, and former-classmate dawrahs. Some dawrahs have names, most do not. Some are attended by both men and women; outside of family dawrahs, most are not. Some meet weekly, others fortnightly or

79. From the point of view of Iran and the Iranian, this has been very *formal* and in describing such politics in terms of *in*formality we view it from a Western frame of reference. In this sense, informal as used in this section is a culture-bound term. We, nonetheless, use the term since it connotes a certain looseness of organization despite the fact that in an Iranian's mind this may be quite formal indeed.

80. Important exceptions here are the Bahā'ī and Zoroastrian religious and the Armenian and Jewish ethnic organizations. Even Freemasonry in Iran is not as highly organized and tightly knit as similar organizations elsewhere.

81. *Dawrah* is a Persian word usually translated as "cycle." Strictly speaking then a dawrah is a cyclical meeting which gathers periodically rotating the place of meeting. The dawrah as treated here is a largely urban phenomenon although the peasants and villagers do have periodic informal meetings at the local teahouses, etc.

82. The gambling dawrah has become one of the most popular kinds of dawrah. Gambling clubs sprung up all over Tehran in the 1960s and by 1970 there were close to 100 of them. For two interesting articles in this regard see Shāhrukh Jinābiyān, "Rīshah-hā-yi Ravānī va Ijtimā'ī-yi Qumār dar Īrān" [The Psychological and Social Roots of Gambling in Iran], *Masā'il-i Īrān,* 3rd yr., Nos. 8-9 (1965–66): 237-42, 286-90.

monthly. Some meet only for one purpose (for example, to gamble), most do not. Some dawrahs have closed membership, others are open to friends of the members. Some Iranians belong to only one dawrah, many Iranians belong to several dawrahs, few urban inhabitants of Iran belong to no dawrahs. All of the personalities at the power points in the Pahlavi political elite have dawrahs and this includes the Shah himself.[83]

The dawrah system is deeply rooted in Iranian history where it took differing and fluctuating forms. Among the more general manifestations of this phenomenon were loose gatherings of clerics and businessmen. For example, there would be regular meetings of all the Shīrāzī businessmen residing in Tehran (Shīrāzīhā dar Tehran). There have also been the famous *khāngāh*s which were a type of continuous dawrah where the darvīshes and Ṣūfī leaders would sit and preach and different groups would come and go. The *qahvahkhānah*s and *chā'īkhānah*s (coffee and teahouses) were important meeting places and still are throughout Iran. Coffeehouses first became prevalent in Iran during the Ṣafavī period when they served as centers of recreation, story-telling, and social and political discussion. During the nineteenth century, the emphasis of coffeehouse organization shifted to a greater concern for commercial and business affairs. Today, there are well over two thousand coffeehouses in Tehran and many tend to be attended according to an identity of occupational interest. For example, bricklayers, butchers, masons, musicians, painters, plasterers, real estate dealers, tile workers, and cobblers each have particular coffeehouses that they attend regularly. In south Tehran, coffeehouse attendance and guild membership often overlap as less formal and more formal group formations intertwine.[84]

It is the dawrah system and informal net of groups which has been the scene of important business, political or otherwise. The dawrah system can be considered both as a kind of web-system itself and as the vehicle through which the rivalries and conflicts pass. The important bargaining, negotiating, and decision making takes place at the card table, in the garden, or on a hike. Dawrahs in the form of *farāmūshkhānah*s (nineteenth-century Masonic groups) and various *anjuman*s ("societies") were vital to the constitutional movement. In the realm of contemporary politics, the present political elite and other high-ranking civil bureaucratic officials have been to a surprising degree staffed by members of two dawrahs formed since the

83. Iranian kings have a tradition of dawrahs and during Qājār times they met in what was called the *khalvat*. This was a social gathering of the Shah and his closest male advisors. Nāṣir al-Dīn Shāh's *khalvat* met practically every day when they would read history, French newspapers, and carry on extended discussions. Shāh Muḥammad Riẓā Pahlavī also has his dawrahs which include, among others, a family dawrah, bowling dawrah, and gambling dawrah.

84. Khusraw Khusruvī, "Muṭāli'ah-yi dar bārah-yi qahvahkhānah-hā" [A Study of the Coffeehouses], *Kāvish,* 1st yr., No. 9 (Bahman, 1341/February, 1963): 84-92.

mid-1950s.[85] These are the older *Gurūh-i Īrān-i Naw* (New Iran Group) and the more recently established *Kānūn-i Taraqqī* (Progressive Club). Both dawrahs were made up of highly trained and educated middle- and upper-class members. The New Iran Group represented names such as Āmūzigār, Rām, Anṣārī, and Farmānfarmāiyān and nearly forty percent of its membership were employed at one time by the United States Point IV program. Its members have been slowly working their way into the political elite ever since. The Progressives have worked faster and have gained more high positions largely because their dawrah became the core of the Iran Novin Party. The Progressives were organized by former Prime Minister Manṣūr and represent names like Huvaydā, Nahāvandī, and Hidāyatī. The story of these two dawrahs highlights the significance of informal relationships not only to the constantly changing political elite but to the entire Iranian political system as well. It is also vitally important to note that both of these dawrahs were staffed largely by individuals of the new professional middle class. Here they made close contact with the upper class represented by the Manṣūrs and Farmānfarmāiyāns and then proceeded to move themselves into the ruling class.

The relationship between the formal political system, for example, and the dawrah system has been extremely important. In times of particularly overbearing political systems, the dawrah system would spread its tentacles which would continue to grow and multiply. At times, the leaders of the formal system would strike out hacking at the dawrah system which they would not tolerate.[86]

The leaders of other formal political systems in Iran have tried to debilitate the dawrah system by infiltrating it and eating away at it from the inside. This has been the method of Muḥammad Riẓa Shāh through the medium of a crowded secret police organization. In 1961, for example, eight middle-class Iranian friends and scholars met and formed a dawrah to discuss sociopolitical issues. They agreed upon certain areas of concern and mimeographed a confidential one-page statement presenting their mutual opposition to corruption, injustice, and oppression. Each member took a copy and the rest were locked away. Five months later, the Chief of the Secret Police called in one of the men and confronted him with a copy of

85. The individuals at points 17, 24, 25, 26, 28, and 30 of figure 6 were members of these dawrahs while four times this number hold other high posts in the system.

86. This was the prevalent method under Riẓā Shāh. Even dawrahs of Iranians that met outside of Iran felt the effects of this campaign. During this period, a group of socially conscious but frustrated individuals formed a dawrah they named *Ḥizb-i Khar* (The Jackass Party). They argued that the knowledgeable in Iran were being constantly punished, therefore it was best to pretend to be donkeys. One former member explained that a donkey even though it has some intelligence is forever considered an ass. Many prominent scholars and intellectuals were members of good standing in the *Ḥizb-i Khar*.

the statement. It was one of the original eight copies. The dawrah broke up immediately. This kind of occurrence explains a great deal about the secret police and the dawrah system, but it also sheds light on one of the major reasons why social interaction in Iran is extremely informal. In the episode described, there was one real element of organization and formality—the printed statement. And this was the evidence that was used to destroy the dawrah and to threaten the lives of its members. These tactics have, in fact, tended to wither some of the strands of the dawrah web or have steered discussion in other strands away from politics. Despite this, however, such activities have yet to damage the web seriously.

It is evident that the systemic tensions of the Pahlavi web flow in stabilizing informality with each power point constantly constructing its own informal network. This tends to keep many of the rivalries hidden which in itself lessens dangerous encounters and imbalances. Mechanisms like the dawrah encourage plotting and omnipresent interlaced antagonisms but discourage concentrated and shattering confrontations. Finally, a system of such informal politics thins and splinters opposition although it at the same time covers and hides the same.

The above study of the relationships that compose the Pahlavi political elite-web-system is closely related to the shape of the Iranian class structure. As was concluded in the case of the Ṣafavī administration, the critical impact of the web-system upon the class structure has been interclass movement and mobility. Of the thirty members of the political elite other than the Shah, fifteen are of upper-class origin and fifteen are of low-middle- and middle-class origin. This indicates that one-half of the elite was absorbed from classes other than the ruling class. Even those of upper-class background are relatively newly arrived here as would be expected in a dynasty two men deep. Muḥammad Riẓā Shāh himself is just one generation removed from the lower classes. Pareto's and Michels's theories on elite circulation take on interesting significance when viewed in terms of such class structures where there is much more than circulation at stake. The described tensions and rivalries within the elite include all levels and cross class lines as power points seek to reinforce their positions while at the same time members of the lower classes seek to better theirs. The Islamic-induced channels described above are in fluctuating availability, while the elite members strive to create personal webs by assisting lower-class individuals to join them and thus the ruling class. Unremitting tensions within the political elite demand this while interclass tension facilitates it (the intellectual or bureaucrat pushing for an elite position). The extremes of this are represented by the Shah who is an unparalleled master of controlled mobility and individuals such as the Mardum Party official who in February 1967, stated before a large gathering in northern Iran: "We Iranians have two

Gods. One is the heavenly God and the other is the earthly God. The latter is our almighty Shāhanshāh."[87] This is all part of systemic patterns that are intertwined and interlaced, but are always in flux and which serve to knit together a class structure that would otherwise be very brittle. The dawrah system is another indicator of this since members of all classes have their dawrahs. Although the dawrah system often follows the class structure and membership is drawn from only one social class, there are many other examples of dawrahs that draw membership from more than one class. Interclass dawrahs are especially common between the middle and upper class and they can always be found in cases where the major organizing principle has been religion, ethnic similarity, or school camaraderie. Such interclass dawrahs are of deep significance for in themselves they represent the web-system's effect on the class structure.

Irano-Islamic Class Relations and Political Change

Class relationships in Islamic Iran have been characterized by reciprocal power exchanges in which the conflicting aggregates remain hierarchically imbalanced. A special resiliency has been built into this structure through personal and group relationships that have been termed the web-system. The latter represents a situation where the power advantage continually shifts back and forth between competing groups and individuals. These relationships have been at the heart of Ṣafavī politics no less than Pahlavi politics and have covered the class structure in the manner of a net-like screen. Class relationships themselves have been shaped and molded by this as an instinctively (and sometimes consciously) controlled movement-mobility has always been in evidence.[88] This has resulted in a structure in which classes are reciprocally related and incessant conflict is filtered and softened. Thus it is that the symbol of Islamic Iran, the wise 'Alī, can speak in the same breath both of the inevitability of a class structure and the extraordinary importance of the principles of equality and social mobility.

---

87. Speech by the Director-General of Organization for the Mardum Party, Bandar Pahlavī, February 17, 1967.

88. At the same time, much of what has been explained in terms of the Iranian class structure may very well apply to other Islamic countries and possibly to other Asian societies as well. In an analysis of Thailand's politics and administration, for example, Fred W. Riggs describes the traditional Thai social structure as a "sticky class system"—a term that seems tailored to the Iranian situation. Professor Riggs writes: "The Siamese system seems to have been neither a caste-like closed system, nor open enough to encourage easy mobility." See F. W. Riggs, *The Ecology of Public Administration* (London: Asia Publishing House, 1961), p. 66.

In relating the various post-Ṣafavī dynastic changes to power relationships, one can come to understand a great deal about both. Emphasis will be placed upon relating the rise and fall of dynasties to the changing pattern of class relationships.

The relationships of reciprocal and balanced exchange transactions have dominated the political system in each of the five dynastic periods. This has already been demonstrated in depth with regard to the Safavī and Pahlavi systems (see figures 4 and 6). Toward the end of the rule of particular dynasties throughout Iranian history, these patterns snapped as political forces shattered the traditional relationships. Challenging individuals or groups overturned the delicate power balance through the accumulation of capabilities enabling them to overwhelm and absorb their competitors. They at the same time threatened that force who stood as the preeminent guardian of these traditional patterns—the Shah. The accumulation of aggrandizing power led directly to tension with the monarch as successive triumphs in political engagements could only concern the one who traditionally protected the division of power. However, it was often the very failure of the Shah to perform this function effectively that led to the disruptive imbalance. The periods when the traditional patterns broke down around the personality of a particular Shah were times of violence, bloodshed, and war.

The falls of the Ṣafavī, Zand, and Qājār dynasties were preceded in each case by demands of several key power points against the Shah. These individuals or groups became very powerful and refused to accept their roles as passive emanations of a King. They confronted the monarch concerned in a reciprocal relationship while the monarch sought to retain a unilateral relationship. In Ṣafavī times, the key forces involved were located in the religious structure as well as in the ḥaram. The challengers in the Zand period were factions in the tribal group itself, while the Qājārs were beset by the numerous groups that fought the Tobacco Concession and demanded a constitution. The pattern of the brief Nādirī period was somewhat different as the monarch himself subordinated rule by maneuver and balanced tension to rule by naked force. Much of the reason for this was that his reign marked a campaign of conquest which could brook little internal dissension. All potential political contenders were indiscriminately subjected (even the heir apparent was blinded) and the period came to an end with the assassination of Nādir Shāh himself.

The fall of each particular Iranian dynasty involved a breakdown of the traditional patterns of balanced and reciprocal tension. This occurred when particular networks of competing individuals clustered about the person of the Shah disintegrated as power linkages broke. It is of vital importance to note, first, that in every case these traditional patterns reasserted themselves with the establishment of a new dynasty and political elite. Second, although certain *group* and *individual* relationships snapped, class relationships remained fundamentally unchanged. Thus, *at the class level,* linkages never shattered despite the fact that certain vital personal political relationships were torn. When the Sāsānian Empire crumbled, however, class relationships also ruptured and the period of violence that followed was marked by class upheaval.

As was the case in the four preceding dynasties, the Pahlavi political system has been dominated by power networks preserved by reciprocity and stabilizing conflict. Although Iranian politics are still governed by this type of relationship, there have been series of crises in which new forces have entered the system. These forces include new classes that now challenge the traditional relationships and do so at the crucial class level. The political elite has responded to this threat in many ways, including a concerted attempt to convince the members of these classes that the traditional relationships work to their advantage. More dramatic has been the Shah's move to strengthen those classes and forces that tend to support the traditional web-system. The White Revolution must be seen in these terms. The following chapters will analyze such questions and policies in depth as our study focuses upon one of these new classes—the professional-bureaucratic intelligentsia.

chapter two

The Professional-Bureaucratic Intelligentsia: The New Class

Through the centuries, the Irano-Islamic class structure was knit together in a persistent pattern of reciprocal, uneven relationships. Despite periodic breakdowns of individual and group power patterns, classes interacted with one another according to an enduring linkage of imbalanced tension. With the turn of the twentieth century, however, occasional harbingers of a new class began to appear on the social scene. During the constitutional movement, a small number of personalities representing new values came to the fore. These men boasted a modern education (at that time, necessarily foreign), stressed liberal goals, and demanded radical reform. Although these voices were soon smothered, the founder of the next dynasty, Riẕā Shāh Pahlavī (1925–41), planted seeds that were to grow and to blossom unexpectedly into a new social class. By the middle 1940s and early 1950s, this class was well enough formed to have become a critical and explosive new force in the Iranian class system.

Riẕā Shāh Pahlavī was a nonrevolutionary reformer who strove to introduce enough change to make Iran a more respected society in the world community. It would at the same time become a society worth ruling. He never intended that there be fundamental change, for the traditional class structure had to remain. The only major modification was that the Pahlavi family be at the center of the new ruling class. Although there were any number of dramatic programs and spectacular reforms, the changes that had a continuing, accelerating, and largely unintended effect were in the related areas of administration and education.[1] It was in the field of education, however, where the vital step was taken, for even the administrative reforms were based on changes in that area. Riẓā Shāh determined that Iran should break away from its traditional system of education which centered on the cleric-controlled *maktab*s and *madrasah*s. The former were nongraded elementary schools stressing reading, writing, and the Koran, while the latter represented higher education and concentrated on Arabic, religious law, rhetoric, and the Koran. Method was rote memorization.

Under Riẓā Shāh, a system of public education was established. In 1928, the Majlis passed a law providing that one hundred top secondary school students be sent abroad annually to acquire a university education. These returnees, who totaled more than six hundred, helped staff the newly established Tehran University. They were the core of a new middle class.

By way of introduction, it is necessary to point out that the professional-bureaucratic intelligentsia is a new class composed of individuals who rest their power position upon employment utilizing those skills and talents which they possess thanks to a modern education. This is a nonbourgeois middle class many of whose members relate themselves to the other classes and the system through function, performance, and service rather than through material wealth, family ties, or property. The members of this class are engaged in professional, technical, cultural, intellectual, and administrative occupations and are by and large a salaried middle class.[2]

---

1. See Amin Banani, *The Modernization of Iran, 1921–1941* (Stanford: Stanford University Press, 1961).

2. There has been an unfortunate proclivity in available English literature on Iran to deny, ignore, and belittle the appearance of any middle class in that society. In 1963, Donald Wilber chided "foreign commentators" who wrote that "the urban middle class of Iran holds the key to the future of Iran." He went on to argue that "the Iranians themselves have given almost no attention to the subject." See *Contemporary Iran* (New York: Frederick A. Praeger, 1963), p. 159.

By far the most prescient study concerning the important Iranian middle class was introduced by T. Cuyler Young in "The Social Support of Current Iranian Policy," *Middle East Journal* 6 (Spring 1952):128-43. For an excellent analysis of the role of the middle class in a provincial Iranian setting, see Paul Ward English, *City and Village in Iran: Settlement and Economy in the Kirman Basin* (Madison: University of Wisconsin Press, 1966), pp. 74-76, 80-81, 98-99. In 1963, we called special attention to the significance of the professional-bureaucratic intelligentsia in Iran. See J. A. Bill, *Middle East Journal* 17: 400-18. For the most extensive study of this new middle class and its role in Middle Eastern politics, see M. Halpern, *The Politics of Social Change in the Middle East and North Africa* (Princeton: Princeton University Press, 1963), pp. 51-78. For one of the earliest analyses of the importance of the new middle class in the developing areas, see V. V. Aspaturian, "The Challenge of Soviet Foreign Policy and the Defense of the Status Quo" (paper prepared for delivery at the 1961 Annual Meeting of the American Political Science Association, St. Louis, Missouri, September 6-9, 1961).

The new middle class is profoundly different from the traditional middle classes not only in composition but also in the relationships that link it to all classes in society. In the Afro-Asian world, the basic distinction is the one that separates this professional middle class from the better-known and publicized bourgeois middle class. In the West, it was the bourgeois middle class that first dominated a transforming social structure. When the intelligentsia became for the first time the majority of the middle class, it was heralded with uncertainty and dismay.[3] In the countries of Eastern Europe and the Soviet Union, this class has taken a particular shape that is alternately termed "intellectual" and "bureaucratic." Most of the time it is referred to as the "new class."[4]

In the nonindustrialized world, this new class has developed either in conjunction with or in place of the entrepreneurial middle class. During the 1955 session of the International Institute of Differing Civilizations held in London, the topic of discussion was "Development of a Middle Class in Tropical and Sub-Tropical Countries." The studies of North Africa and the Middle East indicated that the professional-bureaucratic intelligentsia was becoming a vital and expanding force in those areas. The situation in Latin America was shown to be quite similar in this respect, while in sub-Sahara Africa the signs of an indigenous middle class of any kind are only now beginning to appear. Southeast Asia's middle classes are still dominated by entrepreneurship and trade, although the professional class has been steadily expanding among the indigenous groups.[5] The developing societies are marked by the increasing growth in absolute and relative size of this professional-bureaucratic intelligentsia. This class is steadily surpassing the

---

Some interesting literature exists in Persian concerning this professional middle class. Among the most stimulating writings, one would have to include the following: Jamshīd Bihnām and Shāpūr Rāsikh, *Muqaddamah Bar Jāmi 'ahshināsīyi Īrān* [An introduction to the Sociology of Iran] (Tehran, 1344/1965), especially pp. 54-57; Jalāl Āl-i Aḥmad, "Rawshanfikr Chīst? Rawshanfikr Kīst?" [What Is an Intellectual? Who is the Intellectual?], *Jahān-i Naw,* Nos. 4 and 5 (Shahrīvar-Mihr, 1345/1966):15-32 and "Rawshanfikr Khudī-ast yā Bīgānah?" [Is the Intellectual One of Us or an Outsider?], *Jahān-i Naw,* (Ābān-Bahman, 1345/1966): 89-112; Riẓā Durūdiyān, "Masā'il-i Rushd-i Ṭabaqah-yi Mutavassiṭ" [Problems of Development of the Middle Class], *Masā'il-i Īrān,* 4th yr., No. 2 (1345/1966):28-33; and Dāriyūsh Humāyūn, "Ṭabaqah-yi Mutavassiṭ Kāfī Nīst" [The Middle Class Is Not Enough], *Masā'il-i Īrān,* 1st yr., No. 10 (1342/1963):488-90.

3. For a scholarly account of the development of this new middle class in Western society, see Hans Speier, *Social Order and the Risks of War* (New York: George W. Stewart, 1952), especially pp. 68-85. Another serious study in this regard is C. Wright Mills, *White Collar: The American Middle Classes* (New York: Oxford University Press, 1951).

4. See, for example, Milovan Djilas, *The New Class: An Analysis of the Communist System* (New York: Frederick A. Praeger, 1957).

5. Empirical evidence supporting these conclusions can be found in *Development of a Middle Class in Tropical and Sub-Tropical Countries, Record of the XXIX Session Held in London from 13-16 September 1955* (Brussels: International Institute of Differing Civilizations, 1956).

entrepreneurial middle class in growth and importance for many reasons. In a large proportion of the developing societies, the bourgeois class is dominated by foreigners and minority groups. This discourages and deflects the entry of the indigenous majority who seek mobility and advancement through other channels. Second, ruling classes (whether landlord-oriented or industrial-oriented) create demands and require services that are more the preserve of professionals and technicians than businessmen. This has become especially true in a world of increasing industrialization and specialization. Third, the growing demand for literacy and education has spiraled upward in a manner that has resulted in a proportionate and absolute increase in graduates at all levels. Finally, traditional education has tended to be primarily oriented toward the production of religious clerics and bureaucratic clerks. In contemporary Iran, for example, many young people are being deflected from these traditional occupations and are increasingly moving into professions such as law and teaching.

Despite this accelerating trend, the middle classes still generally account for less than ten percent of the total population in the developing areas.[6] The professional middle class is, of course, an even smaller percentage of this. In many ways then, the Iranian case is important, for in Iran the professional-bureaucratic intelligentsia has grown extremely rapidly. Despite the dynamic growth in urbanization and economic development which fosters bourgeois middle class expansion, the intelligentsia has managed to keep pace. As we will discover below, it has been expanding at a slightly more rapid rate than even the burgeoning bourgeoisie. The implications of this in terms of the political system and processes of change are profound. This middle class has created new relationships, demands, and imbalances which when analyzed may explain much, not only about Iran, but about the processes of change underway in other developing areas as well.

The Essence of the New Class

The new middle class is deliberately referred to as the "professional-bureaucratic intelligentsia" for several reasons.[7] Each term (i.e., "professional," "bureaucratic," and "intelligentsia") describes and explains this class and each emphasizes certain characteristics that are a part of it. The concept "professional" stresses the important characteristic of being highly skilled in a particular area or field. The fact that the members of this class rest their

6. *Ibid.*, p. 447.

7. The term "professional-bureaucratic intelligentsia" has been borrowed from the vocabulary of V. V. Aspaturian.

power on skill and talent rather than ownership, for example, distinguishes them from the bourgeois middle class. Also, the members of the "professions" are an important integral part of this new class. Thus, the term "professional middle class" will also be used to refer to this class.

The term "bureaucratic" also carries with it the idea that the members of this class are basically a nonentrepreneurial middle class. Although not members of the professions, bureaucrats are indeed an important part of this new middle class. Holding modern educations, they possess a certain amount of technical skill and dominate an important section of the governmental apparatus.

"Intelligentsia refers to all those who have obtained or are in the process of obtaining a modern higher education."[8] In this sense, students, although not yet professionals, are part of the intelligentsia. The term "intelligentsia" has been used rather than "intellectual" because this is not a class of intellectuals. The Iranian intellectual deals primarily in ideas and he "examines, ponders, wonders, theorizes, criticizes and imagines."[9] Although the intellectuals are a very important part of the intelligentsia, there are other vital groups involved. There is a "nonintellectual" intelligentsia that is more concerned with acting and doing and this includes technocrats, administrators, managers, and clerks. The intellectuals, on the other hand, are represented by students, teachers, professors, writers, and artists. The term "intelligentsia" will be used interchangeably with "professional-bureaucratic intelligentsia" and "professional middle class" to refer to this new class.

The following are five major characteristics that mark the Iranian intelligentsia.

1. *The members of a growing part of this class refuse to accept the traditional power relationships that dominate Iranian society.*

As such, they stand within Iranian society, but outside the key relationships that have characterized that society. This alienated intraclass group has, therefore, initiated a period of incoherence on the important class level and stands as a threat to the ongoing political system. In terms of our study, this is the principal and crucial characteristic and it will be discussed in more depth in the pages that follow.

---

8. Edward Shils defines *intellectuals* as "all persons with an *advanced modern education* and the intellectual concerns and skills ordinarily associated with it." For our purposes, this is much too broad a definition of intellectual even when applied to the "new states." See Shils, "The Intellectuals in the Political Development of the New States," *World Politics* 12 (April 1960): 332.

9. This phrase is Richard Hofstadter's. See *Anti-Intellectualism in American Life* (New York: Alfred A. Knopf, 1963), p. 25.

2. *The members of the intelligentsia possess or are in the process of acquiring a higher education (i.e., a modern or "new" education as opposed to the traditional maktab-madrasah education).*

This is an important characteristic for it was through the establishment of a new educational system that this class was born. Such a system did much to form the outlooks and to shape the relationships that characterize the members of the intelligentsia. The educational system has become the lifeline of this class. The manner in which this class has come into existence and the rapid growth that has marked it can be seen in statistics that reveal the burgeoning growth of Iranians studying in modern institutions of higher education in Iran.

The figures in table 1, however, tell only part of the story for an extremely significant part of the modern educational system is located outside of Iran. One out of every four Iranian college students is studying abroad. Of these, forty-one percent are in the United States, twenty-eight percent in West Germany, twelve percent in Great Britain, eight percent in Austria, seven percent in France, and six percent in Turkey.[10] Table 2 indicates the increasing trend in this regard and also reveals the extraordinarily high percentage of Iranians abroad as compared to four other Asian-Middle Eastern countries. M. Borhanmanesh writes that "Iran, with a population of six million less than that of Turkey and Egypt, has about three times as many students in the United States as either of these two countries."[11] This

TABLE 1

Number of Students in Institutions of Higher Education in Iran, 1922–70

Year	Number of Students
1922	91
1933-34	795
1943-44	2,835
1953-54	9,996
1963-64	24,456
1970	67,268

Sources: 1. Ministry of Labor, *Barrasī-hā-yi Masā'il-i Nīrū-yi Insānī* [Investigation of the Problems of Manpower] (Tehran, 1964), 3:2033, 2037. In Persian.
2. *Iran Almanac—1962* (Tehran: Echo of Iran, 1962), p. 303.
3. *Iran Almanac—1964-65* (Tehran: Echo of Iran, 1965), p. 508.
4. Ministry of Science and Higher Education, *Āmār-i Dānishjūyān-i Īrānī* [Statistics Concerning Iranian University Students] (Tehran, 1970), p. 5. In Persian.

10. Government of Iran, Ministry of Science and Higher Education, *Āmār-i Dānishjūyān-i Īrānī* [Statistics Concerning Iranian University Students] (Tehran, 1970), pp. 74-75.

11. Mohamad Borhanmanesh, "A Study of Iranian Students in Southern California" (unpublished Ed.D. dissertation, University of California at Los Angeles, 1965), p. 47.

TABLE 2

Number and Rate of Increase of Students Abroad from Five Near Eastern and Asian Countries in Eighteen Host Countries from 1955–61[a]

Country	Population	Number of Students Studying in Major Host Countries		Increase in Students from 1955-56 to 1960-61		Number of Students Abroad per 100,000 of Population
		1955-56	1960-61	Number	Percent	
Iran	20,678,000	2,818	7,610	4,782	170	37
Philippines	27,455,799	1,740	1,954	214	12	7
Thailand	26,257,916	1,004	1,428	424	42	5
Turkey	27,818,248	1,308	2,533	1,225	93	9
United Arab Republic	26,085,326	1,568	3,826	2,258	144	14

[a]Host Countries: Australia, Austria, Belgium, Canada, Czechoslovakia, France, India, Italy, Japan, Netherlands, Poland, Senegal, Spain, Switzerland, United Arab Republic, United Kingdom, United States, and West Germany.

Source: *Study Abroad,* Statistical Tables, UNESCO, 1955 to 1960–61, quoted in Mohamad Borhanmanesh, "A Study of Iranian Students in Southern California" (unpublished Ed.D. dissertation, University of California at Los Angeles, 1965), p. 44.

domestic-foreign division is an important one for although the modern Iranian educational process has meant a decided break with the old system of language, religion, rhetoric, and memory, it nonetheless still carries some of the traditional traits which are not present outside of Iran. A 1964 survey of one hundred Iranian secondary school students yielded interesting results concerning the break involved here. To the statement that "schools instead of concentrating on hypothetical subjects and memory should pay more attention to scientific techniques," ninety-six percent of the sample agreed. However, seventy-eight percent also accepted the next proposition that "for a person to succeed well in his studies memory is more useful than logic and reasoning."[12] The contemporary Iranian educational system is an eclectic model of Iranian, French, and American traits and, although confused and shaky, it nevertheless represents a radical departure from what went before. The products of this new system, along with the graduates of foreign universities returned to Iran (numbering nearly five thousand between 1955–65 alone), have composed the rapidly expanding professional-bureaucratic intelligentsia. This nontraditional education has contributed to many of the characteristics that stamp this new class as profoundly different from any of its predecessors. Some examples follow.

3. *The power position of the members of this class resides primarily in the skill or talent that they possess due to their modern formal education.*

It does not rest on the ownership of property or the possession of wealth and it rests less and less upon connection or manipulative ability. When these considerations are still the overriding ones, then it is often the upper class (and, in some instances, the bourgeois middle class) that is involved. A corollary of this characteristic involves the fundamental issue of merit versus *pārtī* ("connection" or "pull"), for it follows that advancement for the members of this class must be determined by amount of skill and degree of achievement. Although this problem will be discussed in following chapters, it is quite clear that rewards and priorities commensurate to talent and achievement might very well be expected by the members of this class.

4. *The members of the professional-bureaucratic intelligentsia have been exposed in varying degrees to outside philosophies, thoughts, and ideas.*

In many cases (perhaps most), the understanding of non-Iranian and non-Islamic fields of thought has not been very deep. Nonetheless, there has

12. This survey was directed by the Institute for Educational Research and Studies in Tehran. A random sample of one hundred completed questionnaires was graciously provided for purposes of our analysis.

been an awareness and an open-mindedness to alien systems of thought that has in itself been a profound switch from the days when the middle classes were anchored to a final revelation. The great and sudden awareness of other sociopolitical systems and philosophies was quite dramatic and created a backlash that led to expressions such as *fukulī* ("he who wears a tie") and *gharbzadigī* ("western-struck"). *Fukulī* was a pejorative term borrowed from the French to refer to those Iranians who dressed in Western clothing, but understood little either about Iran or about the West. A *fukulī* was an Iranian "dude."[13] Many members of the Iranian intelligentsia became so obsessed with Western ideas and culture that certain writers turned on them and thus Āl-i Aḥmad's well-known book, *Gharbzadigī.* During the 1940s and early 1950s, the influence of Marxist philosophy dominated the thinking of the intelligentsia. At the height of Tūdah influence, he who carried the Tūdah newspaper *Mardum* was considered an intellectual. The members of the new middle class are alert and aware and their interests are wide-ranging.

5. *The members of this class are free of any rigid religious dogmatism and of any blind worship of past history.*

The Iranian intelligentsia has very decidedly discarded old values and value systems. Indeed, one result of this has been an intellectual wandering in continuous search of a new framework. That which was sacred to the traditional middle classes is either ignored or attacked by the new class which is little impressed by either history or prophets. It is perhaps natural that the secularization of the educational process would result in a different view of Shī'ī Islam. The result has been a sharp move away from this most basic of value systems which organized all phases of a Muslim's life. Thus, a mujtahid stated in 1967 that whenever he spoke and worked with university students, he left his *'ammāmah* (turban) at home and wore only a plain suit. The students of today, he pointed out, had little respect for the cleric.[14] Within the intelligentsia in general, there is a deep sense that Islam represents an alien intrusion forced upon Iranians by foreign invaders. It is often stated that the social problems of Iran stem from the Islamic intrusion.

In the move away from Islam, large numbers of the intelligentsia have embraced Bahā'ism, a religion that demands great commitment but at the same time claims progressive and liberal goals.[15] Others have turned not only against Islam but also against religion and any idea of a Deity. Perhaps most of them maintain a vague loyalty to Shī'ism, 'Alī, the Prophet, and

13. Khosrow Mostofi, *Aspects of Nationalism* (Salt Lake City: University of Utah Research Monograph No. 3, 1964), p. 46.

14. Personal interview, May 16, 1967.

15. Bahā'ism is a religion born in Iran in the mid-nineteenth century. It has always been considered a dangerous heresy by practicing Shī'ites.

the Divine. At the same time, however, they readily admit that they are not "practicing Shīʿīs" and that they neither fast nor say the daily prayers. The members of the professional middle class are no longer bound by dogmas and certainties and having severed all such ties they represent a searching and floating force. They have little interest in a past they were never a part of and less interest in the gods of that past.

These are five major traits of the Iranian intelligentsia. Some are shared with other contemporary classes, but no other class possesses all five. There are many other characteristics that mark this new class and this will become evident as this study unfolds. Among them is a basic concern for education, justice, security, and efficiency. This class has also exhibited an extraordinary growth rate and this requires brief examination.

The Size of the New Class

The first comprehensive statistical surveys of Iranian society were begun in the mid-1950s. These studies provide information that is indispensable in ascertaining the size and growth of the professional middle class. Table 1 which offers a fifty-year view of the growth of higher education in Iran tells the more general story of the development of this class. Although the trend revealed here is quite accurate, the reference is nonetheless indirect and incomplete. Two comparative analyses, therefore, will provide us with a more reliable understanding of the size and growth of the new middle class. The first rests on two detailed studies of Iranian government employees carried out in 1956 and 1963.[16] These surveys examine the educational background of government employees of the various ministries and agencies and allow one to compare the growth of the professional middle class in the bureaucracy. The other comparison is based on information drawn from the 1956 and 1966 official censuses and reveals the approximate size of this class in Iranian society.[17]

The greatest concentration of the professional-bureaucratic intelligentsia is found in the governmental apparatus and especially in the Ministry of

---

16. Ministry of Interior, General Statistics Office, *Nashrīyah-yi Āmār-i Kārmandān-i Dawlat* [Publication of Government Employee Statistics], Tīr 1335/1956; and Plan Organization, Iranian Statistical Center, *Natāyij-i Āmārgīrī-yi Kārmandān-i Dawlat* [Results of the Census of Government Employees], Āẕar 1342/1963. Hereafter cited as Ministry of Interior, *Government Employee Statistics, 1956* and Plan Organization, *Government Employee Statistics, 1963.*

17. The two census reports are: Ministry of Interior, *National and Province Statistics of the First Census of Iran: November 1956,* vol. 2; and Plan Organization, *National Census of Population and Housing: November 1966, Advance Sample.*

Education which employs most teachers and professors in Iranian education. In 1956 and 1963, the number of government employees was reported as 200,000 and 260,000 respectively. These figures were quite conservative since they either grossly underreported or completely neglected employees of the police, gendarmerie, and security organizations. In any case, these figures cannot be considered as a lump segment of the professional middle class because a sizable proportion of civil servants (*kārmandān-i dawlat*) are doormen, teaboys, janitors, and errand boys. In 1963, over twenty percent of the *kārmandān* were illiterate and/or without any formal schooling. In 1956 the figure was thirty percent and the illiterates outnumbered those with higher education by more than four to one.[18]

Table 3 reveals the growing number and percentage of employees with higher education in the Iranian civil service between 1956–63. This group is represented by all those who possess a degree of modern higher education and this means any post-secondary school training or study. This includes the Teachers Training Colleges, Polytechnic Institutes, the various educational centers associated with the ministries, and the compact training programs sporadically instituted to meet new tasks. The figures in table 3 refer to twenty-one agencies that accounted for ninety-one percent of government employment in 1956 and seventy-five percent in 1963. They have been selected because of the accuracy of their figures (when checked against other sources) and because they can be compared through the seven-year period.[19] This particular period was especially important since it was during this time that the various reform programs were begun. The Ministry of Economy tripled in employment while the Ministries of Education and Agriculture doubled in size during these seven years. The great demand for skilled and educated personnel to implement the new reforms resulted in most of the employment increase being taken up by the professional-bureaucratic intelligentsia.

The percentage of employees with higher education in the civil service tripled between 1956 and 1963, while the absolute number quadrupled. In 1956, less than one-twelfth of the bureaucracy had received any kind of higher education whereas in 1963 nearly one-fourth could claim such train-

18. Ministry of Interior, *Government Employee Statistics, 1956,* n.p.; and Plan Organization, *Government Employee Statistics, 1963*, pp. 134-42.

19. In the 1963 tables, for example, the figures representing the number of employees in the gendarmerie, police, and Tehran Municipality are grossly underpresented. According to the figures given, the police membership decreased from 22,368 to 3,201 between 1956 and 1963. The gendarmerie decline on paper was even more dramatic, falling from 22,346 to 207! Although these improbable figures accord with the usual tendency of official Iranian statistics to underpresent the size of military-security forces, the numbers provided here are so obviously false that there must be another explanation. These kinds of figures are omitted from our twenty-one agency analysis.

TABLE 3

Government Employees with Higher Education in Twenty-One Comparable Agencies, 1956–63[a]

Agency or Ministry	Higher Education[b]		Total Employees		Percent with Higher Education	
	1956	1963	1956	1963	1956	1963
Ministry of Court	8	8	345	371	2.3	2.2
Prime Ministry	11	51	91	174	12.1	29.3
Ministry of Information	17	71	218	264	7.8	26.9
Plan Organization	573	494	3,981	3,221	14.4	15.3
Ministry of Education	4,593	32,326	48,409	92,777	9.5	34.9
Ministry of Economy	226	1,078	2,961	10,988	7.6	9.8
Iran Carpet	4	7	262	238	1.5	2.9
Ministry of Health	1,684	3,428	10,051	15,673	16.7	21.9
Ministry of Post, Telegraph, and Telephone[c]	412	2,756	10,097	11,593	4.1	23.8
Ministry of Finance	850	1,378	22,369	21,742	3.8	6.3
National Insurance	81	98	629	744	12.9	13.2
Ministry of Justice	1,158	1,723	4,163	5,926	27.8	29.1
Accounting Office	314	1,388	2,931	3,848	10.8	36.1
Ministry of Roads	248	424	3,622	6,040	6.8	7.0
Iran Railroad	535	4,057	22,121	29,481	2.4	14.0
Ministry of Labor	197	267	714	960	27.6	27.8
Ministry of Agriculture	711	2,873	4,305	9,497	16.5	30.2
Ministry of Interior	186	106	2,326	1,864	8.0	5.6
Statistics–Records	147	272	3,146	2,419	4.7	11.2
Municipalities	71	122	9,177	12,660	0.8	0.9
Ministry of Foreign Affairs	294	343	525	672	56.0	51.0
Total	12,320	53,270	152,443	231,152	8.1	23.1

[a]The 1963 statistics contained a "Not Stated" column. Since the number of employees in this category was less than two percent of the total, the 1956–63 figures are compared directly.

[b]Higher education refers to both those with university degrees and those with degrees from "special *āmūzishgāhs*" or training/vocational colleges. The latter include, for example, the Junior and Senior Teachers Training Colleges, the Agricultural Institute, the PTT College, the School of Accounting, the Finance College, the Railroad Institute, and the Institute of Technology.

[c]Due to office and agency changes, we have had to combine and subtract in order to ensure that the comparisons refer to the same units. For example, there was *both* a PTT Ministry and a Telephone Company in 1956. In 1963 they were both combined into the Ministry.

Sources: 1. Ministry of Interior, General Statistics Office, *Nashrīyah-yi Āmār-i Kārmandān-i Dawlat* [Publication of Government Employee Statistics], Tīr, 1335/1956.
2. Plan Organization, Iranian Statistical Center, *Natāyij-i Āmārgīrī-yi Kārmandān-i Dawlat* [Results of the Census of Government Employees], Āẕar, 1342/1963.

ing. Thus, the proportion had increased from eight percent to over twenty-one percent, while the actual number had risen from 12,000 to 53,000. It is important to note also that during this period the total number of *university graduates* employed in all governmental agencies increased from 12,561 to 23,142.[20]

This absolute and relative increase in the number of government employees with higher education during a recent seven-year period is a strong indicator of the more general growth of the intelligentsia in Iranian society. Although the percentages will be higher and the trends more intense in the bureaucratic setting than in the society as a whole, the sharp accelerative increase in university-educated government employees is intertwined with the growth of the professional middle class in general.

In a detailed study of the 1956 official Iranian census, we called attention to the expanding size of the "bureaucratic-intelligentsia."[21] With the appearance of the 1966 census results, it is now possible to analyze the growth of this new class during a crucial ten-year period. The information provided in table 4 supports the trends indicated in table 3 concerning the extraordi-

TABLE 4

Growth of the Iranian Professional-Bureaucratic Intelligentsia, 1956–66, Employed Members Age Ten and Over[a]

	1956	1966
Professional-Bureaucratic Intelligentsia Total	332,000	513,400
Professional, Technical, and Cultural Total	93,200	212,200
Government Employees	54,800	143,200
Self-Employed	22,800	18,500
Private Employees	15,600	50,500
Administrative, Managerial, and Clerical Total	175,900	197,900
Government Employees	146,500	134,900
Self-Employed	17,000	10,700
Private Employees	12,400	52,300
Commerce and Retail Total	62,900	103,300
Government Employees	2,100	2,700
Private Employees	60,800	100,600

[a]The figures in this table include members of the bureaucracy who lack a higher education but are employed in administrative, technical, and managerial positions. The teaboys, doormen, and errand boys in the government apparatus are not included in these figures since they are listed under the census category *service* occupations. The statistics in this table also include private employees who represent the white collar and sales personnel in commerce and industry. Any overestimation that may occur here, however, is compensated for by the statistical absence of the intelligentsia employed in military and security organizations. All figures in this table have been rounded off to the nearest hundred.

Sources: Ministry of Interior, *National and Province Statistics of the First Census of Iran: November 1956,* 2:309-10.
Plan Organization, *National Census of Population and Housing: November 1966, Advance Sample,* Bulletin No. 3, p. 35.

20. Ministry of Interior, *Government Employee Statistics, 1956;* and Plan Organization, *Government Employee Statistics, 1963.*

21. J. A. Bill, *Middle East Journal* 17.

nary growth of the professional middle class in Iran. In the ten years between 1956–66, the new class increased in size by over sixty percent. By the mid-1960s, over one-half million employed Iranians were part of the professional-bureaucratic intelligentsia. With the acceleration of reform programs and the continued growth of the educational system, there is every indication that this class will continue to burgeon and develop rapidly. Although it still represents a relatively small percentage of the total Iranian population, its relative increase has been great. In 1956, approximately one out of every seventeen Iranians belonged to the intelligentsia. Ten years later the proportion had come to be one in twelve.

With the great economic prosperity and increasing urbanization of the 1960s, the bourgeois middle class also witnessed an exploding expansion. Table 5 reveals the details of the 1956–66 growth of this middle class which now also includes almost one-half million employed Iranians. This high growth rate of the bourgeois middle class is profoundly related to the role that the intelligentsia will play in Iran and will be examined in these terms in coming chapters. Table 6 compares the growth of the professional and bourgeois middle classes in terms of the percentage of total employed population in the years 1956–66. Both middle classes increased at approxi-

TABLE 5

Growth of the Iranian Bourgeois Middle Class, 1956–66, Employed Members Age Ten and Over

	1956	1966
Bourgeois Middle Class Total	298,900	471,500
Employers Total	34,700	110,100
Professional-Technical	600	3,400
Managerial-Administrative	3,200	15,400
Commerce and Retail Selling	9,700	36,800
Mining and Minerals	500	1,000[a]
Construction, Manufacturing, Crafts and Transport	17,200	40,800
Service	3,000	10,300
Unidentified	500	2,400
Self-Employed Total[b]	264,200	361,400
Commerce and Retail Selling	264,200	361,400

[a]In the 1966 figures, the category "Mining" is subsumed under "Agricultural," therefore the figure presented is an estimate based on the overall percentage increase of the bourgeois middle class.

[b]This category includes those who are self-employed in commerce and retailing who hire no paid employees. The members of this group constitute the lower bourgeoisie. The figures of self-employed presented here do not include the self-employed in crafts, processing, mining, transport, and service occupations since they are considered part of the working class.

Sources: Ministry of Interior, *National and Province Statistics of the First Census of Iran: November 1956,* 2:309-10.

Plan Organization, *National Census of Population and Housing: November 1966, Advance Sample,* Bulletin No. 3, p. 35.

mately the same high rate, although the intelligentsia grew slightly more rapidly. By the mid-1960s, the bourgeois and professional middle classes together accounted for nearly seventeen percent of the employed Iranian population.

TABLE 6

The Professional and Bourgeois Middle Classes: Percentage Growth of Total Employed Population Age Ten and Over, 1956–66[a]

	Percent of Total Employed Population		Percent Increase
	1956	1966	
Bourgeois Middle Class	5.6	7.9	2.3
Professional Middle Class	6.2	8.6	2.4

[a]The figures in this table have been calculated by dividing the total employed population into the number of employed members of both the professional and bourgeois middle classes for the years concerned.
Sources: Ministry of Interior, *National and Province Statistics of the First Census of Iran: November 1956,* 2:309-10.
Plan Organization, *National Census of Population and Housing: November 1966, Advance Sample,* Bulletin No. 3, p. 35.

This type of accelerating growth of the professional-bureaucratic intelligentsia is highly significant since as this class grows so also do its demands. To the degree that it is a new force concerned with different relationships, its expansion represents all the more deadly a challenge to the old system. As it grows, it can confront the former relationships on increasingly more fronts. At the same time, it will have more forces available for concentrated assaults at vital points in the traditional system. In this sense, numbers are important and a growing force carries with it implications quite different from one that is diminishing and declining. Size, however, is only one variable, and as we will discover, there are several others of even more profound import.

The Origins of the New Class

One of the ablest of class analysts, T. H. Marshall, once stated that the best way to understand classes and to stimulate hypotheses was "to stress the differences within classes instead of those between classes."[22] Although this

22. T. H. Marshall, ed., *Class Conflict and Social Stratification* (London: LePlay House Press, 1938), p. 97.

seems to be a very strange thing for a class theoretician to say, it nonetheless calls attention to the important relationship between intraclass and interclass interaction. Within the Iranian intelligentsia there is a great deal of division and conflicting tension which flows between individuals and groups. Throughout our study, the new middle class will be divided into various groups and group relationships will be analyzed in terms of their impact on class structure.[23] The following intraclass division is introduced immediately since it not only helps define the intelligentsia but also it will be constantly referred to in later analysis.

It makes a significant difference in terms of this study where the members of the professional-bureaucratic intelligentsia originate. The intelligentsia can thus be divided according to the various classes of social origin of its members. In general, they represent all the traditional classes for they are the sons (and daughters) of landlords, military officers, clerics, shopkeepers, bureaucrats, servants, and mule drivers.

In the beginning, i.e., the first thirty years of this century, the members of this class were recruited almost entirely from the upper classes. Only the latter were able to provide their offspring with a modern education. In an important and much-discussed article that appeared in a Persian journal in 1966, Jalāl Āl-i Aḥmad, a well-known contemporary Iranian intellectual, traced the origin of his class in Iran. He named the nobility, clerics, and landlords-tribal chieftains as representing the first three birthplaces of the intellectuals. He traced the ills of the intellectuals to these beginnings and argued that, as a result, the ruling class was still easily "buying" the intelligentsia. Āl-i Aḥmad pointed out, however, that there is now a fourth birthplace and this is the urban middle class. It is the intellectual of this background, he concluded, that is the hope of the country.[24]

Since the 1940s, there has been a discernible trend whereby an increasingly larger percentage of individuals from lower- and middle-class origins has become part of the growing intelligentsia. This trend has accelerated rapidly in the 1960s with the rationalization of university entrance examination procedures whereby the prime criterion for acceptance has become merit. Another reason has been the establishment of institutions of higher education, such as Tehran Polytechnic, and training institutes and colleges attached to various government ministries. The vital catalysts for this trend have been both the demand of the masses of secondary school graduates who press for more education and the political elite's need for such talent

23. Those who question the existence of a new middle class in the Middle East do so by stressing the divisions that exist within this class. In so doing, they assume that class analysis disregards group activity. The most explicit presentation of this viewpoint is Amos Perlmutter, "Egypt and the Myth of the New Middle Class: A Comparative Analysis," *Comparative Studies in Society and History* 10 (October 1967): 46-65.

24. Āl-i Aḥmad, *Jahān-i Naw,* Nos. 4 and 5 (1966): 25-32.

to plan and operationalize the numerous projects continuously generated. A 1966–67 survey of students at Tehran and National Universities indicated the following with regard to social class origin.[25] Table 7 reveals that although the upper class is still well represented in the university system in Iran, students of non-upper-class origin are now in the definite majority. The largest percentage consisted of those listed under "Professional Middle Class" principally because the offspring of all government employees (*kārmandān-i dawlat*) were included in this category.[26] This conclusion is supported by a 1966 survey of two hundred Tehran University students which indicated that fifty-five percent of those interviewed were the sons and daughters of government employees.[27]

Although those of upper-class origin represent only one-sixth of the students sampled in Iran, they represented closer to one-half of a one hundred student sample taken of Iranian students studying in the United States.[28] However, since the lower- and middle-class Iranian students resident abroad usually study in Germany, it is reasonable to estimate that one-fourth to one-third of Iranian students abroad are of upper-class background. In any case, it is quite clear that there is now a high percentage of Iranian youth in higher education who are not of upper-class background and who in fact represent all classes in society. This is a sharp difference from the first days of modern education in Iran when "only the children of the nobles and aristocrats (*a'yān va ashrāf*) could participate."[29]

Other indications of this important trend can be seen through two other surveys that we made of important sectors of the professional-bureaucratic intelligentsia. The Syndicate of Journalists and Writers was established in 1962 by a group of professional writers in search of some protection in what is a hazardous occupation in Iran. In 1967, this Syndicate had 245 members. All were of lower- and lower-middle-class origin with but nine exceptions.

---

25. This information is drawn from a statistical survey directed by an Iranian scholar at Tehran and National Universities in 1966.

26. As such, this figure is slightly distorted. The figure provided does not necessarily mean that all are members of the new middle class.

27. 'Abd al-Ḥusayn Nafīsī and Iftikhār Ṭabātabā'ī, *Barrasī-yi Masā'il va Mushkilāt-i Javānān-i Dānishjū va Dānishāmūz-i Ṭihrān* [An Examination of the Problems and Difficulties of Tehran Secondary and University Students] (Tehran: Plan Organization Publication No. 4 of the Health and Social Welfare Planning Group, 1966), p. 3.

28. Borhanmanesh, "A Study of Iranian Students in Southern California," pp. 80-82. We combine Borhanmanesh's categories "upper class" and "upper middle class" in this figure. In the latter category, he includes, for example, "high ranking government officials," "factory owners," and "landlords."

29. Ministry of Labor, *Barrasī-hā-yi Masā'il-i Nīrū-yi Insānī* [Investigation of the Problems of Manpower] (Tehran, 1964), 3:2032. This is a prodigious three-volume, 2,438-page national manpower study carried out in 1963–64. Hereafter cited as Ministry of Labor, *Problems of Manpower, 1964.*

TABLE 7

Class Origin of a Sample of Fifty Students of Tehran and National Universities, 1966–67

Class	Number	Percent
Upper Class	9	18
Bourgeois Middle Class	6	12
Cleric Middle Class	3	6
Professional Middle Class[a]	18	36
Working Class	5	10
Peasant Class	2	4
Unemployed	2	4
No Answer/Not Clear	5	10
Total	50	100

[a]Includes the offspring of all civil servants *(kārmandān)* except those at the highest level who were considered upper class.

Only one member of this articulate group could be considered of upper-class background for the other eight were for the most part of wealthy bourgeois origin. A study of another group of the new middle class produced similar findings. A survey of 307 college-educated *bakhshdārs* (district governors) revealed that only seventeen were from upper-class background and nearly all of these were local (provincial) landholding families.

This group division according to social origin will be utilized in studying class relationships linked with specific problem areas. This division is a significant one for explaining and understanding such processes.

The Divisions within the New Class

Bertram Wolfe, in a splendid description of the Russian intelligentsia at the beginning of the twentieth century, says much that is relevant to our analysis of the new Iranian professional middle class.

> The Russian intelligentsia is a specific formation of nineteenth-century Russia, not to be identified with the "educated and professional classes" of the Western lands, or with the officials, technicians, and managers of present-day Russia. It was extruded out of a fixed society of medieval estates into which it no longer fitted, an ideological sign that the old world of status had been outgrown. It was recruited simultaneously from the more generous sons and daughters of the nobility and from the plebeian youth: from above and from below. Its members were held together, neither by a common social origin and

> status, nor by a common role in the social process of production. The cement which bound them together was a common alienation from existing society, and a common belief in the sovereign efficacy of ideas as shapers of life. They lived precariously suspended as in a void, between an uncomprehending autocratic monarchy above and an uncomprehending, unenlightened mass below. Their mission as independent thinkers was to be critics of the world in which they had no place and prophets of a world that had not yet come into being, and might have no place for them either. They were lawyers without practice, teachers without schools, graduate clerics without benefices and often without religion, chemists without laboratories, technicians, engineers, statisticians for whom industry had as yet no need, journalists without a public, educators without schools, politicians without parties, sociologists and statesmen rejected by the state and ignored by the people.[30]

The Iranian professional middle class has entered the traditional web-system, but important sections of this new class refuse to become a part of that system. These refuse to relate according to ongoing patterns of conflict and personalism, and as a result stand as a constant and growing reminder of system transformation. Those groups within the intelligentsia that strongly reject the dominant patterns of the web-system feel that their skills and sacrifice entitle them to advance and not be bound in any uneven relationship. They refuse to bow in deference to the more powerful and at the same time hesitate to set aside their tools of technical skill for the old tools of maneuver and intrigue. Traditional relationships are strongly criticized on the grounds that they hamper efficiency and impede projects.

There are other groups within the professional middle class, however, that support in varying degrees the traditional patterns. In all, there are four groups within the intelligentsia and each maintains a different relationship in regard to conflicting power patterns. These four groups will be presented as ideal-types since stances continually shift and commitment comes in many shades. The groups to be analyzed are termed the Uprooters, the Technocrats, the Maneuverers, and the Followers.

The Uprooters are the initiators of transformation. They are the ones who criticize the old patterns the most severely and refuse to be bound by such relationships. They universalize their complaints and criticisms and increasingly strive to rip the old web. These are a new breed of rebels who center their attack not only on individuals but on the relationships as well. The Uprooters are often the members of the new middle class who can be most

30. From *Three Who Made a Revolution: A Biographical History* by Bertram D. Wolfe. Copyright © 1948, 1964 by Bertram D. Wolfe. Reprinted by permission of the publisher, The Dial Press.

accurately called intellectuals. They are primarily drawn from the ranks of teachers, professors, students, and writers. This group is by and large alienated from the present political system.

The Technocrats are primarily concerned with carrying out the particular tasks for which they have been trained. They are intent on modifying and repairing the existing system in order that they might go on with their various activities. As such, the Technocrats are alienated on grounds of procedure and include administrators, managers, and many professional people.

The Maneuverers are the defenders of the traditional power network. They are the manipulators who for a multitude of reasons favor the ongoing relationships. Their modern education and formal skills are reserve power handles since they understand the traditional web best. They suffer in disadvantageous patterns of competition only temporarily, and because of personal ties they know that they can always maneuver into better power positions.

The followers are those individuals who float in the safest and smoothest direction. They are the trailers of power who gravitate toward the strongest personalities, groups, and classes.

As is the case of all Iranian groups and classes, these four groups overlap and interlock. There are Uprooters who are also Technocrats and vice versa. Individuals shift from one group to another group as times and pressures vary. Thus, the new middle class which has begun to shatter the traditional Iranian class relations is itself the locus of division and discord. The struggles going on within this class are intimately related to the political system and interclass relationships as well. In order to understand the challenge, it is necessary to analyze these four groups in depth. Who are they? What is their relationship to one another, to other classes, and to the political system? What are their demands? What relationships are they defending or attacking and why? How does this affect the traditional patterns and what does it mean in terms of change?

chapter three

The Uprooter: Ideological System Alienation

Perhaps the most serious challenge to the existing Iranian political system is represented by those members of the professional-bureaucratic intelligentsia who can be most justifiably termed intellectual. These would be the best-educated and most highly sensitive among writers, artists, teachers, professors, and students. Because they demand radical change in the traditional web system, the members of this group are termed the Uprooters. They oppose the system not only for reasons of procedure and spite, but in many instances for ideological reasons as well. Indications and signposts of this alienation have been many during the past two decades and merit investigation.

The two great recent opposition movements, namely the Tūdah Party and the National Front, have been organized, led, and for the most part manned by these segments of the professional middle class.[1] Teachers and professors dominated the leadership ranks of these movements, while stu-

1. The fact that the professional-bureaucratic intelligentsia was the backbone of the Tūdah movement is supported by information drawn from two studies of Tūdah membership produced by the Iranian government. Military Governorship of Tehran, *Sayr-i Kumūnīzm dar Īrān az Shahrīvar-i 1320 tā Farvardīn-i 1336* [The Evolution of Communism in Iran from September 1941 to March 1958] (Tehran, 1958) and *Kitāb-i Siyāh* [The Black Book] (Tehran, 1955). In English, see Sepehr Zabih, *The Communist Movement in Iran* (Berkeley and Los Angeles: University of California Press, 1966), pp. 187, 204, 249, 256-57.

dents were the catalysts and moving forces in the important mass element vital to low-level organization and street activity. When these two organizations were finally crushed, the intellectual opposition continued although most of it has trickled underground. Strong evidence of this attitude continues to bubble ominously to the surface. It threatened to destroy the system during the Amīnī Period as students and teachers responded to a slight release of government pressure by full-scale organization and demonstration. Under Minister of Education Darakhshish, teachers throughout Iran formed perhaps the closest-knit grass roots organization since the days of the Tūdah Party. Between 1967 and 1971, Iranian universities were the scenes of numerous cases of student discontent.

On April 10, 1965, an attempt was made on the Shah's life. Fourteen young men were subsequently brought to trial for complicity in what has come to be called the Marble Palace Plot. The accused individuals, who averaged twenty-seven years of age, were all members of the professional middle class, and half of them were either students or teachers. In 1968, another group of fourteen was apprehended and charged with communist ideological leanings and conspiracy. The individuals concerned all held university educations, and the average age of the group was twenty-nine. Early in 1971, eighteen young men were sentenced and imprisoned for "anti-state activities." Among the members of this group were twelve students, three civil servants, and a pharmacist. The members averaged twenty-five years of age. In January 1972, the Iranian government announced the discovery of three extensive networks of individuals who were plotting terrorist activities against the regime. An examination of the membership of these groups indicates that once again the professional-intelligentsia was assuming its place at the forefront of the alienated opposition.

The Writers and Alienation in Print

In a society such as Iran where political and ideological criticism is choked and muffled, there is an area where one can look to find the attitudes and stances of young Iranians. It is possible to examine both what they write and what they read. Here one can see how in masterful esoteric manner the Iranian writer presents the situation of himself and his class. One first begins to sense the gap between the Iranian intellectuals and the Iranian traditional sociopolitical system when he studies their writings and, in particular, their fiction and poetry. The following is a brief analysis of recent Iranian writers and writings and is meant to reveal the gap between the Uprooters and the system.

From the abdication of Riẓā Shāh through the Muṣaddiq Period (i.e., 1941–53), Iranian poets, novelists, and short story writers produced a mass of literature that analyzed and criticized the contemporary social and political scene. Not only was this a time when they could write with relatively little censor restriction but also it was a period when their class enjoyed sporadic political participation. They openly attacked existing social conditions, criticizing the oppression, injustice, poverty, and discrimination they witnessed in their society. Novelists like Buzurg 'Alavī and journalists like Hidāyatullāh Ḥakīm-Ilāhī and Muḥammad Mas'ūd sensitively portrayed the sociopolitical scene.[2] A few of these writers such as Ṣādiq Hidāyat and Sayyid Muḥammad Jamālzādah acquired international reputations, but all of them became famous in Iran where they were well known to the members of all classes.

Following the events of 1953 and the fall of Muṣaddiq, the climate in which such persons wrote changed drastically. They themselves refer to the period since that time as the "Period of Strangulation (*khafaqān*)." Their reaction can be seen in terms of a four-group division.

The members of the first group have opted out. They have either given up writing or they have refused to publish. Some like M. Bihāzīn have switched to translation while others including Buzurg 'Alavī have left Iran.

The second group consists of those writers who have turned away from many of their old ideas and have joined the system. They continue to write, but their former criticism has given way to indiscriminate praise. This group although relatively small in number is nonetheless very much present. A relevant case in point is Firaydūn Tavallulī's recent book *Pūyah.* Better known examples of this include 'Alī Dashtī and Muḥammad Ḥijāzī whose messages have for years changed with the political winds.[3] Perhaps under-

2. Buzurg 'Alavī was one of the fifty-three Iranians jailed by Riẓā Shāh in 1937 for Marxist activities. He was among the founders of the Tūdah Party and is a well-known Persian writer. His *Chashm-hā-yash* [Her Eyes] and *Panjāh-u-sah Nafar* [Fifty-three Persons] sharply criticize the conditions of Iran during the rule of Riẓā Shāh, while *Nāmah-hā* [Letters] contains selections about the difficulties of the lower classes and the inefficiency of the bureaucracy. Muḥammad Mas'ūd's two best projects were his *Gulhā'īkah dar Jahannam Mīrūyad* [The Flowers that Grow in Hell] and *Bahār-i 'Umr* [The Spring of Life] where he portrayed the life of the lower and middle classes and severely attacked the educational system of the day. Between 1941 and his assassination in 1947, he published the controversial newspaper, *Mard-i Imrūz* [The Man of Today], where he attacked the wealthy and the powerful with great vengeance. Mas'ūd attacked anyone and anything that he considered evil and in the end it cost him his life. Ḥakīm-Ilāhī is perhaps less known than the other two despite the fact that he wrote a series of journalistic studies revealing the horrible conditions in the mental institutions, prisons, red-light districts, and schools of Iran. He fought communism in Iran in the 1940s and began a long campaign to reform and clean up the Ministry of Justice.

3. Both Dashtī and Ḥijāzī along with greater intellectuals such as Riẓāzādah Shafaq found high positions in the political arena because of this ability. These three found their reward in the Senate.

standably, the leading Iranian journalists, newspaper editors, and directors also must be considered members of this second category.

The third, and in terms of talent and audience, most important group consists of those who continue to do social writing but have changed their method and style. In order to present their ideas they resort to symbolic and esoteric writing. The members of this group include the most famous contemporary Iranian writers such as Jalāl Āl-i Aḥmad, Aḥmad Shāmlū, Ṣādiq Chūbak, Siyāvush Kasrā'ī ("Kawlī"), Mahdī Akhāvān-i S̱āliṯ, Hushang Ibtihāj ("H. E. Sāyah"), and Ghulām Ḥusayn Sā'idī. These are the writers who are read and cherished by the young intellectuals of Iran and who in their writings bitterly and powerfully portray their place in a system they feel no part of. A survey of fifty poems by Akhāvān-i S̱āliṯ, Shāmlū, Kiyānūsh, Farrukhzād, and Ramzī reveals an extraordinary emphasis upon such themes as "walls," "loneliness," "darkness," "fatigue," and "nothingness."[4] These poems deplore the situation of the Iranian intellectual and obliquely criticize and condemn the existing sociopolitical system in which the intellectual is chained. Dāvūd Ramzī echoes a theme common to nearly all of these writers when in his *"Ākharīn Īstgāh"* [The Last Station], he writes:

High walls
Very high
As high as the world
I am surrounded
Foolishly I try to make a path
Dead ends everywhere
Every escape blocked

Even the great poetess Furūq Farrukhzād occasionally left her usual themes of love and nature to cry out against the conditions of her class. In *"Āyah-hā-yi Zamīnī"* [Earthly Passages], she particularly blames the intellectuals themselves and in scorching language describes their degrading position.

Swamps of alcohol
steaming with acrid poisonous gases
dragged down to their depths
the inert mass of intellectuals
and the verminous mice

4. The poems came from Akhāvān-i S̱āliṯ' *Az īn Avistā* [From This Avesta], Kiyānūsh's *Dar Ānjā Hīchkas Nabūd* [There Was No One There], *Shabāvīz'* [The Herald of Dawn] and *Shabistān* [Nightroom], Shāmlū's *Havā-yi Tāzah* [The New Climate] and *Quqnus Dar Bārān* [The Rain-Drenched Phoenix], Farrukhzād's *Barguzīdah* [Selections], and Ramzī's *Jidāl* [Conflict].

gnawed through the pages of gilded books
stacked in ancient closets [5]

Perhaps the greatest collection of poems condemning the system politically and ideologically is Aḥmad Shāmlū's *Havā-yi Tāzah* [The New Climate] which contains seventy selections written between 1947 and 1956. It is this same writer who in his own terms describes the situation of Iran's intellectuals before and after 1954. In 1950 in his poem *"Sarguzasht,"* he referred to the Iranian intellectual as "the Phoenix rising from the flames." In 1966 he titled a collection of his poems "The Rain-Drenched Phoenix."

Besides the three groups described above, there is a fourth group of younger Iranian writers who have grown up in the post-1953 environment. They seldom write socially, but concern themselves with pure poetry usually imitating foreign poets and styles. They have no goals and make up opium and heroin circles where they write for one another, sporadically publishing their work in scattered magazines. They have opted out in a very special way, namely by turning their backs on the sociopolitical system and by trying to escape from a situation they label hopeless. These writers and poets number nearly one thousand and are perhaps the most alienated of all, their most common reaction being "bi-man chah" [What's it to me?].[6]

Finally, in terms of class origin, it is important to realize that despite notable exceptions such as Ṣādiq Hidāyat, the overwhelming majority of writers come from lower- and middle-class background. They have moved up into the professional-bureaucratic intelligentsia and in such cases as Muḥammad Mas'ūd they have never forgiven the ruling upper class.

Thus, through the work of the poets and writers it is possible to see the extreme alienation that exists between the system and important groups in the intelligentsia. The demand to uproot is expressed esoterically but repeatedly in their writings. In order to understand the conflict and its implications, it is necessary to concentrate on one of the points in the system where these forces collide and where the professional middle class is being channeled and fed into the system. The university is such a point.

5. This translation by Karim Emami cannot be improved upon. Miss Farrukhzād died in a tragic automobile accident in February 1967. Her life represented the dramatic and perilous lives of all young Iranian writers and perhaps of the professional-bureaucratic intellegentsia as a whole. She had several other brushes with death including two automobile accidents and one attempted suicide. She was Iran's leading poetess and one of its greatest modern poets.

6. A powerful novel revolving about a young poet and heroin was written by Nuṣrat Rahmānī and meaningfully titled *Mardīkah dar Qubar Gum Shud* [The Man Who Disappeared in the Dust]. Selected passages of this novel can be found in English in *Kayhan International,* June 11, 1965. A young intellectual's desperate search for opium is vividly described by Jamāl Mīr-Ṣādiqī in a moving short story that appeared in the best Iranian literary magazine *Sukhan* in May 1967 (*Shab, Shabī Tārīk* [A Night, a Dark Night]), *Sukhan,* 17th yr., No. 2 (Urdībihisht 1346):173-83.

Pahlavi University as Locus of Conflict

> His Imperial Majesty has ordered that every possible means be employed to expand and improve all facilities at this university so that it may rank among the best in the world.
>
> —Asadullāh 'Alam, Chancellor,
> Pahlavi University, October 12, 1966

Pahlavi University in Shīrāz represents the most serious attempt to establish a quality institution of higher education in modern Iran. The idea was developed by Iranian and American authorities in the late 1950s and the United States Agency for International Development (AID) became the responsible American agency. In August 1962, AID signed a contract with the University of Pennsylvania whereby the latter was to work with Pahlavi as an academic partner in an advisory capacity. Among other things, Pennsylvania agreed to send a number of instructors and professors to Pahlavi better to ensure the latter's chances of becoming a "quality university." Pahlavi University officially came into being in June 1962 when it took the place of what was formerly Shīrāz University.

The Iranian political elite strongly favored the establishment of a Pahlavi University for it seemed to promise many benefits and few risks. First, such a university would pose a threat to Tehran University and would provide a balancing force against it. Not only had Tehran University often been a base for serious activities against the system, but also it had been stagnating academically and this to a degree that defied reform from within. Placing a rival in the south and providing it with unlimited resources would very possibly heighten Tehran University's academic standards while at the same time lessen its political threat. Second, such a university would cut down on the "brain drain" by providing some solid education at home. The government's demand for the skilled and educated had been rising at an alarming rate as new reform projects and programs were constantly being generated. A new university would keep needed talent in Iran. At the same time, it would siphon off a few more from the threatening masses of secondary school graduates clamoring to get into a university. Third, recent history had shown that the greatest threats to the existing system were the university students. At Pahlavi they would be far to the south where a "scholarship" system would be set up to ensure a little more responsibility and loyalty on their part. Finally, there was a certain amount of prestige involved in being termed the academic counterpart to an American university the calibre of Pennsylvania and in having your graduates contractually termed "the academic equals of Pennsylvania graduates." There would, of course, be risk involved in establishing a liberal American-type institution on Iranian soil but this risk could be greatly reduced by the right kind of administrative control.

For the United States government, wholehearted financial, intellectual, and technical support made a great deal of sense for such a venture. Not only was it important to build good education in countries like Iran but also it was of benefit to have a hand in helping to educate coming Iranian generations. Furthermore, United States military and other aid programs to Iran had been under fire for years. Here was an opportunity to support an important and much-needed educational project. Outside of financial considerations, the University of Pennsylvania saw the contract it had acquired in terms of prestige. Possessing a foreign affiliate or counterpart had come to be an important symbol in university circles.

The first five years of Pahlavi University history were marked by numerous indications that a new university stressing quality and excellence was developing in Iran. No effort was spared to provide the most modern facilities as buildings and building complexes sprang up throughout Shīrāz. Early estimates indicated that such facilities would be constructed at a cost of sixty million dollars. The faculty was hired at salaries double and triple those paid by other universities. Scores of talented young Iranians with degrees and jobs abroad were recruited and joined Pahlavi. The American government backed the project while an American university joined the experiment with representatives on the spot. The Shah continually let it be known that he personally desired that Pahlavi University become an academic institution of the highest calibre. The picture was completed when the political elite selected the administration that was in fact to make the university work.

The Administrative Web

From the beginning, the Pahlavi University administrative system has represented a network of relationships of conflict and bargaining in which connections and maneuver are the means of survival. This has meant that in the first place the Chancellor must be an individual who is accomplished at utilizing and preserving such relationships. In May 1961, the old but relatively progressive Chancellor was suddenly dismissed introducing a year in which nine different Chancellors were appointed to head Pahlavi University. In April 1962, Dr. Luṭfullāh Ṣūratgar became Chancellor and served in this capacity until January 1964. During this crucial time in the life of the new university, the administration was developed along the line of the traditional web-system and the inevitable clash occurred as the new forces challenged old methods. Resignations by key members of the newly hired Iranian faculty coupled with a strong stand by outside advisors resulted in the Chancellor's dismissal early in 1964. He was replaced by Asadullāh 'Alam.

Mr. 'Alam was a member of the political elite and the most trusted of the Shah's inner circle.[7] He rebuilt and reinforced the old patterns that had been threatened during the latter stages of Dr. Ṣūratgar's chancellorship. With the help of his trusted lieutenant, Amīr Muttaqī, 'Alam locked the Pahlavi administration into the central political authority—a policy that has been pursued at Tehran and National Universities as well.[8] Neither 'Alam nor Muttaqī have had much experience in formal education and none in educational administration. They have both, however, proved themselves skillful masters of maneuver within the traditional Iranian web-system. For the central political authority, it is a question of priorities and at the top of the list is loyalty, tranquillity, and control. The 'Alam administration was able to deliver this at Pahlavi, but only through great effort and cost. In October 1966, Chancellor 'Alam assured the Queen of the administration's goals and successes in this area.

> In this institution more than anything else all efforts were concentrated toward training the students in the knowledge that they are Iranians. . . . We are proud to say that they leave this institution ranking among the most loyal and patriotic citizens of the country.[9]

Woven into this administration have been the old Shīrāz families and names like Qavāmī, Lashkarī, and Dihqān in the university structure reveal this influence. As late as 1966, only one department had an Iranian chairman who was not a holdover from old Shīrāz University. 'Alam and these

7. This was done despite a Pahlavi University statute stating that the Chancellor should not be a government employee and must not accept any other job. He was required to devote all his time to the university and not to receive salaries from any other source. 'Alam failed on all these counts. See *Kayhan International,* February 20, 1964.

8. The situation at National University has reflected this policy better than any other. The first Chancellor was inconsistent but dynamic and he laid the foundation of a quality institution. In so doing he made numerous enemies who forced his resignation. His successor was a professional politician who at the time he was appointed Chancellor was a Minister without Portfolio. The third Chancellor was best described as "a political trouble-shooter who fills posts wherever a loyal and trusted man is needed." As a result, National University has deteriorated to such an extent as an academic institution that it is now being compared to the provincial schools.

9. Speech at Pahlavi University, Shīrāz, October 11, 1966. Chancellor 'Alam constantly made speeches to assure the political authorities that first and foremost Pahlavi University was turning out loyal subjects. In a speech in Tehran on February 23 of that year, he made this point several times and spoke about the students' "duties to their country and to its symbol the Shāhanshāh"; that the students were being "taught to be loyal"; about their "devotion to their King and country"; their "enthusiasm to work, devotion to the King"; and that "they feel unquestionable loyalty to His Imperial Majesty and consider him as belonging to them." Such statements represent the language of the environment of the web-system.

members of the local Shīrāz elite shared the upper class-aristocratic characteristic and the fact that they administered Pahlavi University was a fact not lost upon the young faculty.

The Pahlavi University administration operates in much the same manner as the Safavī and Pahlavi political elite networks analyzed in chapter 1. It rests on balanced forces of tension with all spheres of authority blurred and uneven. A typical example of the uncertainty of authority occurred in 1966 when the university Provost was at the same time chairman of the Department of Mathematics and dean of the College of Engineering. Just as enigmatic as the fact that each of the three positions was a full-time job were the authority patterns that emerged. As Provost he was *superior* to the dean of the College of Arts and Sciences; as dean of the College of Engineering he was *equal* to said dean; and as chairman of the Department of Mathematics he was *subordinate* to this same dean.

The Entering Faculty

The administrative web that has been imposed on Pahlavi University has been threatened from many sides, the principal challenges being posed by the Pennsylvania Team, the students, and the young returnee professors. The first two forces have been disposed of with surprising ease. It has been the faculty that has refused to accept all the rules of the game and has resisted to a degree that has shaken the web to its core. Just as fast as resisting individuals and small pockets of individuals have been broken and wiped out, new pockets have sprung up and spread.

In the fall of 1966, over fifty Iranians holding M.A. and Ph.D. degrees were recruited and returned from the United States to join the Pahlavi faculty. In the years preceding this dozens of others had already returned. Many of these returnees were among the most competent and talented of the younger intelligentsia. Upon entering the Pahlavi web-system, they soon became entangled and found that they did not necessarily see priorities as the administration did. Many held quality education as their first goal. They further resented the politically picked administration and the fact that positions of authority were filled by upper-class, old family personalities. Many also found it very difficult to work in an unpredictably irrational system where favoritism and influence outstripped merit and talent.

As the members of this new middle class were injected into the Pahlavi web, they initially determined not to become involved in the politics and maneuver but to concentrate only on their teaching and research. Without exception, however, they were all sucked into the web by virtue of the fact that they had to deal (and bargain) with the administration on such issues as salary, facilities, student affairs, and faculty organization. The clash was perhaps inevitable while the pressures were practically unbearable.

As the intelligentsia has entered the Pahlavi web and has sought to defend and improve its position, it has split into different groups depending upon the relationship the individuals have adopted vis-à-vis the traditional relationships. The instructors and professors at Pahlavi University can be divided into the four categories: the Followers, the Maneuverers, the Technocrats, and the Uprooters.[10]

In most cases, the Follower has acquired his *license* in Iran and has gone abroad where he has earned his graduate degrees. He has then returned to Iran and to Pahlavi University. This man does not entertain grandiose plans for himself but is satisfied with some material luxury and prestige. He wants a television set and an automobile in which he can take his family for their Friday picnics. His vision is limited and at times of confrontation he will follow the easiest path with little resistance. The Follower tends to gravitate toward the nearest and strongest personality. He links himself in whatever relationship that is present and as such he fills in the spaces in the web-system. The majority of the faculty at Pahlavi University are Followers.

The Maneuverer has also often received his graduate education abroad. He, however, is extremely clever and intelligent, if not always in terms of formal education, always in terms of understanding the intricacies of the web. Unlike the Follower, this person has the biggest possible plans for himself. He is a man of big ideas and infinite expectations and he will do anything to realize these expectations. This means relating himself in great deference to the most powerful and influential, while at the same time expecting to be shown deference by those in inferior positions. With his closest competitors and approximate equals, the Maneuverer relates in personal and competitive bargaining, and uses all methods available to gain the submission of the other. He is constantly engaged in constructing new connections and building personal ties and is more interested in power than in either profession or perfection. The web-system has been spun by the Maneuverer and he knows all of its strands and channels. He holds virtually all high administrative positions at Pahlavi University as he does in the society. If not a member of the upper class, he has sought such membership by becoming an extension of it.

The Technocrat has received his graduate education either in Iran or abroad. He is very much in evidence at Pahlavi University where he concentrates upon his own specialty or skill. When procedures hinder this work, he complains and occasionally calls for reform. He is quite content to work

10. This classification was first formulated after an intensive study of personnel at Pahlavi University in January and February 1967. The scheme has been devised according to how the faculty has reacted during periods of stress, e.g., during the struggle between merit and influence. Like all typologies, it is altogether too neat, for as one young biology professor said: "I belong to all four categories depending upon the situation." Nonetheless, the scheme is a useful ordering device that will help us to understand the dynamics of Pahlavi University and then to build hypotheses about the relationship of the professional-bureaucratic intelligentsia to the traditional web-system.

within the traditional system which he struggles to modify through time. When the Technocrat sees the implementation of his occupational activities threatened by the web-system, he responds by seeking reform through repair. The emphasis is upon modifying change.

The Uprooter in the Pahlavi University environment has in nearly all cases received his undergraduate education abroad, usually in the United States. He is competent, courageous, and noncorrupt (although he may be corruptible). This man is in the very definite minority at Pahlavi although his numbers have been growing. His goal is to transform the web itself and he will stand and fight for what he believes in. The Uprooter desires quality education and realizes that it cannot be provided by the ongoing pattern of ascriptive manipulation. He is under constant pressure since his very existence is a living threat to the web-system and to the Maneuverers. The Uprooter favors decisions based on merit rather than influence.[11]

Issues and Conflict

With the above typology in mind, one can study in general terms the basic struggle that has characterized the existence of Pahlavi University. In the beginning, Pahlavi seemed to have an excellent chance not only to become a high quality educational center but also to become the first Iranian academic institution where the old web of political-personal-influence relationships would be torn. The Shah had stated more than once that Pahlavi was to be above all else a first-class academic center and he supported his words with action when he dismissed several early Chancellors who were local Maneuverers of the first order. Pahlavi also possessed an inbuilt advantage that promised an efficient and rational institution and that was the University of Pennsylvania Team. If they could not directly support the Iranian Uprooters, they could at least provide example and encouragement through their own activities.

Despite continual confrontation and conflict, the Maneuverers have managed to protect the old system largely through their control of the administration. In major encounters the Maneuverers have prevailed. Since 1962, the Chancellors have guaranteed the persistence of the past and challenging Uprooters have been defeated. In the early history of Pahlavi University, the greatest challenge to the old web-system was represented in the personality of Dr. Yūsif Hātifī.

Hātifī was a brilliant scientist with an international reputation in biochemistry and he stood as an Uprooter of great integrity. His return to Iran as a member of the Pahlavi University faculty was of major import to the prestige and success of the newly formed university. As acting dean of the College of Arts and Sciences in fall 1962, Hātifī, with a number of other

11. This typology is essentially the same as the ideal-types introduced at the end of chapter 2.

young educators, prepared a curriculum that was to transform old Shīrāz University into a modern institution stressing academic excellence. Just prior to the beginning of the fall semester, the Chancellor suddenly announced an admission seventy percent higher than had been planned. This arbitrary act not only admitted a number of students of doubtful calibre into the newly developing university but also it destroyed all hopes of introducing the new curriculum. During the 1962–63 academic year, the administration sabotaged several other projects initiated by Hātifī and other members of the faculty. In the summer of 1963 Hātifī returned to the United States.[12]

Four months after Hātifī's departure, Prime Minister 'Alam became Chancellor of Pahlavi University. 'Alam recruited Hātifī from the United States and the latter returned to Iran as Provost for the 1964–65 academic year. At the same time, 'Alam moved Amīr Muttaqī into the administration thus ensuring the persistence of traditional patterns and control. The inevitable clash between Uprooters and Maneuverers occurred and Hātifī refused to compromise with the administrative web. In fall 1965, Dr. Hātifī did not return to Pahlavi University. During his year as Provost, he had worked to rationalize the administration and improve the curriculum. The Chancellor and his assistants, however, ignored and bypassed the office of Provost and traditional power relationships prevailed on all levels. The best indication of this occurred in the fall of 1964 when the Shah made two visits to Pahlavi University. The Pahlavi administration directed by Muttaqī dipped deeply into the university budget to build elaborate decorations and to repair reception halls for the Monarch's visit. As a result, the education budget floundered and attempts to build academic excellence ceased for lack of funds. The Muttaqī, 'Alam, Shah chain of deference took precedence over all other relationships and goals including the professed aim of building Pahlavi University into a center of quality education.

There are several reasons why the Maneuverers have been able to control and direct Pahlavi University affairs. First of all, when the Shah appointed 'Alam (and as a result Muttaqī) to head Pahlavi, he chose an especially able and adept traditional administration. In so doing, he perhaps unwittingly destroyed any immediate chance that Pahlavi might have of becoming a high calibre educational institution. Second, the "inbuilt advantage" (the Pennsylvania Team) referred to above proved to be more of an "inbuilt disadvantage." In the first place, only a few members of the "Penn Team" were from the University of Pennsylvania. Although certain members of the Penn Team were told that they were at Pahlavi only to teach, they found that by not becoming involved in anything else they were in fact very much

12. For a rare view of the Pahlavi University web-system and a typical Maneuverer in action, see Leo Vaughan, *The Jokeman* (London: Eyrie and Spottiswoode, 1962). This novel is based on the author's own experiences while teaching at Shīrāz University and his "Dr. Marvasti" represents the Maneuverer-Chancellor described in our text.

involved. In spring 1967, one Iranian Uprooter explained that when he had approached the Penn Team for support and assistance he had found them to be a "pillar of sand."[13] The situation was further aggravated by internal divisions within the advisory apparatus and an apparent lack of communication between Philadelphia and the team in the field.[14]

Besides its financial and facility control, the administration has often used the students against the faculty while at the same time working to divide and split the Uprooters. By providing an elaborate system of "scholarships," the administration attempted to buy student loyalty.[15] Students were in fact paid by the administration to cooperate with the system. In this way, many of them developed ties with the administration and work in the classroom became a secondary concern. This undercut university discipline and allowed students to bargain for grades and privileges. They would use the administration against the faculty over issues of grading and at the same time continued to demand more and more lucrative scholarships. In February 1967, this method of dividing and buying resulted in a period of crisis when students went on strike over grading. The administration at first attempted to pacify the students, but when this failed a firm stand was taken and the strike was broken. Prior to 1967 also, the administration was generally able to isolate and divide the forces of Uprooters. The only area where a small group had been able to join hands and acquire some position and rank was in the Medical School. The Departments of Physics, Engineering, and Mathematics were centers of some challenging members of the intelligentsia, but these individuals were all relatively new at Pahlavi and were of low rank.

Despite the control that the Maneuverers have been able to maintain, the struggle has continued to bubble ever since Hātifī's departure. There has been a continuing influx of new faculty, many of whom refuse to bow to the more powerful. By mid-1967, they had developed another threat to the old web. For the first time in Pahlavi's short history the young faculty had begun to organize faculty meetings, seminars, and picnics despite frantic efforts by the Maneuverers to prevent it. By this time also they had found an issue about which they could rally. The university Book of Regulations had laid down certain demanding conditions for appointment and promotion especially concerning publication. Assistant professors would not be

13. Personal interview, January 31, 1967.

14. One of several key examples of this occurred in early 1967 with the signing of the Pennsylvania-Pahlavi contract. At least two members of the Penn Team in Shīrāz told us that Philadelphia ignored its field staff in the entire matter. This lack of coordination was always noted by the Pahlavi administrators who used it to undermine the authority of the Pennsylvania team in Shīrāz.

15. According to various estimates, between 60 to 90 percent of Pahlavi University students received scholarships during the 1966–67 academic year. These scholarships ranged from 100 to 250 tomans (13 to 31 dollars) per month.

eligible for promotion to associate professorship unless, among other things, they had published "an article in at least one reputable scientific journal." Associate professors had to have published three such articles to qualify for full professorship. According to Note Two, Article One of Chapter One, this meant an article in an *"internationally* reputable scientific journal" and not "theses, abbreviated notes, general writings, letters, case reports or any work of this kind."[16] The Maneuverers fought these regulations bitterly for they were too busy manipulating to write such papers. They were joined in their protest by the Followers most of whom lacked the ability and/or initiative to produce such articles. The Uprooters stood up against great pressures and in a struggle that went right to the top put their positions on the line. The Regulations were not changed but the struggle had only begun. From all this, it is quite evident that as long as this professional-bureaucratic intelligentsia keeps entering the web, the pockets of Uprooters will continue to crystallize and challenge the traditional relationships.

The Politics of Confrontation

The Pahlavi University analysis reveals significant relationships between Iranian politics, the traditional web-system, and groups within the professional middle class. It becomes immediately evident that the central political authority views the Iranian university more in terms of control and as a center for producing the skills needed to carry out its programs than as a serious center of learning. Therefore, it has been important for the political authority to extend and protect the web-system in all universities. The universities have been deemed important enough to merit direct personal connection with the national political system and the figure of the Shah. The various chancellors, therefore, have often been either members of the political elite or faithful servants of the Shah. In this way, one web is intertwined and interlaced with another and the tentacles of traditionalism gain reinforcing support.

In order that the university system operate according to ongoing patterns, it is essential that university administration be directed by those who are loyal to such relationships. These are the Maneuverers. They are not always easy to discover since they try more and more to disguise themselves as Uprooters.[17] This recognition by the Maneuverers that they should

---

16. *Ā'īnnāmah-yi Intiṣābāt va Tarfī'āt-i Kārkunān-i Āmūzishīyi Dānishgāh-i Pahlavī* [Appointment and Promotion Regulations of Academic Employees at Pahlavi University], Chapter I, Article 1, Note 2 and Chapter II, Articles 4-5. In Persian. (Mimeographed.) Italics mine.

17. This became especially true in the 1960s when the Shah began to use revolutionary language to describe his programs and reforms. This language was immediately adopted by all members of the political elite.

appear like Uprooters is of singular importance since traditionally it was the Maneuverer-Manipulator who was most admired and imitated. This attempt to appear as champions of change represents an important shift in attitude that may very well lead to unintended long-range effects.

The Uprooters struggling in the Pahlavi University web-system tend to possess an American undergraduate education through which they have acquired certain achievement values. In a sense, their entire existence and identity have become tied up with the skills and knowledge they have obtained through such an education. By their very existence in the system, they pose a threat to the web-system and the Maneuverers who buttress such a system. The latter expend great effort in splitting and dividing the Uprooters who are relatively few in number and thus must coalesce in order to defend themselves and achieve their goals.

Due to the nature of the traditional power patterns (i.e., the Maneuverer controlled and directed), there is much more movement from Uprooter to Follower than from Follower to Uprooter. Many join the system as Uprooters, but after a little time and much pressure they become Followers. The trends are such, however, that movement in the direction of the Follower (and the Maneuverer) is a transient phenomenon while in the long run the Uprooter is becoming more and more common. An important part of the reason for this is that the forces of change support the Uprooters whose numbers and skills increase in importance with each new project, department, or school. As the intelligentsia itself increases, the Uprooters keep entering the web-system at an increasing rate, thus heightening the risk for the old patterns and the Maneuverers who direct them.

The webs of the traditional power network are woven together in a manner that allows key Maneuverers to be active in more than one web. Chancellor ʻAlam was not only involved in the Pahlavi University web-system but also he was an important part of the Shīrāz municipal web, the Fārs provincial web, and the national political web. In the latter, he stood in subservient service to the Shah; in the Pahlavi system, he considered everyone else as his own servants; and in the Fārs provincial system he stood in direct conflict with the Governor-General and the Commander of the Second Army whose headquarters were in Shīrāz. Through the person of the Chancellor, therefore, Pahlavi University was fastened into the intricate network of intertwining web-systems. The Maneuverers controlling the Pahlavi University administrative system possess power at the university level because they have been active in the other webs. The Uprooters, however, have power precisely because they are in the university. This is the heart of the conflict between the Uprooters and the Maneuverers, between the challengers and the defenders of the traditional pattern of power relationships.

The Student Uprooters

> The Iranian student must be courageous and willing to sacrifice. He should and can form student unions and organizations. He should not, however, build these into anything political. That is not his business.
>
> —Prime Minister Amīr 'Abbās Huvaydā,
> Personal Interview, May 29, 1967

One of the fundamental parts of the university structure is of such importance to this inquiry that it merits separate analysis. This is the student group. The students are located at the key birth-point of the professional-bureaucratic intelligentsia for all members of this class were at some time students. They with the writers who are in fact "extended students" are the most alienated section of the new middle class as well as one of the most politically volatile. The student problem is complicated and combined with the situation of youth in general. In developing areas, at least, this problem has received too little scholarly attention.

Fifty percent of the population of Iran is under twenty years of age. Thirty-three percent is between the ages of fifteen and thirty. These figures become even more staggering when it is pointed out that the trends indicate an even higher percentage of young people in years to come.[18] Student and youth affairs have been slowly becoming a primary concern of the political elite who have begun demanding investigations, studies, proposals, projects, and conferences in this regard. Here it is necessary to examine the elite policy vis-à-vis this group as well as to analyze the demands that Iranian youth have been making. Alienation and its political implications along with class relationships and change will also be investigated.

The Demands

The Iranian student-youth has been concentrating his demands in six main problem areas: family, sexual, educational, economic, occupational, and political. All six areas are intertwined and interrelated in the sense that difficulties in any one of them may mean the same in any of the others. *Sexual* demands may mean parent-child *(family)* division which may lead to no money *(economic),* resulting in no *education,* and therefore no job *(occupation),* hence *political* resentment and alienation. There are innumerable combinations of such relationships and the one described is very common. The goal here is not to present a long analysis of each problem

18. Ministry of Labor, *Problems of Manpower* 1 (1964): 567-70.

area but rather to pinpoint them and to examine briefly a few of the vital demands.[19]

A 1966 questionnaire distributed to Tehran and National University students provided the following information regarding the demands and priorities of Iranian university students.[20] From the response, it is evident that these students felt that the two listed problems demanding greatest attention were inequality-injustice and the educational system. Almost one-half of them chose the former and one-third the latter. Other evidence supports these findings including a survey of the contents of the more serious magazines and journals that the students read such as *Firdawsī* and *Jahān-i Naw.* The demand for equality and justice has definite political implications and the student demands here can be seen in the popularity of such novelists as Chūbak, Hidāyat, Ṣā'idī, and Afghānī. The writings of these men tend to concentrate upon the inequality and injustice suffered by the lower and middle classes in Iran.

Below are some of the important problems facing the people of this country. There are different opinions concerning which of these should be the government's main task. In your opinion to which of these problems should the government pay the most attention? Select only one.

Problem	Reply Percentage
Bettering the spiritual and moral level of society	2
Controlling and regulating business	0
Eliminating inequality and injustice	46
Improving conditions for your family	4
Planning and expanding economic development	14
Raising the general level of education and increasing educational opportunities	30
No reply	4
Total	100

19. In his book *Javānī-yi Purranj* [Suffering Youth], Iranian psychologist Dr. Nāṣir al-Dīn Ṣāḥib al-Zamānī lists and discusses sixteen problems that plague Iranian youth: problems of work, education, independent study, recreation, acceptance and recognition, sex, mate-selection and divorce, military service, generation-clashing, togetherness without understanding, conflicting values, disharmony between home and school, too little or too much independence, lack of guidance and leadership, fear of rivals and lack of social ideals. Ṣāḥib al-Zamānī's study is the most serious analysis of the situation of Iranian youth. The book is well researched and well documented. *Javānī-yi Purranj* (Tehran, 1965), pp. 22-23. In Persian.

20. The original questionnaire was drawn up by Seymour Martin Lipset and was translated and administered by an exceptionally competent Iranian social scientist. This survey will hereafter be referred to as the Tehran-National University Survey.

The response to this question carries with it even more extraordinary implications, however, since two of the fundamental issues for any traditional Islamic society ranked at the bottom of the students' concerns. Less than five percent of those surveyed felt that "bettering the spiritual and moral level of society" and "improving conditions for your family" were problems deserving most immediate government attention. This indicates a sharp break with tradition and reveals that the young Iranian may very well be a new man. Bearing these findings in mind, we will briefly examine three of the demands of youth. They concern education, organization, and class.

Education. Few areas in Iran have occasioned more criticism and less constructive activity than the system of education. The Iranian student himself becomes particularly demanding at two points during the educational period—at the entrance and exit points. These are two dangerous and narrowing bottlenecks and crucial junctions in the life of today's young Iranian.

Late every summer, thousands of Iranian secondary school graduates gather to take the university entrance examinations. This has become a time of tremendous pressure and fearful apprehension for the youth of Iran. Table 8 indicates the approximate number of applicants who have sat for the examinations in recent years and it also reveals the number who have been actually admitted into the university. According to these figures, the situation has been such that approximately one out of eight university applicants is accepted. In the 1966 Pahlavi University entrance examination, only one out of every fourteen examinees was accepted. Another study has shown that less than seven percent of Iranian grammar school graduates ever get into the first year of college.[21] An annually increasing number of

TABLE 8

University Entrance Examinations: Number of Examinees and Number and Percentage Accepted, 1963–69[a]

Year	University	Examinees	Accepted	Percent Accepted
1963	Tehran and Affiliated[b]	13,600	2,000	14.7
1966	Tehran and Affiliated	35,000	4,000	11.4
1969	Tehran and Affiliated	60,000	8,000	13.3

[a]The figures quoted are estimates rounded to the nearest hundred. They were gathered from various Iranian newspapers and magazines.
[b]Also Mashhad, Tabrīz, and Isfahān Universities.

21. Ṣāḥib al-Zamānī, *ibid.,* p. 60.

secondary school graduates signals the growth of the reservoir of resentment that exists here. One answer has been to build several new universities and technical-vocational schools, but this has neither taken up much of the slack nor has it touched any of the important qualitative questions.[22]

Thousands of these youths in the end seek employment, but here also they encounter acute competition and great pressures. Foremost Iranian scholars have warned of the dangers involved in the high rate of unemployment among youth. Every year two-thirds of all secondary school graduates join the masses of unemployed and in 1965 this meant close to 15,000 graduates.[23] Many of these have been absorbed in the military service, but each year also finds large numbers of released soldiers entering the job market. One effect of the formation of the famous Literacy Corps and other such organizations has been to take large numbers of these unemployed high school masses off the streets and to scatter them throughout the countryside. One Iranian journalist satirically wrote that even if Iranian youth had political parties, heroin, and gambling it would not be a bad idea if they could also find employment. He quoted former Minister of Labor Khusruvānī as saying: "What are these people going to do because they cannot find work? Kill themselves?"[24] Some have done just that while others have released their frustrations in a multitude of other ways.

Another particularly acute pressure point in the formal education of youth occurs after the schooling has been completed and the graduate must search for a place in society. The most serious facet of this situation and one which has received a great deal of attention (but little analysis) in recent years concerns the Iranian educated abroad. The political elite has become very sensitive to the need to convince their educated intelligentsia to return. The Shah and recent Prime Ministers have spoken on this point many times stressing the cost to Iran in foreign exchange, not to mention the subsequent loss of scarce skills and talent. In urging the graduates to return, the Iranian government has prepared movies, published special magazines, and offered many attractive financial and occupational inducements.[25] It is not accidental that it was an Iranian who directed the highly publicized United Nations

---

22. The Plan Organization's "Introductory Report to the Third Educational Plan" indicates that, in 1960, less than four percent of all students were enrolled in vocational schools. This percentage has been slightly increasing.

23. Ṣāḥib al-Zamānī, *ibid.,* p. 33.

24. Khusraw Shāhānī, "The Pain of Youth and Its Cure," *Khvāndanīhā,* 27th yr. No. 4 (5 Mihr 1345/1966): 18.

25. An example of one such widely distributed movie is Majīd Muḥsinī's "Parastū-hā bi-lānah-hā-shān bar mīgardand" [The Swallows Return to Their Nests]. Muḥsinī has been a deputy to the Twenty-first and Twenty-second Majlises and has traveled to Europe to try to convince Iranian students to return. In 1966, the Prime Minister's Office began putting out a high-quality literary magazine entitled *Talāsh* and has distributed it to Iranians throughout the world. The magazine refuses to touch political issues and ignores social problems as well.

Special Fund study of the "brain-drain." Nearly 30,000 Iranians are now studying abroad and in 1966 alone 18,000 young Iranians seeking assistance to study in the United States filed through the office of the American Friends of the Middle East in Tehran. It is estimated that Iran is losing close to 1,000 educated Iranians per year to foreign countries and that 900 and 600 Iranian doctors are practicing in New York and Munich respectively.

This exodus of young Iran and the subsequent reluctance to return indicates a much deeper problem than can be explained away in terms of the great financial-vocational-industrial inducements afforded by the West. Once returned, it is the foreign-educated Iranian who often becomes the most alienated member of his class. The struggles and difficulties the returned Iranian witnesses can be seen in such literary works as Jamālzādah's *Rāhābnāmah* (1948) and Esfandiary's *Identity Card* (1966). It may be recalled that Ṣādiq Hidāyat wrote his *Būf-i Kūr* [The Blind Owl] in the mid-1930s after returning to Iran from his first trip to Europe. Much of the frustration is traceable to problems of readjusting to the old web-system of personalism and influence as well as employment, political, and ideological difficulties. Many also returned to Iran expecting only the highest positions and salaries. This type of returnee often feels he is entitled to influential posts in the system.

In 1963–64, the only serious study of the educated Iranian returnee was carried out under the auspices of UNESCO. This extensive study, based on a preliminary sample of 1,174 graduate returnees educated in the United States, France, and England, was accompanied by identical studies of Egyptian and Indian returnees. In the end, 253 subjects were selected and the tabulated results of the interview-questionnaire are revealing.[26] Nine percent of the Iranian returnees were "happy to be home again." With respect to employment, 6 and 14 percent of Egyptian and Indian returnees experienced "difficulties in finding a job." In Iran, the figure was 31 percent. Ninety-eight percent of the Iranian returnees felt that they needed assistance in their professional field in terms of placement and working conditions. Egyptian and Indian returnees of the same mind counted 75 and 57 percent. Seventy-six percent of the Egyptian returnees surveyed felt that

---

26. The man who directed the Iran study was Dr. Morteza Nassefat of the Institute of Social Studies and Research of Tehran University. The statistics of the following two paragraphs were drawn from his manuscript "Les Situations des Étudiants Iraniens à l'Étranger et Leur Rôle dans l'Échange des valuers Culturalles entre l'Iran et Leurs Pays Hôtes" (Tehran, 1965) and from United Nations document UNESCO/SS/COM/5 Rev.-PRIO, Oslo, November 1964. The sample was selected with regard to age, date of return, country of study, branch of study, period of residence abroad, type of student (scholarship), level of education, and sex. All those questioned returned between 1955 and 1962 and had been studying in France, England, or the United States. In the Egyptian and Indian surveys, the host countries were Germany, England, and the United States. The study itself is a very scholarly one and the Iranian section is particularly well done.

they could utilize their foreign training "to a great extent" on their present jobs. The Indian and Iranian figures were 48 and 36 percent respectively.

In the ideo-political realm, the survey raised the following question and produced instructive results.

> *In your opinion, what institutions, ways of living, values, and ideas of your former host country do you consider it would be valuable to introduce into your home country?*

	Percent for Each Home Country		
	Egypt	*India*	*Iran*
No specified answer	5	10	3
Educational system	18	51	23
Attitudes toward world	42	32	55
Social welfare and security	27	27	48
Reorganization of state	17	1	10
Administration/government procedure	17	15	17
Women's rights	9	0	17
Family life and child rearing	24	2	10
Leisure time activities	18	4	4
Individual freedom and rights	6	12	28
Emphasizing national character	53	15	7
Others	31	1	33

Many more Iranian returnees than either Egyptian or Indian feel that their country would do well to introduce from the West values and ideas of "individual freedom and rights." The groups surveyed indicate the same with regard to "social welfare and security schemes."

The fact that Iranians seem to have special problems of readjustment may say things both about the Iranian system and about the personality and alienation of the returning intelligentsia. In this vein, it is relevant that the UNESCO study shows that sixty-one percent of the Iranian returnees felt that they had changed "to a great extent" while abroad. Only thirty percent of the Indians and thirty-eight percent of the Egyptians felt the same way. It is for this reason perhaps that a perceptive young journalist has referred to this part of the intelligentsia as "the uprooted."[27] In some cases the resulting frustration has had political roots; in many cases it has led to dramatic political acts; and in all cases it has had strong political implications. In the following way, a Western-educated Asian has described what returning home has meant. Her words are reechoed ceaselessly by Iranian returnees.

27. See Alfred Bakhash, *Kayan International,* February 27, 1963.

> We acquire split, two-layered souls. Underneath are deep emotions, taboos and compulsions, repulsions and loves unexplained and dark. Above, a glut of glib words, theories whose meaning disappears in the presence of limitless want, ideas intellectually acknowledged and emotionally important, behavior rational but suddenly forgotten when the sea begins to roar. . . .
>
> It is not easy to cut out great pieces of oneself. For whatever the West had done, some of us had loved it for one thing: that delicate reality, frail and hard to handle, gentle, and strong in tenderness—spiritual liberty. . . .[28]

Thus, two of the demands that young Iran voices in the area of education are the right to acquire that education as well as the right to use it. Some of the implications and struggles this has occasioned are analyzed above. There are of course innumerable other demands that are made during the educational period itself and one of these will be discussed next. This moves the focus of concentration closer to the political system and concerns a certain freedom to organize. The case to be treated here is student organization and group activity.

Organization. Despite their many efforts, the youth of Iran have few organizations of their own. Since 1954, student groups have been closely supervised and tightly controlled by the government and there are no open youth groups formed without Security Organization investigation and permission. The manner in which student affairs have been handled in Iran has increasingly contributed to student apathy and resentment. In 1967, there were thirty-three Iranian organizations that dealt with affairs of youth and, with the possible exception of three minority-religious-ethnic societies, they were all highly ineffective. On April 22, 1967, a special committee on youth problems affiliated with the Ministry of Labor and the Prime Ministry met to analyze the general situation. At this meeting, discussion centered upon the need to coordinate all the various youth organizations. It was also proposed that a different environment be created for the youth of Iran—one in which democracy would be stressed as the prime value. This group concluded its meeting by asking for two and one-half billion rials to begin needed programs in the area of student and recreational organization.[29]

The youth themselves have all but boycotted the existing government organizations. A summer 1966 survey of four hundred university students and secondary school seniors revealed that eighty-eight percent of them did not belong to any youth organization and of the few who did one-half

28. Han Suyin, *A Many-Splendored Thing* (Boston: Little, Brown and Company, 1952), quoted in Mostofi, *Aspects of Nationalism,* p. 45.

29. Personal copy of the minutes of the April 1967 meeting.

named the Iran America Society. Three out of the four hundred were members of the major government-sponsored youth organization—the Youth Guidance Organization. Concerning the administration of youth organizations, eighty-seven percent demanded that youth itself be in charge while four percent favored government administration.[30]

While this very survey was being carried out, the government took what was called a major step in meeting the demands of youth. An elaborate "Youth Palace" was built and offered olympic-sized and heated swimming and diving pools, a 250-seat theatre, air-conditioning, and exquisite marbled architecture. The location of this palace is north of Tehran significantly at the site of the former Security Organization Club. Theoretically, the members themselves are supposed to direct the organization, but many students consider several of the supervisors as security police agents.[31] One student of lower-middle-class background described it as "a luxurious haven in the midst of nothing filled with government agents inviting us to come in." The Youth Palace is viewed by most young Iranians as belonging to the sons and daughters of the upper-class elite anyway.

The situation of university student organizations is even more barren, for with the exception of the tiny Ābādān Institute of Technology, there is no Iranian institute of higher learning that has a student council or government. There is only one student organization found in most Iranian schools and that is the closely supervised *Anjuman-i Islām* (Islamic Council). The Tehran-National University Survey indicated that close to ninety percent of the respondents considered "university student government" a valuable need. A recent attempt to establish a student council occurred at Pahlavi University when the administration suddenly appointed a student representative. Student protest reached such a state that the administration consented to elections for a student organization. Twenty-two representatives were elected and in less than six months all had resigned. They had believed they were to represent the student body, but the administrators considered these representatives as their own.

In the end, the students have not only been demanding organizations and associations but also they want groups in which they and not the government provide the direction. The government's long record of failure and inefficiency in this area has just served to aggravate the problem.

---

30. Nafīsī and Ṭabāṭabā'ī, *Barrasī-yi Masā'il va Mushkilāt-i Javānān.*

31. In a personal interview, the Prime Minister vigorously denied this. There are probably few such agents in the Youth Palace, but it immediately inherited this reputation as its predecessor, the Youth Guidance Organization, was well staffed with such agents. To counter the criticism that the Youth Palace belongs to a privileged few, Iranian authorities have recently established a dozen more Youth Centers throughout the country. It is also important to note that a conscious effort is being made to separate the Youth Palace organization from formal government affiliation.

Group-Class Relationships. From what has been presented above, it is possible to recognize certain group-class tensions and relationships that exist in the student ranks. In terms of class, the Tehran-National University Survey produced some interesting results. From the following figures one can gain an insight into the attitudes of the Iranian student toward other groups and classes. The question posed was as follows:

> *If a person who forms part of the groups indicated below occupied a high position in government, what degree of confidence would you have that he would place the interests of the nation above those of his private interests?*

	Answers in Percent				
	Much	Some	Little	None	No Answer
Businessmen	4	24	30	20	22
Union Leaders	12	34	24	10	20
Religious Leaders	6	28	22	22	22
Workers	8	28	30	8	26
Large Industrialists	8	22	26	22	22
Large Landowners	6	14	24	34	22
The Military	4	28	22	22	24
Professionals	64	8	8	0	20

These figures show that the students place a relatively strong trust in their own class. This is quite remarkable in light of the deep distrust and cynicism that characterizes Iranian youth. After the professionals, most confidence is placed in the workers and union leaders while least is placed in large landowners, businessmen, and large industrialists.[32] From this, it can very plausibly be hypothesized that the university students place much more trust in the lower classes than they do in the upper. To a question raised about "the struggle between employers and workers," forty-six percent replied that, in general, they thought that the workers were right while six percent considered the employers right.

One-third of these students did not see any chance that social classes could get along at all together. Over forty percent believed that social classes will always exist in Iran, while another thirty-five percent saw them disappearing only when the political system changes. It is clear that the students are very much aware of class realities and that they have very little confidence in the Iranian upper class. Even among themselves there is important tension based upon differences of social class origin and this affects them in many ways.

32. This is particularly interesting since only one-sixth of the students sampled were of lower-class origin.

It is the offspring of the lower and middle classes who suffer the most at the time of entrance examinations described above. These are the ones whose parents cannot for the most part afford to send them abroad and therefore they must either succeed in the Iranian entrance examinations or forego a higher education. It can also be proposed that the great majority of university students in Iran are of lower- and especially middle-class background. Of the minority of upper-middle- and upper-class origins studying in Iran, most are at National University where tuition charges are relatively high. Among privately supported students abroad whose families represent the lower-middle and middle class, some fifty percent do not return to Iran where because of limited family connections, they face "meagre work prospects and a consequent inability to better themselves."[33] Similar students of upper-class origin return at a much higher rate estimated to be seventy-five percent. Finally, whatever organization and activity that do exist for young Iran exist for those youths of upper-class origin. The elite here is called in Tehran the "jet-set" and they have their own clubs, clothes, and cars. The Youth Palaces that are built are by their very titles and nature off limits to the youth of lower- and middle-class background.

In brief summary here, Iranian students do view themselves as members of a new middle class and they are in many ways more alienated from the existing upper class than from the lower. Yet there are still differences and tensions among them traceable to their social origins. It is the youth of lower- and middle-class origins who are most alienated because they are losing the most. It was such a youth who assassinated Prime Minister Manṣūr in January 1965 and it was also such a youth who attempted to assassinate the Shah that same year.

The Alienation

The alienation of the Iranian student can be seen almost as clearly as that of the writer described at the beginning of this chapter. Indeed, the young writer has recently been a student and has only extended his former way of life and state of mind. The overlap is easily seen in the cases of educated young journalist-writer R. I'timādī who wrote a novel depicting the agony of the younger generation. Students purchased the book, appropriately titled *Sākin-i Mahallah-yi Gham* [Resident of the District of Sorrow], in such numbers that two editions were sold out almost immediately. The third edition was confiscated and the author brought to the Criminal Court

33. Habib Nafisi, "The Brain-Drain: The Case of Iranian Non-Returnees" (paper presented at the Annual Conference of the Society for International Development, New York, March 17, 1966), p. 7.

for "promoting a philosophy which encourages Iranian youth to rebel against the established social and moral norms."

In general, the young people of Iran have become more and more preoccupied with opium, heroin, and alcohol and the suicide rate among Iranian youth is alarmingly high.[34] The Iranian youth himself speaks of a great loneliness, emptiness, and insecurity and even coins colloquialisms to describe this experience. When he says he is *hapalīhapaw,* he means that the ground is constantly shifting beneath him and that there is nothing he can grasp to keep himself from falling. Much of the difficulty is the overwhelming force and challenge of change and this too has helped twist and alienate him. The following analysis of Iranian youth reveals the relationship between these forces of change and the depth of alienation he feels. These are personal impressions recorded in 1966 after a series of discussions with Iranian student friends.

> There are more and more parties taking place in urban Iran. A short time ago this did not exist for the young. Now they exist but have little meaning. Such activities and recreation are only being imitated. The young do not understand the philosophy behind such pastimes. They just dress up and go.
>
> This reflects the shallowness and emptiness in the lives of the young people. They battle their conservative families to do things they themselves do not understand. As such the present generation is the battered victim of change. They are the living wedge of shock troops that are being mangled by a situation that has exploded upon them. The forces of yesterday give ground grudgingly.
>
> But even when the forces of yesterday become more pliable and openminded, the battle has still only begun. Change that is aimless and baseless must be given meaning and anchored in the world in which it takes place. What good are new clothes and styles if there is no place to go? What good are places to go if that is all they are? Why imitate surfaces without understanding substances? Why destroy without building?
>
> Yet, who can be dynamic, inventive, and constructive in a system where problems of family, sex, money, education, and employment sap one's every energy? The battering that the young Iranian absorbs from such fundamental problems takes its effect upon him. He is lost, distrustful, insecure, and cynical. He is a young man and an old man. But

---

34. There are many relevant statistics but their reliability is very questionable. It can be said with reasonable certainty though that seventy-five percent of the suicides in Iran are committed by young people between the ages of fifteen and thirty. In the early 1960s, there were half a million reported cases of opium addiction in Iran. It is estimated that after the United States Iran has the largest heroin addict population in the world. Heroin is the near monopoly of young people in Iran while opium is more common among the older generation. See Ṣāḥib al-Zamānī, *ibid.,* pp. 203-4. See also note 6 above.

tomorrow the real task begins. He must lead Iran. His training ground has been a slippery one but he has survived. In so doing, however, the young Iranian has often blunted the tools of initiative, optimism, and creativity so necessary to the tasks now at hand.[35]

Political-Elite Policy

The entire subject of youth and student problems has had severe ideo-political implications and much of the resentment continues to flow in this direction. The policy of the political-elite and government in responding to this situation will have an important effect not only upon the future direction this alienated group takes but also upon the future of Iran.

As was briefly indicated in the discussion of youth organization, the approach of the government has contributed to making a bad situation worse. The major reason has been that the system has decided to infiltrate the ranks of Iranian youth in order that it may both observe their activities and control them as well. The universities are a case in point.

After 1955 (Āẕar 16), when three students were shot to death on the Tehran University campus, the government promised that troops would never again enter university grounds. The students came to trust this immunity and such was the situation until January 1962 (1 Bahman 1340) during the stormy days of Amīnī's Premiership. In a surprise attack that day, the commandos moved across the university grounds destroying property and beating the students. Following this episode, the Security Organization openly moved into the universities, and at Tehran University a military general sat in the Secretariat with files on every student.[36] The government now adopts a hard line toward the students although techniques vary from university to university. At Tehran University the method has been force and open intimidation. At Pahlavi University the method has been bribery in the form of scholarships. At the Ābādān Institute of Technology an entire class was dismissed. Besides this, there are several hundred students who are in the employ of the Security Organization. These are the "professionals" who frequent the government-sponsored youth organizations and who march and demonstrate in the streets on proregime holidays. They get an education out of it and afterwards become the latest Maneuverers in the system.[37] In attempting to harness the students of Iran to the present system, one university dean suggested the government form a

35. Personal interviews, March 7, 1966.

36. This particular man was also active in local government, the Boy Scout Organization, and in many welfare groups. There is little doubt that he controlled student affairs at Tehran University. Another military-security man held a somewhat similar position at National University.

37. More than one Minister in recent years has moved up to cabinet rank along this route.

"white guard" made up of students and then relate it to the Shah's "white revolution."

Combined with this force and bribery, there has been a genuine effort to improve the situation of youth in certain areas. Both the Shah and the Queen have emphasized the need to assist the Iranian student in many critical realms. Queen Farah has taken a personal interest in the problems of Iranian youth and has strongly indicated her intention to do something about solving these problems.[38] Unlike most members of the political elite, the Empress continues to hold the trust and confidence of this generation whose members view her as an especially enlightened and human force. In November 1970, the Shah himself spoke to the issue of student problems at the first graduation ceremony of Aryamehr University. He stated that the lack of youthful protest is unnatural and that all legitimate student demands ought to be granted even when they are not vocalized. Despite this high level concern, however, elite policy towards youth remains essentially unchanged.

The three-pronged policy of intimidation, bribery, and selected concession has succeeded in some degree to quiet the students down. It has not succeeded in diminishing their opposition nor can it build commitment. As was shown at the beginning of the chapter, there are many forces involved and many struggles in process. Whenever there has been the slightest relaxation of pressure or misdirected bribery the students have exploded. The Iranian political elite as well as Iran needs the commitment and support of its youth. It is getting neither and as a result was recently warned by leading psychologist Dr. Maḥmūd Sanā'ī:

> The future of the youngsters of this community does not concern bridges and roads and asphalt which if cheated on only involve a material loss and can be rebuilt with new capital. If the life of the young generation of this country is lost it is not obtainable again.[39]

The Politics of Alienation

The Iranian student Uprooter represents the most alienated, volatile, and threatening force within the new middle class. He exists as an uprooted Uprooter who is primarily concerned with rejecting and ripping the web-system. He battles relationships of personal conflict and deference in many arenas and on family, religious, and educational levels. He feels little com-

---

38. Personal interviews, October 13 and November 18, 1970. Between these two interviews with the Empress was a private interview with a Deputy Director of the Security Organization. This particular agent, who held an M.A. in political science from Tehran University and boasted thirteen years service in the Organization, was in charge of youth and student affairs. The meeting took place in a small unmarked building in northeast Tehran on November 12, 1970. The security agent argued that there were no roots to student discontent in Iran but that this dissatisfaction was merely the fashion. He concluded that problems have a way of disappearing and that the youth situation was no exception.

39. "New Plan for the Organization of Schools," *Sukhan,* Shahrīvar 1, 1341/1962, p. 77.

mitment to traditional power linkages and endeavors to sever them as they surround his existence.

The Maneuverers as guardians of the old web-system attempt to neutralize the threat of the student Uprooter by means of intimidation, manipulation, and sporadic concession. This policy meets with varying degrees of success as a number of students always join the web-system and relate according to the dominant patterns of that system.[40] Many do not, however, and they react in many ways. A large group decides to opt out. Many flee Iran and never return, while others return only to leave once more. Others flee spiritually; i.e., they are physically present but mentally absent as they retreat into environments of apathy, opium, and alcohol. A tiny but growing minority resorts to suicide which represents the ultimate means of opting out. This policy of isolation, separation, and retreatism is coupled with a more positive response which involves active resistance. This usually involves a revolt against the deference relationship as students resist the dictates of father, teacher, and mullā. The same conflict is initiated vis-à-vis the Shah and the political elite. Many Iranian students are no longer willing to exist as the extensions of anyone else's personality. This is attested to by deepening father-son fissures, religious rejection, and political demonstrations.[41]

Since the system is composed of interrelated and interwoven webs with Maneuverers and Uprooters active in many webs, frustration and alienation in one web is swiftly channeled into other webs as well. Student unrest in the university, for example, feeds directly into the national political system. Threats to the university administration become threats to the basic relationships that mark the political system. Situations of upheaval in one web can be easily transmitted to other webs. For these reasons, the political authority attempts to preserve and protect the fundamental patterns in other vital areas such as the educational, economic, and religious systems. This is done by placing members of the political elite in key positions within these systems. This in turn increases overlapping and interlocking which, although it may provide temporary reinforcement, at the same time eases the task for long-run destruction. As the Uprooters among the intelligentsia (e.g., the students) increasingly threaten local webs and destroy traditional relationships, other interrelated webs, including the central political system, immediately feel the impact.

---

40. As this chapter has briefly indicated in several places, the student group is also the scene of many Maneuverers, Technocrats, and Followers. Since this chapter, however, has emphasized the general role of the Uprooter and since there are a larger number of Uprooters among the student group than perhaps any other, it is the student Uprooter who has been stressed. The following two chapters will concentrate upon the role of the Technocrat and of the Maneuverer.

41. For a penetrating discussion of the struggle between tradition and modernity in terms of the Iranian value structure, see William G. Millward, "Traditional Values and Social Change in Iran," *Iranian Studies* 4 (Winter 1971): 2-35.

chapter four

The Technocrat: The Politics of Procedural Disaffection

Chapter 3 analyzed the alienation of the most highly educated and sensitive groups in the professional middle class and indicated that much of this has taken an ideological and political coloring. It also revealed that part of this opposition has resulted from disaffection with the procedures and methods that marked the very being of the web-system. This section will treat the alienation that stems from procedural disaffection as members of the intelligentsia attempt to go about their business rationally, efficiently, and creatively. These are the groups who are disaffected and frustrated on procedural grounds, but are not supporters of fundamental change in the national political system. Administrators, middle-ranking bureaucrats, and professionals, such as physicians and engineers, dominate this category.[1] These are the Technocrats who strive to perform their tasks and to in-

1. The physician-engineer problem will not be discussed separately in this chapter. What is generally said concerning the bureaucrat-technocrat also holds true for them. With regard to physicians, suffice it to say that in Iran there are 4,000 to 6,000 physicians while there are approximately 2,000 Iranian physicians practicing abroad (one-half of those in Iran practice in Tehran which represents less than one-tenth of the country's population). There are more American-trained Iranian doctors in New York than in all Iran. For these and other relevant statistics in this area, see Ṣāḥib al-Zamānī, *ibid.,* p. 57; G. Henderson, "Foreign Students: Exchange or Immigration?" *National Association of Foreign Student Advisors Newsletters* (New York: November, 1964); and "Doctors Urged Return Home," *Kayhan International,* January 20, 1966.

troduce rationality into their working environment. They are set against the traditional power relationships analyzed in chapters 1 and 3 and their alienation is documented largely in technical reports and plans. They have found that their talent and work is seriously hampered by the influence-wielding, red tape, nepotism, and favoritism that surround them. Much has been written about these relationships, but there has been little analysis linking them either to the classes that must deal with them or to the processes of change that challenge them.

The Procedure Challenged

> It is hereby announced that despite the huge numbers of influence-wielders, the dispensers of influence have no more positions open. . . . Bringing influence will not bring a job.
>
> —Advertisement, Tehran Bus Company,
> *Iṭṭilā'āt* Newspaper, April 12, 1967

The Persian language is rich in terms and expressions that explain how the old personal web operates. Such expressions as *pārtī, pārtībāzī, dastah bandī, bandbāzī, kāqazbāzī, rushvah, ḥaqq-i ḥisāb, āvurdan-i tawṣīyah, nān qarz dādan, rafiqbāzī,* and *zad-u-band* refer to levels and means of maneuvering and manipulating in order to improve one's own position in the system. These are everyday expressions that explain how goals are achieved and work gets done. Such terms cannot be properly translated into English for their closest equivalents carry a pejorative connotation that is not always present in the Persian usage. The closest translations would be such expressions as "connections," "influence-wielding," "cliquishness," "ganging up," "red tape," "bribery," "paying off," "pulling strings," "pork barrelling," "favoritism," and "manipulating." In order to appreciate the subtleties of these expressions, it would be instructive to explain a few of these terms in more detail. The following interpretations have been developed from extended discussion concerning the history and meaning of these terms with Iranians from all walks of life. *Āvurdan-i tawṣīyah* means to bring influence to bear and implies the use of connections to achieve a certain goal. *Nān qarz dādan* literally means to loan bread but always implies a deal whereby favors are exchanged. The process is one of logrolling and back-scratching. *Zad-u-band* is a compound of two terms meaning manipulation, maneuverability, and more. *Zad* connotes the idea of striking, pounding, and softening while *band* means to tie, bind, or bend.

In its original and deepest meaning, *zad-u-band* refers to the act of making something (or someone) more malleable by consistent pounding and hammering. The more resilient and elastic object is next twisted and bent to suit the purpose at hand. People who engage in *zad-u-band* are individuals who practice this kind of manipulation. They are the "wheelers and dealers" who in this study are synonymous with the category Maneuverers.

The most common of these expressions is *pārtī* which means to have connections, to be able to pull strings, or to have "pull." *Pārtī* symbolizes the traditional system and is the best single expression to describe its dynamics.[2] The Ministry of Foreign Affairs has traditionally been staffed with members of a few select families. Other organizations such as the Municipality, the Ministry of Finance, and the Customs Organization are known throughout Iran as the most developed centers of favoritism and influence-wielding. In Ṣādiq Hidāyat's *Ḥājjī Āqā* (1945), Ḥājjī advises his youngest son on how to succeed in Iran:

> Do not be afraid of abuse, humiliation or slander. . . . When kicked out of one door enter with a smile from an other. . . . Be impudent, insolent and stupid, for it is sometimes necessary to pretend stupidity—it helps. This is the type of man our country needs today. . . . Be an opportunist. Try to establish connections with the holders of high offices. Agree with everybody, no matter what his opinion is so that you may attract his utmost favor.[3]

This kind of personal interaction has spread and affected organizational relations as well. Organizations cooperate with one another only to the degree that close personal relationships exist between and among the personnel that staff the particular units. Thus, the picture is one of bitter competition and conflict between universities, hospitals, ministries, youth organizations, military-security organizations, and professional clubs and societies. Particularly intense conflict, for example, has marked the following organizations: National University-Tehran University, Ministry of In-

2. Pārtī and personalism exist, of course, in all human societies. As chapter 1 indicates, however, Iranian society with its lack of institutions is *built* on such principles and most important business is carried out this way. For the best analysis in English of pārtī and its institutionalization in Iranian society, see Ali Nasseri, "The Ecology of Staffing in the Government of Iran" (unpublished M.A. thesis, American University of Beirut, 1964), especially pp. 64-72.

3. Hidāyat, *Ḥājjī Āqā,* quoted in H. Kamshad, *Modern Persian Prose Literature* (Cambridge: University Press, 1966), p. 193. For the best English analyses of this system, see Norman Jacobs, *The Sociology of Development: Iran as an Asian Case Study* (New York: Frederick A. Praeger, 1966); and Esfandiary's *Identity Card.* In Persian, besides Hidāyat's *Ḥājjī Āqā,* see also Ḥājj Zayn al-ʿĀbidīn's *Siyāhatnāmah-yi Ibrāhīm Big* and Muḥammad Ḥijāzī's *Zība.*

terior-Tehran Municipality, Security Organization-Military Intelligence Organization, and Nimāzī-Sa'adī Hospitals. A detailed 1966 Plan Organization study of the development of Gīlān Province revealed that there were thirteen government agencies competing on local level development projects alone in that province.[4]

This traditional system is being challenged by the new groups of technocrats that constantly appear. These young men are of quite a different cast than their predecessors for they are interested in achievement.[5] With industrializing and reforming processes underway, achievement and occupational competence have become of greater and greater import. The technocrats have as a result been able to establish a foothold in the system and their impact has been very evident in certain areas. They have made their greatest progress in the following organizations: the Central Bank, the Sifīd Rūd Dam Authority, the Khūzistān Water and Power Authority (KWPA), the National Iranian Oil Company (NIOC), and the Plan Organization. The struggle against favoritism, vested interest, personalism, and pārtī, however has just begun and even in these organizations success has been limited. In the cases of the NIOC, the KWPA, and the Plan Organization, the old patterns have managed to reassert themselves many times with the result that the technocrats have often become discouraged and cynical.

The NIOC, KWPA, Plan Organization, and the Reassertion of Pārtī

The National Iranian Oil Company has been one of the more exceptional organizations in Iran in the sense that ability and talent have been important factors in appointment and promotion. Behind this, of course, lay fifty years of foreign training and, as a result, the establishment of certain patterns. However, from the time of Muṣaddiq, when the oil industry was nationalized, until today, the NIOC has slowly moved deeper and deeper into the web of pārtī and favoritism. Muṣaddiq needed men he could rely upon and as a result many of the most experienced and skilled Iranian oil men lost their positions. With the fall of Muṣaddiq, this trend continued and the three chairmen of the NIOC (Bāyat, Intiẓām, and Iqbāl) have been intertwined with the central political elite. They brought their friends along with them to the NIOC and in this way the old web-system continually rein-

4. Plan Organization, Social Affairs Planning Group, *Barrasī-yi Muqaddamātī-yi Mushkilāt-i Ustānī Kardan-i Būdjah va Barnāmah dar Ustān-i Gīlān* [Preliminary Examination of Ustan Budgeting and Planning Difficulties in the Province of Gīlān] (Tehran, April 1966), p. 14. (Mimeographed.)

5. For rare insights into this group, see articles by "Shapur Rahbari" in *Kayhan International,* 1964–67. The young man who writes these columns is himself such a technocrat.

forced itself. This pattern, of course, breeds cliques and in the NIOC there are several such phenomena. The most important and pervasive of these has been the one that surrounds Dr. Riẕā Fallāḥ, the Director in charge of Technology and International Affairs. Fallāḥ is a very knowledgeable and able oil man and during his years with the Oil Company he has built up a clique of some two hundred men who are committed to him (even more so than to their jobs). In NIOC circles, these employees are known as "Fallāḥ-men." At the same time, the highest echelons of the Oil Company are well staffed with members of the Iranian upper class. Besides Chairman Manūchihr Iqbāl, there are many others such as Manūchihr Farmānfārmāiyān, Fatḥullāh Nafīsī, Āqākhān Bakhtiyār, 'Abbās Iqbāl, and Khusraw Hidāyat who are members of the upper-class elite.

Despite these inroads of personalism and politics, the Oil Company is still an organization where talent and merit count for a great deal. The competent and dedicated young technocrat or petroleum engineer who has no pārtī and few connections can succeed better here than in almost any other Iranian organization. The oil business is an extremely technical field. Each job has special qualifications and a certain type of education and experience is necessary. Thus, even the Farmānfārmāiyāns and Nafīsīs must possess a certain skill and ability (the two mentioned above, for example, are qualified engineers). Those individuals, chosen on personal-political grounds, have at times found life difficult and as a result the members of the upper-class elite have often found it easier to move in the direction of the government when seeking a career. The NIOC is an interesting place to observe the interaction and struggle between pārtī and the need to hire and promote the best talent available in order to make an advanced and technical industry succeed.

Two other organizations that have had strong records of rationality and efficiency in the midst of great irrationality and inefficiency have been the Khūzistān Water and Power Authority and the Plan Organization. Both were established with direct American assistance and advice and both became centers where the best-trained and dedicated technocrat-administrators gathered. Over the years, however, these organizations were slowly drawn into the political web as the politician began making decisions that undercut the technocrat's effectiveness and position. The dramatic example of this occurred when top technocrat-planner Abul Ḥasan Ibtihāj was cut out of the Plan Organization for opposing the establishment of a Petro-Chemical Plant near Shīrāz.[6] In taking such a stand, Ibtihāj confronted the highest ranking politicians and a personal business web of the top echelon of the Iranian political elite. Ibtihāj's fall symbolized the precarious position of all achievement-oriented forces.

6. This particular issue was the last of a series where Ibtihāj had threatened vested personal and political interests.

The Abādān Pocket of Efficiency

With the fall of Muṣaddiq and the signing of the 1954 Oil Agreement, several hundred foreigners were brought back to help get the Ābādan Refinery back on its feet. Although the Oil Company had always operated under foreign supervision, local political considerations ruled the refinery, which international oil men labeled "the most unrealistic refinery in the world." Part of the reason for its establishment was to provide employment and economic viability for the province of Khūzistān and by 1949, the Ābādan Refinery employed 46,000 people. Other refineries of roughly the same construction and complexity managed with four to five thousand employees. Even by 1966 the manufacturing cost of one barrel of oil at Ābādan was 60 cents while at other prewar factories the same could be done for 40 cents. Postwar factories processed one barrel of oil for 28 cents and new refineries can now do the job for 15 cents.[7]

In the postnationalization period, however, the oil consortium launched an all-out attack on this inefficiency and expense. By 1967, the number of employees at the refinery had been cut to 17,000 and, most importantly, the number of foreign staff had been reduced to only eighty men. At Ābādan, there are Iranians who are now considered among the best managers, administrators, and businessmen in the world. One high ranking consortium official stated that "this refinery has taught a few hundred Iranians the meaning of business."[8] For the first time, the General Refinery Manager is an Iranian and he is one of the most capable and efficient technocrats that Iran has ever seen. The top fifteen Iranians at the refinery average forty-five years of age and have been with the company for an average of two decades. Thirteen of them have B.Sc. degrees, the equivalent, or higher, and all of them are respected for their talent and dedication. In the last few years there has been a pressing demand for Iranians who have moved ahead because of skill and merit and everyone has rushed to the consortium and refinery for recruitment. Needless to say, even the few there are inadequate to begin to meet the demands of gas plants, steel works, aluminum industries, and the multimillion dollar petro-chemical industries being established in Iran. These are industries that must compete internationally and in such business there is little room for pārtī and influence-wielding.

There are certain relevant reasons why the refinery has become a pocket of efficiency and talent in the Iranian system. First of all, it has been established and controlled by foreign experts and administrators. These are men who have known very well the importance of talent, dedication, and

7. These figures were gathered during a series of interviews with consortium officials in Ābādan in February 1967.

8. Personal interview, February 22, 1967.

experience and have worked hard to build this into the Iranian oil industry. Even more important is the fact that they have not been as vulnerable to political intervention by the Iranian elite and herein lies the big difference between the Consortium-Refinery and the NIOC. Second, this has been a business that has had to stand up to international competition and this leaves little room for pārtī. Only the most capable will do for as one English oil man said: "The Consortium has 150 tankers each month waiting to be filled with oil to be sold in an internationally competitive market. We cannot take a chance on some aristocrat's semiqualified son-in-law to direct such an operation."[9] Finally, in 1955–56, a rigid grade classification system was introduced and this has been religiously applied. This twenty-grade scheme was imposed in a culture of bargaining and flexibility and as a result was universally hated by the Iranian staff. This classification system was built into the oil company operation and in many ways discouraged personal bargaining and maneuvering. This, along with the foreign presence, provided an inbuilt mechanism which the higher-ranking Iranian managers could use as legitimate excuses to resist personal pressures and requests.

The Ābādan Refinery has thus in many ways been isolated and insulated from the Iranian web-system. This has been a vital reason why the best Iranian administrators and technocrats have been developed here. Advancement has been based largely upon performance and those Iranians who now direct the refinery operations are eminently qualified. The existence of these men is well known in Iran and the demand for many more like them is becoming greater as new industries, organizations, and projects are initiated.

The Technocrat and the Web-System

Examples such as the oil company organizations are in many ways atypical for they have been partially isolated from traditional power patterns and, in particular, from political-personal intervention. It is not accidental, for example, that the more efficient and successful administrative operations have been several of the regional development authorities. Key examples such as the Sifīd Rūd Dam Authority and the Jīruft Development Authority have been far removed from Tehran and, as a consequence, from much of the political and personal pressures that debilitate initiative and efficiency. In these cases, it has only been distance and inaccessibility that have helped, while in the case of the Consortium, it has also been a certain international barrier.

Most Iranian technocrats and administrators are involved in government and quasi-government organizations and it is here where the capable and

9. Personal interview, February 24, 1967.

dedicated are needed the most. This unfortunately is also where the old linkages are the strongest and where business is characterized by connection and pārtī.[10] In 1964, the Institute of Social Studies and Research of Tehran University completed a detailed and documented study of the Iranian government administration. This analysis, which was presented in mimeographed form for limited circulation, listed nine problems that characterized administrators and administrative relationships:

1. Absence of cooperation between administrators
2. Incorrect philosophy behind the entire idea of administration
3. Bribery
4. Absence of goals or interest in work
5. Prevalence of influence-wielding
6. Lack of respect for the people
7. Use of administrative power for personal benefit
8. Continual absence from work
9. Misuse of government property

Documentation was supplied to support these conclusions which revealed a great lack of commitment and an omnipresent reliance on favoritism and influence-wielding.[11] The latter was also shown in the Tehran-National University Survey by the following statement and response:

There is no politician who will not place his friends and relatives in public jobs.

Response	Percent
Strongly agree	18
Agree	72
Disagree	10
Strongly disagree	0

It is into this kind of system that the educated young Iranians are moving. Many have studied developmental economics and public administration abroad and have returned to put their education into practice. The same four-group classification scheme used in chapter 3 is again relevant here except in this case there are many more Followers and Maneuverers due to the pressures of long-established patterns. Also the number of Techno-

10. A great deal of time, energy, and expense has gone into a new civil service law designed to reform much of the old web-system. This law, however, has been constantly watered down and distorted as the old system has easily twisted and neutralized it.

11. University of Tehran, Institute of Social Studies and Research, *Taḥqīq Dar Bārah-yi 'Ilal-i Tawfīq va 'Adam-i Tawfīq-i Sāzmān-hā-yi Idārī Dar Jalb-i Riẓāyat-i Mardum* [An Investigation into the Reasons for the Success and Lack of Success of the Administrative Organizations in Procuring the Satisfaction of the People] (Tehran, 1964), pp. 25-31. This is an extraordinary document primarily because it supports its conclusions with evidence.

crats who become ideologically or politically alienated is very small due to the fact that they put technology above politics and strive to remain technocrats rather than risk political involvement.

The new technocrats are struggling to press forward ideas of merit and performance. In waging this battle, they refuse to become politicians as well, for given the political system, this would mean an acceptance at one point of something that they as technocrats have been fighting against. One high-level Plan Organization technician terms the system one of "administrative feudalism" in that technocrats are controlled by politicians who have no understanding of what a rational administrative system is. The professional bureaucrats, in order to maintain their effectiveness, generally remain below the rank of Director-General *(mudīr-i kull)* for it is at this rank and above that the pressures of the web-system become most intense. Most Technocrats who move across this point tend to become Followers and Maneuverers. The dilemma that confronts the Technocrats, however, is that in order to press forward ideas of merit and rationality, it is necessary to build new relationships and this demands political involvement.

The Technocrats as described here are alienated, therefore, because of the personalism, favoritism, and influence-wielding that hampers their work as technicians. Yet in order to rise above a certain level in the system they are under tremendous pressure to accept these same methods. It is for this reason that many of the top planners and technocrats leave Iran. When the brilliant Dr. Bahman Ābādiyān left in 1966 to join the International Monetary Fund, Iranian newspapers reported that it was not the economic motive that caused these men to leave but rather the psychological atmosphere in which nepotism and the politicians made the technician's life unbearable. According to the UNESCO study, it is this same atmosphere that frustrates and alienates the returnees.[12] It should be stated here that not all the Technocrats are disaffected procedurally and, as the following chapter will indicate, a certain number of them have moved up to political positions including ministerships. This has meant that they not only have been willing to join the web and what it implies but also that they have had the connections and pārtī necessary to propel them to such positions.

In terms of class origins, most of the Technocrats and middle-ranking bureaucrats are of lower- and middle-class backgrounds. Therefore, they have tended to lack important and influential connections and as a result have not been subjected to the same temptations that those of upper-class background have. It is natural that those with important political ties and connections will be less critical of a system that rests on such relationships. The overwhelming majority of the lower- and middle-ranking educated bureaucrats and technocrats are therefore of lower- and middle-class background and it is necessary to examine a group who work at these levels.

12. See chapter 3.

The preceding sections have shown the varying degrees of intensity that mark the dynamics of the web of pārtī, personalism, and politics. From the Ābādan Refinery to the NIOC to the government ministries themselves, it is possible to recognize the challenge and change that marks the old system. The administrators and technocrats are often alienated from and subverted by this system. The following section will treat the former while the next chapter will analyze the latter.

The Bakhshdār and the Pressure of Provincial Pārtī

> The old civil-military administration smashes and beats at us and our only refuge has been the masses of people.
>
> —26-year-old Bakhshdār,
> June 8, 1967

In analyzing the professional middle class, it is important not to overemphasize those groups with the highest education or those who have studied in foreign countries. The largest number of this class are still those who have been educated at home and who do not speak a foreign language. These people often staff the middle echelons of the bureaucracy and are of lower- and middle-class background. One such group that is intimately involved in the processes of change underway in Iran consists of the educated *bakhshdārs*. The bakhshdār is the local administrative officer in charge of the *bakhsh* or district and as such he is the district governor. On paper he ranks behind the *ustāndār* (governor-general) and *farmāndār* (governor) in the provincial hierarchy and in a constantly shifting situation there are 13 *ustāndārs*, 149 *farmāndārs*, and 452 bakhshdārs throughout Iran. In the national governmental apparatus, these officials are the responsibility of the Ministry of Interior.

The New Bakhshdār

The bakhshdār[13] is the most influential provincial official who is directly in contact with the people. He is concerned with local government and devel-

13. This section is based on observation of the bakhshdārs at work in the remote areas of Iran. Discussions concerning the new bakhshdār and his place in the system were carried out with all related ranks of government officials including the Prime Minister, Minister of Interior, Deputy-Ministers of Interior, Director-Generals, Governor-Generals, Governors, Mayors, Gendarme Officers, and Village Heads. The villagers themselves also described their relationship with the old and new bakhshdārs.

opment and operates at the grass-roots level. In the eyes of the central government, he has traditionally been a very unimportant official and the position has been a kind of "booby prize" to incompetent and local influentials. The bakhshdār has usually been selected by the Ministry of Interior in consultation with the *ustāndār* and *farmāndār* of the particular province and district. The traditional bakhshdārs have been illiterate and/or uneducated, corrupt, and distrusted by the people.

In 1964 a series of events in the Ministry of Interior led to the beginning of fundamental change in the old bakhshdār system. A Tehran University professor and satellite of the political elite invented a program whereby many of the always troublesome students would spend part of their time in the Ministry of Interior in on-the-job training. This led to manpower difficulties and pressures in the Ministry as these students began graduating and demanding full-time employment. The ultimate result was a program whereby these graduates would be sent to the provinces as bakhshdārs. Like so many other reform programs in Iran, the bakhshdār program was initiated quite unintentionally.

By June 1967, four series of *bakhshdār-i līsānsīyah* (bakhshdārs with degrees) had been trained and sent to district governorships in every corner of Iran. Besides their college credentials, most of them also received a special six-week training course at the rural training center of Garmsar near Tehran. Here they took special courses in local government, administration, finance, and development. During this time the new bakhshdārs were able to gain an insight into what was to come in terms of the organizations that they would have to deal with, as representatives of the following groups delivered speeches to them at Garmsar: Investigating Section of the Ministry of Interior, Municipalities, City Councils, Peasant Organizations, Community Development, Municipal Unions, Political Section of the Ministry of Interior, National Police, Gendarmerie, Civil Defense, Literacy Corps, Health Corps, and Extension Corps.[14] Fifty-three were trained from August 1 to September 11, 1964, in the first cycle. The second group numbered 109 and was at Garmsar from October 30 to December 11, 1964. The third cycle included 101 persons trained from January 16 to February 24, 1965, and the last group of 44 was at Garmsar from January 15 to March 3, 1966. In total, 307 educated young people have been trained and sent to replace the old bakhshdārs. These 307 have included 23 women. Fifty percent of them have majored in law, geography-history, or the religious sciences, while most of the rest have their degrees in agriculture, language, or

---

14. The content of these speeches, reproduced in Ministry of Interior Training Publication No. 17 printed in July 1966, reveals that the lecturing officials were very concerned about informing the new bakhshdārs just what their sphere of influence was *not* to be. After a dozen such speeches, the bakhshdārs wondered how there could possibly be a place for them in the official provincial network.

geology. Only 15 have been educated abroad and three have earned a doctorate. The average age is 25 or less than half that of the men they have replaced.

The Struggle and the Sacrifice

The entire bakhshdār experiment has been marked by a great deal of sacrifice and cost largely because of the overwhelming strength of the traditional relations in the provincial administration. Through the efforts of Murtiẓā Varzī who was Director General of both Planning and Administration in the Ministry of Interior and was himself a Technocrat with few connections and little pārtī, a spirit of genuine dedication and enthusiasm has been instilled into the new and educated bakhshdārs. This, combined with two sympathetic Ministers of Interior (Pīrāstah and Anṣārī) and a solid training program, resulted in a force of "new men" that quietly moved out to challenge the old web.[15]

From the very beginning, pārtī and influence-wielding threatened the program. In the Ministry of Interior itself, Maneuverers not only attempted to sabotage the program but worked to select and promote relatives and friends into the project. Although the recruitment process was based on merit and performance, influentials managed to make some favoritism work in terms of placement and later promotion. The then Director-General of Administration, through political and security connections, directed much of this.[16] In general, however, the bakhshdār project has rested on a solid foundation of merit. Besides the reasons provided above, it is important to realize that these young people simply have not possessed connections and pārtī and only five percent of them could in any way be considered of upper-class origin. These twenty individuals, furthermore, have been of *local* big family background and as such have only been a peripheral part of the national political elite. It was, however, significantly in behalf of these persons that the pressures of pārtī were applied at two points in the program.

When the young bakhshdārs first went out to their districts, the members of the provincial bureaucratic web viewed it as some kind of temporary joke foisted upon them by their old friends back in Tehran. This attitude quickly changed when the new men began speaking and acting with grim determination. In Rāmsar in Māzandarān, a husband-wife bakhshdār team let it

---

15. This has been quite a contrast to the highly publicized Literary, Health, and Extension Corps which have been directed by members of the political elite all struggling with one another to gain more political favor and international publicity out of the experiment.

16. This personality later became Director-General of Elections in Iran and supervised the 1967 national parliamentary elections.

be known that the network of bribery presided over by the Mayor, Chief of Police, and Health Officer would have to be broken up immediately. In Jalāq in Balūchistān, a young bakhshdār worked and lived with the people despite the protests of the *farmāndār* in nearby Sarivān. In Haftgil in Khūzistān, a 26-year-old bakhshdār secured advantages for the people from the all-powerful oil company and opened public discussion groups with the population despite the threats of the local Chief of Finance. The reaction of the established groups was deadly. The newly commissioned bakhshdārs found themselves opposed by the entire provincial administration, usually including the *ustāndār* and the gendarmerie. The situation was aggravated by the ominous presence of the replaced bakhshdār who had been given a nominal position in the *ustāndār*'s or *farmāndār*'s office. From here he could block the new man's every step. The result was instructive. The husband of the Rāmsar husband-wife team was waylaid, physically assaulted, and seriously beaten. The local officials in Balūchistān fired their new bakhshdār after numerous harassments had not achieved the desired result. This young bakhshdār immediately sent a letter to the Ministry of Interior asking for confirmation of this action and directions concerning his next assignment. Forty-five days later his letter reached Tehran. The Khūzistān bakhshdār was promoted to *farmāndār* and transferred to Tehran Province. Here he immediately threatened the existing system of corruption centering around the Deputy-Governor and as a result was suddenly transferred out of the province.

Despite the fact that these young bakhshdārs have seemed exposed and defenseless against the old web, they have nevertheless begun to have an important effect. One reason has been the spirit that they have taken into their work with them. They correspond with one another across the country and compare problems and accomplishments. In the spring of 1967, one of their colleagues was killed in a flood in Khurāsān while on the job and as a result he has become a kind of symbol to the rest. Second, not *all* of the established provincial forces have been hostile. Several of the governor-generals, if they have not exactly supported the bakhshdārs, have at least done nothing to hurt them. Among the more cooperative governor-generals when the new bakhshdārs first were dispatched were Pīrniyā of Fārs, Anṣārī of Khūzistān, 'Aẓīmā of the Southern Ports, and Amīnāzād of Kurdistān.[17] It has been in these provinces that the bakhshdārs have been most effective and an example follows.

17. Governor-Generals in Iran are chosen according to the strength of their political and security connections. Many are military men and most of them have close relationships with the Court or Security Organization. The Governor-General of Māzandarān was such a person and was brutal in his treatment of the new bakhshdārs. Yet when the shakeup in Governor-Generalships was made in May 1967, this particular man was promoted to the Governor-Generalship of the critical province of Fārs.

In Fārs Province, a 25-year-old bakhshdār named Muḥammad Rawghanī was assigned to the district of Marvdasht. This man lived with the people of Marvdasht 24 hours a day and with the support of Governor-General Pīrniyā he was able to go about his business without consuming all his time and energy warding off administrative enemies. When he became district governor of Marvdasht in the summer of 1965, there were only 14 schools, with a population of 15,000, in the entire district. In 20 months he initiated 177 development programs including the construction of 63 schools, 20 baths, and 10 bridges; the repair of 14 schools and 25 baths; the construction of 63 kilometers of road; and the installation of three electric generators and three water systems. In all of these projects, he managed to secure the financial and physical participation of the villagers who for the first time believed a government official was on their side. There is little doubt that Rawghanī and others like him are "new men."[18]

In many of the areas of Iran, the bakhshdār has found that everywhere he turns he is faced with hostility, jealousy, and danger. This has caused many of them to turn to the villagers and has as a result created a new relationship between a government official and the people. Most of the bakhshdārs say that they have been able to begin gaining the trust of the people but at the same time they admit that only time will tell. The people had been robbed for years and the new bakhshdārs consider bribery to be one of the greatest problems that they have faced. Traditionally, the money had moved up the administrative ladder from people to *shahrdār* (mayor) to bakhshdār to *farmāndār* to *ustāndār*. The people's money still moves but in many districts it now goes from *shahrdār* to *farmāndār* to *ustāndār*. The program itself has managed to endure because of a dedicated few in the Ministry of Interior along with the bakhshdārs themselves and the hard-fought campaigns they have won. The long-range consequences of the program especially in terms of fundamental change could be extraordinary.

Two years after the first group of bakhshdārs were dispatched, one could easily see what the cost had been. In most cases, idealism and dynamism had given way to apathy and alienation. Whatever success and impact they had achieved was paid for in terms of the punishment they had absorbed. Even the most successful of them looked for new employment and many blamed Tehran for not providing them with necessary support and protec-

---

18. Rawghanī was one of the new bakhshdārs with whom the writer traveled extensively. The difference between the old and the new can be seen in an episode that took place in the village of Haftgil. Towering behind this village were huge salt mounds and every year the seasonal rains washed layers of salt down upon the village. The new bakhshdār went to the *farmāndār* and suggested that a canal be dug to drain away this salt. The old *farmāndār* became very upset and misunderstood the term "canal." He said that he did not want to get involved in the construction of a Suez or Panama Canal for not only would Tehran oppose it but also it could have serious international implications.

tion. By June 1967, only 232 were still on the job as 30 had resigned and another 45 had received transfers.[19] One young bakhshdār who had achieved notable successes in three districts only to be transferred out each time summed it up by saying: "We are being sacrificed." Most of them have been willing to sacrifice but none have wanted to be sacrificed. Their alienation stems from the corruption, bribery, favoritism, and influence-wielding that they have had to work against.

The bakhshdār experience represents many others that occur every day in Iranian society. The educated Iranian with energy, dedication, and commitment is battered into an alienation that stems from procedural disaffection. In the process, however, his impact takes its toll on the old web and thus pockets, such as those described in the section above, slowly appear. The bureaucracy proper is just beginning to be attacked in these terms and the new bakhshdārs were among the first challengers. This kind of man stands for procedural change although he seldom supports fundamental change in the political system. Of the thirty bakhshdārs who resigned, all of them acquired employment in other governmental agencies and ministries. From the Iranian-educated bakhshdār to the American-educated Ph.D. technocrat, the largest group of the professional-bureaucratic intelligentsia is alienated on grounds of what can be best termed "the pārtī procedure." This is what keeps them from using their education and from achieving what they know they can and this is also why the Iranian political elite cannot capture and retain their commitment.

The Politics of Procedural Disaffection

A large section of the professional-bureaucratic intelligentsia is alienated from the existing system on grounds of procedure. This procedure is an integral part of the traditional Iranian relationships of power, pārtī, and personalism. The procedurally disaffected Technocrats are largely administrators, planners, and middle-ranking bureaucrats, all of whom have acquired a modern education. The members of this group have come to understand that their skills are not the keys to advancement and future. They further realize that it is difficult to attain their technical and occupational goals in a system where the irrational and personal prevail. The effect of the pressure of the old web-system on the new technocrat-bureaucrat is one of apathy, cynicism, noncommitment, and insouciance. In a constantly changing situation, therefore, there is movement from idealistic commitment to frustration and apathy but very little of the opposite trend.

---

19. Ten of the forty-five were promoted to *farmāndār.* Most of those promoted possessed connections with Maneuverers in the Ministry of Interior.

The traditional relations are strongest near the central political authority and therefore the most intense pressures and disaffections exist in these environments. The alienated technocrat-bureaucrat tends to be located below the rank of Director-General in the administration since advancement beyond this involves extraordinary pressure to accept the ongoing power patterns. Despite the continuing growth of apathy and alienation among the Technocrats, they have challenged the traditional system and persistently strive to introduce new relationships whenever and wherever they can. The embryonic construction of new relationships, however, has been limited to areas where there has been a certain amount of foreign control or to nonpolitical areas usually involving scattered developmental projects in the provinces. Despite this tendency, however, the Technocrat's efforts to build rationality and efficiency continue to produce a broadening impact that has even begun to penetrate certain echelons of the political system (e.g., the new bakhshdār program). Much of this spreading impact can be explained in terms of the overlapping characteristic of the traditional web-system analyzed in chapter 3. Other factors contributing to this trend include the accelerating growth and improvement of communication which permits increasing contact with other patterns and relationships, whether they exist in foreign environments or in Iran as new and challenging relationships.

In the face of this growing challenge, the political elite pursues a consistent policy of weaving the Technocrats into the web-system via promotion into political posts and economic concessions. By accepting the traditional patterns, the Technocrats surrender their former stress on relationships built upon merit, achievement, and institutions. In order to avoid this, significant numbers of Technocrats consciously seek to ignore and avoid anything political. They constrict their universe to the task at hand and as long as the road is built or the plan is formulated they rest content. This approach cannot fail to have long-term consequences since the persistent development of new relationships at any level involves much more than that level. In the short run, however, this avoidance of the political contributes to the preservation of the traditional relations which are protected and extended by the political authority.

chapter five

The Maneuverer: The Web-System Defended

The preceding two chapters have continually alluded to the existence and activity of a third group in the new middle class. This group is composed of those who consciously and unconsciously support the traditional web-system. They are the Maneuverers and they possess a vested interest in protecting and expanding the ongoing relationships. They are linked into the political system in opportunistic deference and many have become members of the political elite itself. The Maneuverers are related to one another in direct rivalry and move in intense conflict with both the Uprooters and the Technocrats.

The Maneuverers are a major cause of the fissured and divided nature of the professional-bureaucratic intelligentsia. They have built suspicion and distrust among the members of the new class and have weakened and hardened its reputation in the eyes of the other classes in society. Āl-i Aḥmad paints a gloomy picture in this regard and argues publicly that there are only two groups in the intelligentsia: (1) those who turn the wheels of the governing apparatus and prop up the system; and (2) those who spend all their time begging the pardon of those who control the system. He writes that as a result the Iranian intellectuals are "lost and wandering."[1] They

1. Āl-i Aḥmad, *Jahān-i Naw,* Nos. 4 and 5 (1966): 26. Jalāl Āl-i Aḥmad, who was one of the most talented and formidable critics of the Iranian political system, died on September 11, 1969.

have attached themselves to the "purses of oil money" and act as the obedient servants of power and censorship.[2] In disgust, Āl-i Aḥmad condemns the entire intelligentsia and labels them maneuverers and manipulators. This is a rather extreme expression of the views of the Uprooters and Technocrats who generally refrain from such broad accusations. At the same time, however, they criticize and ever fear the members of their own class who are the Maneuverers.

This attitude toward the intelligentsia also permeates the lower classes. A typical voice in this regard was the letter of a *bāzārī* to the editors of *Firdawsī,* the Iranian magazine designed for the student-intellectual audience. The small shopkeeper (by signature Sayyid 'Alī Akbar Libāschī) wrote that his class considered the intelligentsia corrupt and shameful and viewed them with "dislike, disgust and despair." According to Libāschī, a member of the intelligentsia is concerned only with "his profits, his income and expenditures, his own head and face, his automobile, his status, his maneuverings *(zad-u-band-hā),* and his nastiness *(pidarsūkhtigī-hā).*"[3] The actions of the Maneuverers nourish such opinions and increase intraclass and interclass tensions. In the process, such dealings become a catalytic agent in the extension and preservation of patterns of conflict, insecurity, favoritism, and personalism. By operating in a web-system and by heightening group and class tensions, the Maneuverers pressure others not only to relate but to do so according to ongoing processes. Having been forced into confrontation and harried by tension, the Uprooters and Technocrats often turn in self-preservation to the prevailing methodology of power. As a result, the intelligentsia is a fractionating and fluctuating class. The intellectuals cry out against one another while the entire class becomes the target of upper- and lower-class criticism.

The Majlis and the Maneuverers Rewarded

The Maneuverers are located throughout the areas of middle-class concentration but tend to cluster about the formal centers of political activity. Although they are very much in evidence in universities, for example (see chapter 3), their overwhelming drive is in the direction of politics. In recent years this has meant the highest echelons of bureaucracy, the Cabinet, the political parties, and the Majlis. The most reliable major channels for such

2. *Ibid.,* p. 32.

3. Sayyid 'Alī Akbar Libāschī, "Khijālat Bikishīd" [Be Ashamed of Yourselves], *Firdawsī* (Āẕar 16, 1344/1965), p. 7.

advancement have been the military-security organizations and the Iran Novin Party. Maneuvering members of the intelligentsia have consistently joined these organizations in order to gain entry into the highest political posts. Once a member of the Cabinet and/or the political elite, they can no longer be considered members of the professional middle class. Their newly acquired connections and political position have catapulted them into the ruling class. This is also true to a great degree in the Majlis where secret police investigation and approval must be supplemented by the Shah's assent. The King possesses intimate information about each member of the Majlis who are in effect treated as personal servants. The parliamentary candidates accept this situation in word and deed. The Maneuverers excel in this game and therefore the Majlis is one of their natural habitats.[4]

The following is a brief examination of the history of the Iranian Majlis. Through the years it has been dominated by those who have struggled to protect the traditional web-system. It is in the Majlis that one finds the most accomplished of manipulators. They have used the system to attain high political position and subsequently use this position to buttress the ongoing pattern of relationships. By studying the education and occupation of the Majlis representatives, it is possible to see how the Maneuverers in the professional-bureaucratic intelligentsia have gradually seeped into the Majlis.

Table 9 provides a view of the percentage of each Majlis that have held a degree in modern higher education, i.e., a license or doctorate. Table 10 indicates the overall percentage for the three periods—conclusion of the Qājār Period (1906–26), Riẕā Shāh Period (1926–41), and Muḥammad Riẕā Shāh Period (1941–67). The trends here are evident. From the Fourteenth Majlis on (1944–), the percentage of license and doctorate holders has increased steadily. During the Twenty-first Majlis (1963–67), the percentage of college-educated representatives jumped to 62 percent, a proportion far above that of any other Majlis. In this particular Majlis, 121 out of 196 representatives possessed a higher education and of these, 57 were educated outside of Iran.[5]

---

4. For a detailed analysis of the patterns of Majlis politics, see James A. Bill, "The Politics of Legislative Monarchy: The Iranian Majlis," in Herbert Hirsch and M. Donald Hancock, eds., *Comparative Legislative Systems: A Reader in Theory and Research* (New York: Free Press, 1971).

5. Zahrah Shajīʿī, *Nimāyandigān-i Majlis-i Shawrā-yi Millī dar Bīstuyik Dawrah-yi Qānūnguzārī* [The Representatives of the National Consultative Assembly During the Twenty-One Legislative Periods] (Tehran, 1344/1965), p. 238. This survey was carried out under the auspices of the Institute of Social Studies and Research of the University of Tehran. Tables 9-12 have been abstracted from this survey. Although entirely lacking in analysis, this study presents a wealth of reliable data and represents one of the best efforts in Iranian social science. It provides detailed information on the age, education, occupation, and social class origins of the deputies of the First through the Twenty-first Majlises.

TABLE 9

Holders of Advanced Degrees in Modern Education in the Twenty-one Legislative Periods[a]

Constitutional Period	Majlis	Percentage of Degree Holders
First 1906–26	1	19
	2	25
	3	17
	4	12
	5	16
Second 1926–41	6	12
	7	12
	8	15
	9	16
	10	13
	11	13
	12	13
Third 1941–67	13	14
	14	26
	15	31
	16	28
	17	38
	18	43
	19	47
	20	48
	21	62

[a]License, Bachelors, Masters, and Doctoral degrees
Source: Zuhrah Shajīʻī, *Nimāyandigān-i Majlis-i Shawrā-yi Millī dar Bīstuyik Dawrah-yi Qānūnguzārī* [The Representatives of the National Consultative Assembly During the Twenty-one Legislative Periods] (Tehran, 1344/1965), pp. 207, 282.

These figures do not in themselves demonstrate a necessary increase in professional middle-class representation in the Majlis. In the First (and during most of the Second) Constitutional Period, for example, those with a higher education were virtually all members of the upper class. These were most often landlords with foreign education. Recent Majlises, however, have witnessed an influx of professional middle-class individuals who have been either professional-technical employees or middle-ranking bureaucrats. Table 11 indicates the occupational status of the representatives to the twenty-one Majlises. Representation has been dominated through time by landlords and government employees. It is evident, however, that the professional middle class has been consistently gaining membership. Table 12 reveals how the professional-technical group has grown while the cleric class has declined through the three periods. By the Twenty-first Majlis, almost one-fourth of Majlis membership had been engaged in professional-technical occupations whereas the clerics were completely unrepresented.

TABLE 10

Holders of Advanced Degrees in Modern Education in the Three Constitutional Periods[a]

Constitutional Period		Percentage of Degree Holders
First	1906–26	18
Second	1926–41	13
Third	1941–63	36

[a]License, Bachelors, Masters, and Doctoral degrees
Source: Shajī'ī, *Nimāyandigān-i Majlis-i Shawrā-yi Millī,* p. 207.

According to Table 11, 69 percent of the Twenty-first Majlis had been government employees. These were virtually all middle-ranking bureaucrats who had been land reform officials and members of the professional middle class. The government and professional-technical employees together account for a majority of Majlis membership. From these figures, and the educational statistics presented in tables 9 and 10, it is concluded that the professional-bureaucratic intelligentsia has been steadily increasing its membership in the Majlis ever since the early 1940s. The largest increase, however, has taken place in the 1960s with the introduction of the various reform programs. In the Twenty-first Majlis, landlord representation fell to its lowest proportion since 1909. Cleric membership has ceased entirely. The slack is being taken up by middle-ranking bureaucrats and professionals.

Majlis membership does not necessarily mean that an individual is a Maneuverer who supports and thrives on the web-system. Through the years there have been examples of outspoken reformers and occasional Uprooters who have sat in the Majlis. During the 1926–41 and 1954–68 periods, however, this type of individual has been conspicuously absent. These periods have marked the rule of Riẕā Shāh and the more recent years of the reign of Muḥammad Riẕā Shāh. Authoritarian rule was tightened during these periods and the will of the monarchs directly superseded the wills of individuals situated deep in the government.

Beginning with the Seventh Majlis during the Riẕā Shāh Period, Majlis representation was completely controlled by the King. At the beginning of each cycle, the Monarch's hand-picked Prime Minister submitted a list of names to the Shah. The latter would cross out the names he objected to. The Prime Minister then sent the list to the Ministry of Interior and new elections would be announced. For years the Director-General of Elections was M. Firaydūnī who organized and supervised the actual election process. The slate handed down by the Prime Minister with the Shah's approval

TABLE 11

Occupations of Majlis Representatives During the Twenty-one Legislative Periods[a] *(In Percent)*

Legislative Period	Occupation						
	Landlord	Merchant-Trader	Government Employee	Cleric	Professional-Technical	Private Industry	Lower Class
1	21	41	23	20	7	5	0
2	30	9	46	24	19	2	0
3	49	7	47	31	12	5	0
4	45	9	55	23	9	1	0
5	49	4	51	24	15	2	1
6	52	7	48	23	12	2	2
7	56	12	44	17	9	1	2
8	59	15	42	10	13	1	1
9	55	20	42	9	16	2	1
10	54	19	37	8	19	1	1
11	59	18	35	6	2	2	1
12	58	18	32	6	21	2	1
13	59	18	30	6	23	2	1
14	57	13	37	8	21	2	0
15	56	15	49	4	19	1	0
16	57	13	50	2	19	3	0
17	49	9	46	11	19	3	0
18	60	18	40	2	17	2	0
19	59	11	52	0	19	3	0
20	58	8	48	1	22	2	1
21	35	12	69	0	21	16[b]	6[c]

[a]The figures in this table total well over 100 percent per Majlis since certain representatives practiced several occupations.

[b]With the Twenty-first Majlis, the industrial aristocracy first appeared as a category. The statistics for this period reveal that five deputies were "capitalists, industrial shareholders, factory owners, . . ."

[c]This 6 percent includes nine workers and two peasants.

Source: Shajīʿī, *Nimāyandigān-i Majlis-i Shawrā-yi Millī,* pp. 180, 267.

TABLE 12

Occupations of Majlis Representatives During the Three Constitutional Periods (In Percent)

Occupation	Constitutional Period		
	First 1906–26	Second 1926–41	Third 1941–63
Landlord	39	57	57
Merchant–Trader	15	16	13
Government Employee	44	39	46
Cleric	24	11	4
Professional–Technical	12	17	19
Private Industry	3	2	2
Lower Class	0	1	0

Source: Shajī'ī, *Nimāyandigān-i Majlis-i Shawrā-yi Millī,* p. 180.

never lost an election. The Seventh through Thirteenth Majlises were Majlises of Maneuverers.[6] One study of the Riẓā Shāh Period describes this as follows: "The most successful members of the Majlis were those who most admired the Shah and the Pahlavi organization. They were also secret police agents who reported the secrets and discussions of their associates."[7] During this period, "only those who submitted themselves to the Shah and his agents led a decent life."[8]

The present Shah operates in much the same manner and although professional middle-class membership has increased in the Majlis, it has been the Maneuverers (especially since 1954) who have been involved. The 1963 and 1967 election procedures tell the reason why. Each member of the Twenty-first and Twenty-second Majlises had to manipulate his way through the following screen. First, substantial sums of money had to be paid in order to gain party membership while additional fees were involved in assuming candidature for the Majlis. In the case of the 1967 elections, all candidates had to join a party according to the instructions of the Shah. Second, any Majlis hopeful required an important connection or broker who would present the individual's case not only to the party's leaders but to the Shah as well. In the 1963 elections, for example, the most important figures of this kind were Aḥmad Nafīsī and Ḥasan 'Alī Manṣūr. Nafīsī was Mayor of Tehran and presided over the Congress of Free Men and Women which nominated the parliamentary candidates. Manṣūr was the head of the "Progressive Center" Majlis grouping which later became the Iran Novin

6. Four of the key Maneuverers of Continuity in the Majlises during the Riẓā Shāh Period were Ḥusayn Dādgar, Ḥusayn Rahbarī, Abulfatḥ Dawlatshāhī, and Amīr Nuṣrat Iskandarī.

7. *Sharq-i Tārīk* [The Dark East] (Tehran, 1321/1942), p. 141.

8. *Ibid.,* p. 143.

Party.[9] Other personalities who are instrumental channels to Majlis membership are all members of the political elite (see figure 6). Particularly active in this area have been Asadullāh 'Alam and Ja'far Sharīf-Imāmī. Third, all Majlis aspirants have had to be thoroughly investigated and approved by the Secret Police. The latter has been very active in the recommendation and disqualification of candidates. Finally, an individual might succeed in maneuvering through all the above entanglements only to be vetoed by the Shah. There have been many cases in recent years where this King has crossed out would-be candidates in much the same manner as his father had done in the 1930s. Such vetoes have often been cast against Uprooters who have temporarily played the game in order to find a more effective level on which to work. The King, then, stands as the final barrier and allows only the proved and loyal Maneuverers to pass. During the 1967 election period, an Iranian with the pseudonym Jarqah wrote a letter to the editor of an Iranian magazine. In this letter, he criticized the "ruling clique" and the atmosphere of "fawning, flattery and opportunism" that surrounded the elections. He spoke of the cynicism and apathy of the people for the elections and concluded: "The situation is in such a sad state that most of the people have forgotten where the Majlis is situated. The hopeless quiet of the graveyard pervades our society and there is no sign of political activity among the people."[10]

The case of the Majlis is also the story of the Cabinet, the high bureaucracy, and the military-security apparatus. Certain members of the professional middle class have begun seeping into all such organizations. In so doing, however, they have embraced the web-system and have used it for personal advancement. This has helped to buttress and maintain the system.

It is a gross oversimplification to portray all the Maneuverers who have gained high position as servile opportunists. Many have been sincerely committed to fundamental change and have attempted short-term compromise for long-term gain. In the following sections, the two basic types of Maneuverers are analyzed.

The Maneuverers of Continuity

A recent Iranian Prime Minister and long-time member of the political elite once publicly stated that he was the "slave" of the Shah. This statement is the slogan of life and success of the "Maneuverers of Continuity." It expresses the creed of these individuals and their fundamental belief in the

9. Nafīsī was charged with corruption and arrested in December 1963. Manṣūr was assassinated in January 1965.

10. Jarqah (pseud.), "Will it Really be a Free Election?" *Khvāndanīhā* (Tīr 24, 1346/1967).

traditional web-system. Earlier chapters have already referred to the activities and methods of this group, but they have yet to be systematically viewed in context of power relationships.

The Maneuverer of Continuity is represented by the great flatterers and sycophants. They relate in the political system as opportunistic reflections of the Monarch and their subservience, humility, and obsequiousness in his presence is a sight to behold. In their own formal posts, however, they suddenly become "little Shāhanshāhs" and relate to their subordinates in a similar network. This time, however, they see others as extensions of their own personalities and expect them to act as such. Thus, the same man who considered himself the Shah's "slave," expected all his subordinates to view him in the same way when he became Managing Director of the National Iranian Oil Company.

In July 1969, Queen Farah publicly attacked the pervasive patterns of behavior practiced by the Maneuverers. She strongly criticized "those sycophants who try to name every public place after a member of the Royal Family imagining they would benefit by doing so." The Empress argued that "sycophancy" was perverting "all classes of the people." In a private interview in 1970, the Queen argued that her public condemnation of flattery and sycophancy was meant to criticize these practices at all levels of government since they had become tools for personal advancement even at the lowest echelons of the bureaucracy.[11]

The Maneuverer of Continuity is referred to by the Iranians themselves as the proverbial cat *(gurbah)* because of his great ability to survive crises and always land on his feet. Thus, whenever the traditional patterns have been threatened or weakened (e.g., 1906–25, 1941–53), this kind of individual manages to survive and to improve his position. During the Muṣaddiq Period, for example, the Maneuverers tended to stand by the King even though his authority was being undercut. When the Shah emerged victorious, so also did this relationship, and those who had supported it found themselves even more firmly and favorably entrenched within it.

The Maneuverers of Continuity exhibit their deep support for the relationship of according special submission to the key national political figure in many dramatic ways. They compete with one another to exhibit the most imposing and most numerous pictures, busts, and paintings of the Shah. In this game, those pictures with personal autographs are particularly coveted. In a bizarre but significant twist to this emphasis on pictures of the major source of deference, the governor *(farmāndār-i kull)* of Tehran Province in

11. The Queen's public statements denouncing patterns of flattery had a profound impact in Iran and are still discussed in middle-class circles. For a complete presentation of Her Majesty's comments, see *Kayhan International,* July 30, 1969. The author's interview with Queen Farah referred to in the text took place at Niyavarān Palace on November 18, 1970.

1966 continually sold expensive pictures of the Shah to a young bakhshdār who was threatening traditional relationships in the province. The bakhshdār could not afford this process and he finally asked the *farmāndār* to desist. The latter immediately reported the incident to the Secret Police and they investigated the bakhshdār on grounds of questionable loyalty and patriotism. This example sharply depicts how one Maneuverer pressured a threatening individual to conform to the dominant power pattern. In this case, the very symbol of the pattern, i.e., the picture, was used as an instrument by the Maneuverer to protect himself and the ongoing relationships.

The Maneuverers not only strive to mention the Monarch's name in all their discussions but also they expend much effort in planning speeches so that they can publicly elaborate upon his greatness. On October 2, 1966, when the President of Turkey arrived in Tehran for a state visit, the Mayor of Tehran presented him with the key to the city and made a welcoming speech. In this speech which was broadcast over Radio Iran, the Mayor spoke only of the Iranian Shah, stressing his greatness and listing his reforms. More than one Iranian expressed displeasure at this and pointed out that rather than speaking about the guest, the Mayor had spoken only about the host. By going on record as strongly supporting the Shah (and the more lavish the praise, presumably the stronger the support), the Maneuverer proclaims his approval and acceptance of the web-system.

Such approval is also proclaimed in many other ways, including the written word. Poems and books are continually being written in praise of the Shah or on occasion even in honor of other members of the political elite. Many Maneuverers have used such writings to move to more favorable positions in the political web. One recent example was a book written by Manūchihr Hunarmand entitled *Pahlavism.*[12] In this work, the author labels the Shah's actions and programs "a new ideology" and calls it "Pahlavism." He compares Pahlavism to all the great world economic schools and political ideologies. There are sections, for example, on Pahlavism and Democracy, Pahlavism and Socialism, and Pahlavism and Communism. The writer explains in his introduction:

> It is the source of pride for me, the smallest servant of the nation, to call the ideology and political and economic school of the glorious Shahanshah, approved under the nine articles of the Shah and the people, after the name of the Pahlavi Dynasty—PAHLAVISM. I will

---

12. Manūchihr Hunarmand, *Pahlavīsm: Falsafah-yi Sīyāsī, Iqtiṣādī, Ijtimā'ī* [Pahlavism: A Political, Economic, and Social Philosophy] (Tehran, 1345/1966). For an English translation of the opening sections of this book, see J. A. Bill, "Pahlavism: The New School as a Doctrine," *Tehran Journal,* February 28, 1967.

compare it economically and politically to all the progressive schools of the contemporary world and will prove its superiority.[13]

The Maneuverers of Continuity have a vested interest in acting as guardians of the web-system which they defend in many ways. One of the most profitable methods in terms of individual advancement has been to protect the Shah who is the fundamental source of power in the society. By reporting any questionable behavior on the part of their colleagues and competitors to the monarch or his security agents, the Maneuverers often reap huge rewards.

There have been innumerable examples of the preservation of power patterns as practiced by the Maneuverers of Continuity. Many are highly intricate and involve a long series of manipulative acts. Often existing rules are broken and the formal-legal structure is disregarded and distorted in order that traditional relationships may remain in effect and power patterns may persist. The members of the political elite have set the pace in this regard. Although the Constitution has never been seriously revised, it has, however, been alternately twisted, distorted, reinterpreted, and ignored. Thus, Leonard Binder writes: "Constitutionalism, as presently maintained in Iran, is a farce."[14]

A recent example of this persistent drive to preserve the traditional patterns at the expense of rules, regulations, and law has occurred at Tehran University since 1963. This university has always been a dangerous threat to the web-system for it has been the habitat of angry young Uprooters. As such, it has often been the focal point of violent clashes between opposing forces. In June 1963, a leading Maneuverer of Continuity became Chancellor of the university and he immediately began reintroducing the university into the traditional web-system. This Chancellor, who related to the Shah in calculated deference, slowly converted the university into the same kind of relationship. After a long tradition in which the deans of the various faculties were elected, for example, the Maneuverer-Chancellor suddenly abrogated university regulations and began appointing the deans. The Secret Police publicly moved into university offices and began propping up the old system by force and intimidation. Both student and faculty Uprooters were silenced or dismissed. The Chancellor was so successful in this policy that regulations had to be "revised" once more. In 1967, a bill was passed by the Majlis providing that Tehran University become an "autonomous" institution. According to this law, the university is to be ruled by a Board of Trustees which is to possess all power. The members of the Board have

13. *Ibid.,* p. 10.

14. Binder, *Iran: Political Development in a Changing Society* (Berkeley and Los Angeles: University of California Press, 1962), p. 85.

the right to appoint a Chancellor who may then serve a five-year term. This law has had two major effects:

1. The Maneuverer-Chancellor could be reappointed to his position. The old regulations had provided that a Chancellor could only serve two terms and the Maneuverer's second term was due to expire.
2. The entire university would be tightly entwined into the national political web-system. This law of university "autonomy" in fact results in exactly the opposite. The major reason is that the Board of Trustees is composed of politicians and the greatest Maneuverers of Continuity in Iran. These include the Director-General of the National Iranian Oil Company, the Minister of Education, the Minister of Economy, and the Minister of Court. The Chairman of the Board is the Prime Minister.

What has occurred then is that the Chancellor was instrumental in strengthening the power web *within* the university, and at the same time he managed to bind the university into the national political web-system where the traditional relationships are most intense. This has involved continual contradiction and revision of university regulations.[15]

The Maneuverers of Change

In a 1967 interview, the Prime Minister of Iran explained his position with regard to change. He argued that traditional relationships had to be destroyed completely for it was imperative that an entirely new system come into being. The Prime Minister stated that the old patterns had to be torn and uprooted for it was futile to attempt to build the new upon the foundation of the old.[16] This official represents a growing number of Iranian influentials who speak in terms of change and utilize revolutionary language to describe their tasks. This group is made up of the young intelligentsia who decided to accept the general rules of the web-system on a temporary basis in order that they might gradually change this very system.

Contrary to the Technocrats who seek to avoid involvement in politics, this type of Maneuverer struggles to attain an important position in the political elite. He consciously relates to the Shah in deep deference and

15. In 1968, new Chancellors were appointed to each of Iran's eight institutions of higher education. These men averaged approximately forty years of age and were all well-educated members of the professional middle class.

16. Personal interview, May 21, 1967. In another interview with the author in Tehran three years later, Prime Minister Huvaydā was considerably less outspoken about the issue of change. Instead, he bitterly attacked the critics of the regime whom he termed "pseudo-intellectuals." Personal interview, December 5, 1970.

confronts his competitors in relationships of personal competition. In moving for advancement, he often uses the language of the Uprooter against the system, but at some point he compromises with the system in order to gain entree into high position. With the introduction of the reform programs of the 1960s, this compromise became much easier to make since the Shah and political elite began speaking in terms of reform and revolution.

Once having accepted and utilized the traditional methodology of power, the Maneuverer finds himself bound tightly into the web-system. The further he advances in politics, the more ensnarled he becomes in the traditional relationships. Any attempts at radical reform of these relationships lead immediately and directly to personal disaster. Former resolutions and intentions to uproot and destroy old methods quickly disappear and give way to continual rationalization. All that remains is revolutionary verbiage which confuses transformation with modification and which flourishes in an atmosphere created by the political elite in the 1960s.

Whereas the Maneuverers of Continuity have never questioned the permanence of the traditional patterns, the Maneuverers of Change have seriously challenged and criticized them. This challenge, however, has been muted whenever the individual is lifted into the political elite. Here it is essential that the Maneuverer accept and protect the ongoing system, for in so doing, he is also protecting himself. He thus joins the web-system and his actions are scarcely distinguishable from those of the Maneuverer of Continuity. The Maneuverer of Change rationalizes his position by presenting the following types of arguments: "His Imperial Majesty is the most knowledgeable and progressive force in Iran and we are content to carry out his wishes"; "the forces of reaction and corruption are everywhere. The only way to overcome them is to defeat them at their own game. After all, one must protect himself"; "Iran is improving every day. Formerly there was much corruption and no economic development. Today there is still corruption but there is also economic development."[17]

The Shah, who occupies the central position in the web-system which characterizes Iranian politics, has made the task of rationalization much easier for the recent breed of Maneuverer. He encourages revolutionary talk and has introduced a vocabulary of change that calls for transformation but is used for preservation.

The Methodology of the Maneuverers

The Maneuverers are those members of the intelligentsia who support and defend the traditional power relationships. In so doing they divide and

17. Personal interview notes, Tehran, June–December 1970.

weaken the professional middle class. This group bears testimony to the stubborn persistence of the traditional web-system in contemporary Iran.

The most ambitious Maneuverers among the intelligentsia seek high position in the political system and are found in ever-increasing numbers in the Majlis and the Cabinet. Their presence in the political system gives them special importance and provides them with a decided advantage vis-à-vis the Uprooter and Technocrat groups.

The Maneuverers themselves are divided in their approach to traditional politics. A smaller but growing group has at one time demanded fundamental change in the patterns, only to become a force buttressing the old once its members have joined the political system. Compromising has led to rationalizing as manipulation to achieve position has meant manipulation to maintain position.

While an increasing number of the intelligentsia has been absorbed into the political system, the political authority has introduced policies stressing change. By professing a belief in reform and speaking in terms of revolution, the Shah has admitted the need for fundamental change. Although this has eased the conscience of certain Maneuverers of Change and has helped convert other members of the new middle class to the ongoing system, it has also introduced other complicating factors. When individuals speak the language of new relationships while acting in terms of old ones, they contribute to the rise of serious unintended consequences. The following chapter will discuss this and will explain how it will become more and more difficult to preserve the old in deed while praising the new in word.

chapter six

The White Revolution: The Politics of System Preservation

The half century of Pahlavi monarchy in Iran has been characterized by traditional patterns in which the Shah promotes passive servitude in all relationships that others maintain toward him and balanced rivalry in all other personal, group, and class interaction. The former pattern is often buttressed by the latter since forces that are constantly checked by others seldom have time to challenge the strongest force in the system. At the same time, however, those who are always competing in webs of rivalry tend to view all personalities and groups in competitive terms and this can easily come to include even the Monarch.

During the last ten years of his rule, Riẕā Shāh was quite successful in encouraging strong attitudes of submission toward the throne. The same has been true since the mid-1950s during the kingship of Muḥammad Riẕā Shāh. Among the various threats to any such relationship is the one posed by those who overtly appear as competing centers of power. The very presence of such competition questions the right of the original source to exist. This leads directly to a breakdown of the patterns of deference surrounding the particular monarch. This situation also introduces a challenging new relationship into the system since the competitor, at least, refuses to become a passive reflection of the personality demanding such. This type of threat explains in part the tension that gradually built up between the mujtahids and both Pahlavi monarchs. In each case, it was only after the king had solidified the basic relationship and his position within it that he moved against the leading clerics. The mujtahids with their relationship to the Hidden Imām have always represented a special threat to the Shah who ruled demanding complete deference from all.

Even more dangerous competitive threats to this kind of rule have existed, however, and these have grown from within the political system itself. The key example has been the personality of Muḥammad Muṣaddiq who led the movement that resulted in the nationalization of the Iranian oil industry and who was the powerful Prime Minister between 1951 and 1953. Muṣaddiq possessed charismatic qualities of such a nature that the Shah was pushed back into the shadows, a fate particularly debilitating to one who seeks to rule by demanded deference. It is obvious that he who rules in this manner cannot tolerate any competitor for this undermines the basic relationship itself.[1] No one recognized this better than Riẕā Shāh who systematically stifled the development of leadership and put aside all potential competitors.[2]

A closely related threat to such relationships are individuals who do not compete with the monarch by presenting themselves as alternatives, but rather they refuse to be viewed as extensions of a particular personality. The khans of the great tribes have been consistent examples of this kind of challenge. During the Riẕā Shāh period, tribal leaders such as Sardār As'ad and Ṣawlat al-Dawlah paid for this stance with their lives. Other notable individuals who have refused to bend submissively in more recent history have been jailed (Dr. Mihdī Bāzargān), exiled (Muẓaffar Fīrūz), placed

1. Muṣaddiq was a long-time opponent of the Pahlavi dynasty and was one of the few statesmen who voted against Riẕā Shāh as monarch. Throughout his life, Muṣaddiq stood against the Pahlavi pattern of rule. After his defeat in the fall of 1953, he was placed under house arrest in his village of Aḥmadābād. Special precautions were taken to ensure that virtually no public contact or publicity would ever again involve Muṣaddiq. Even when he died in early March 1967, the news was not released until the Shah returned to Tehran from a trip to Khūzistān. The newspapers then made the minimum announcement. Such a policy was essential to the preservation of Pahlavi rule, for as long as Muṣaddiq lived he represented a direct threat. For Dr. Muṣaddiq's own words criticizing Pahlavi politics, see *The Speech of H. E. Dr. Mossadegh Concerning the Nationalization of Petroleum Industry in Iran* (Tehran: University Press, 1951), pp. 25-28. Muhammad Riẕā Shāh expressed his own view of Muṣaddiq as follows: "Those who knew him at close range, as I did, will long remember Mossadegh with pity as somebody who lacked integrity as well as manliness and statesmanship. His three main characteristics were his negativism, his hypocrisy, and his egotism." See *Mission for My Country,* p. 109.

2. This policy often meant exile, as in the case of Sayyid Ẕīā' al-Dīn Ṭabāṭabā'ī, or murder, as in the case of Taymūrtāsh. It sometimes led to domestic exile followed by murder, as in the case of Mudarris, or suicide, as in the case of Dāvar.

under house arrest (Allāhyār Ṣālaḥ, Muḥammad Darakhshish), or assassinated (Taymūr Bakhtiyār).[3]

A deeper and more recent threat to this pattern of expected deference is posed by those who combat the relationship itself. While the above two challenges have been directed against a *particular* relationship, this threat is to the relationship itself. The Uprooters within the professional middle class are aligned against this relationship and represent a fundamentally different challenge to the traditional system. Since it is the members of a new social class that are involved and since these individuals are opposing a system and not a personality, the Shah and political elite cannot respond in the traditional manner. Arrest, imprisonment, exile, and bribery are not enough to silence and conquer a growing social class. This challenge stands as a serious threat to the relationships that have characterized the class structure in particular. Whereas the other challenges are directed solely against a particular relationship involving certain personalities, the appearance of this new social class heralds fundamental change in class relationships. As such, it confronts the traditional web-system at various levels and it pushes for change both in political leadership and social structure. The development of this challenge and the measures taken to contain it viewed in terms of the traditional system explain a great deal about politics and change in recent Iranian history.

The 1951 Land Reform Farmān and the Embryo of Reform

The rule of Muḥammad Riẓā Shāh can be divided into three periods, two of which were dominated by important reform proposals. The first period (1941–51) ended in January 1951 when the Shah issued a *farmān* (decree) stating that he would distribute the crown lands. The second period (1951–53) represented the Muṣaddiq premiership when the former political elite was replaced and the Monarch temporarily lost his advantage in the national political system. The third period (1954–) has been dominated by the events of January 1963, when the Shah announced his six-point reform

3. These individuals have little in common except for their refusal to relate to the Monarch in deferential servitude. Bāzargān is a professor, philosopher, and prolific writer who was dean of the Faculty of Technology at the University of Tehran. Fīrūz was a Qājār Prince who was very active in politics in the late 1940s when he worked first with Sayyid Ẓīā' al-Dīn and then with the Tūdah Party. Bakhtiyār was the first head of the Security Organization (SAVAK). Ṣālaḥ was a Muṣaddiqist and Darakhshish was Minister of Education in the Amīnī cabinet. Bāzargān, Bakhtiyār, and Fīrūz probably would have liked to establish their own political systems with themselves at the controls.

program. Although both the 1951 and 1963 reforms centered primarily upon land distribution, they differed from one another in depth and direction and were influenced by the challenges that confronted the politics of the day.

Between 1941 and 1950, Iran was the scene of political chaos as opposition groups of every hue sprang up to challenge the system. The Allied occupation artificially guaranteed relative order for much of this time, yet few members of the political elite escaped scathing attack by one or another of the many pamphlets, magazines, or newspapers that had blossomed with the fall of Riẕā Shāh. The Communist-oriented Tūdah Party was at the height of its influence in Iran and its members vociferously attacked the political elite of the day. In the face of persistent opposition, the young Shah was unable to get loyalty and obedience and was confronted by numerous competing and conflicting forces. On the class level, patterns of personal and direct rivalry also prevailed as persisting class relationships remained secure. It was during this period, however, that traditional power patterns even at the class level could no longer be taken for granted. An embryonic professional middle class appeared on the social scene and it was from this direction that much of the opposition came. The violence and upheaval of the 1940s culminated in an attempt on the life of the Shah in February 1949. Later that year, the King made his first trip to the United States where, instead of receiving economic assistance, he was advised to begin reforms.

On January 11, 1951, Muḥammad Riẕā Shāh called a meeting of the Iranian political elite and told them that the last nine years had witnessed a great deal of talk but no action. He stated it was time for reform. A few days later, the newspaper *Dāryā* carried a powerful article entitled "Nine Years of Talk." The following excerpts from this article reveal the pressures that were being applied at that time for general reform and land distribution.

> Nine years had passed when Muḥammad Riẕā Shāh summoned the Majlis deputies to his residence and told them that the situation was dangerous. He said: "We should prepare to defend our borders. We should meet the demands of the nation. We should establish social justice [*'adālat-i ijtimā'ī*]. We should collect direct and inheritance taxes. We should equalize property. Unfortunately, I have talked for nine years without taking this into attention. . . ."
>
> It seems that once again the clarion of danger has been blown. The rein-holders of the country feel that perhaps their interests are in danger. Thus, they speak about defense of the homeland. The Shah discussed such subjects and talked about social justice and the necessity of equalizing wealth. He talked about removing the sources of discontent. . . .

> It seems that the smell of gunpowder had had an effect on the minds of these people and they realize that a dangerous future faces them. . . .
>
> The Shah should begin. He should instruct that all those 1500 villages which are for the moment among the Pahlavi endowments be immediately distributed among the peasants. Then His Majesty should summon all the big landowners of the country and say: "I started myself. You must imitate me." Then he should have the government present a land distribution bill to the Majlis. . . .[4]

Less than a month after this editorial, the Shah of Iran handed down his decree calling for the distribution of the Royal lands. He argued that it was not a question of giving away the land, but rather of selling it to the local peasants on favorable terms and over a long period. During the next twelve years, certain areas of the Crown lands were slowly and sporadically divided. No serious general land reform program, however, was ever begun.

The upheaval of the 1940s represented an uprising of individuals. Despite the fact that scattered evidences of a new social class were very much in evidence, the opposition crystallized primarily against the Shah and not against the traditional web-system. The threats that developed did so within the framework of intensely personal competition and the Monarch was forced to defend himself from the challenges of individuals such as Qavām al-Salṭanah and Muẓaffar Fīrūz.

The biggest organized threat to the political elite was posed by the Tūdah Party which drew its membership from the disaffected of all classes. The leadership, however, was dominated by members of the newly developing professional middle class.[5] Nonetheless, even the Tūdah Party in its own organization was to a large extent established according to personalism, pārtī, and omnipresent rivalry. Not only were the leaders divided among themselves but also there was a gap between the leadership and the mass of party regulars. Tūdah leaders such as Sharmīnī, Qāsimī, and Kiyānūrī worked to build circles of sycophants about themselves while the more frequent relationship was intra-Tūdah personal opposition. The party developed two wings with the students and young people generally on the left and the leadership and masses largely on the right. This internal division

---

4. *Dārya,* 25 Day 1329/1951.

5. Eight of the eleven members of the Tūdah Central Committee organized in the early 1940s were members of the professional-bureaucratic intelligentsia. Individuals such as Alamūtī, Iskandarī, Buqrātī, Bahrāmī, Rādmanish, Kāmbakhsh, Kishāvarz, and Gunābādī were teachers, judges, journalists, and physicians by profession. S. Zabih writes that of the fifty-three individuals jailed in 1937 for Communist activities, thirty-five percent were teachers, twenty-five percent were government employees, fifteen percent were students, fifteen percent were workers, and ten percent were of other professions. See *The Communist Movement in Iran,* p. 67.

resulted in indecision at critical points in the life of the Tudāh Party and in the end contributed to its defeat.[6] When analyzing the Tūdah movement in terms of power relationships, it becomes less difficult to understand how individuals who were avid Tūdah members in the 1940s have in the 1950s and 1960s become members of the political elite and the Shah's secret police. They have, after all, been consistently operating within the same web-system.

Since the opposition that bubbled to the surface in the 1940s related in the traditional patterns, there was no threat to either the class structure or to the ongoing relationships. The response of the Shah in 1950, therefore, was intended to strengthen a personal position by announcing a personal program. At that time, he could not afford to alienate the upper class by instituting broader reforms. The upper class would always support the web-system even though certain members refused at the time to relate with the Monarch in a subservient obedience.

As the *Dāryā* quotation indicates, the reform announcement itself followed a great deal of pressure for just such a program. During a churning period of political upheaval, the reform proclamation was followed by the assassination of Prime Minister Razmārā and the rise of Muṣaddiq. This ushered in a new period and a new challenge to the Iranian web-system.

During the Prime Ministership of Dr. Muṣaddiq, the traditional system was confronted by a much more serious challenge than any that had occurred in the 1940s. Spurred by a wave of nationalism and oil nationalization, the Iranian middle class rallied around the Muṣaddiq banner. At the same time, Muṣaddiq promised radical social reform and pledged to revolutionize the Iranian political system. His movement cannot be adequately explained in terms of personalities alone since it was based on the support of entire social classes.[7] At the center of this support was the rapidly crystallizing professional-bureaucratic intelligentsia. The latter was part of a class alliance in which the bourgeoisie was also a vital force. The traditional system survived the Muṣaddiq crisis when this bourgeois middle class deserted the movement due to the pressures of economic well-being and the threat of growing Tūdah influence.[8] Muṣaddiq's important support in the bāzār began to crumble when business declined and religious tenets were

---

6. The prevalence of the traditional power pattern even within the Tūdah organization has been indicated in a series of personal interviews with four former active Tūdah Party members. Further investigation of this crucial assertion needs to be carried out.

7. For an example of one of the few Westerners who recognized this fact at the time, see Blair Bolles, "Egypt, Iran, and U.S. Diplomacy," *Foreign Policy Bulletin* 31 (August 15, 1952): 3. See also Cottam, *Nationalism in Iran.*

8. The United States also threw its support behind the traditional web-system in Iran and participated actively in the events of August 1953 that enabled the Shah to reestablish the shaken relationships. For a scholarly account of this episode, see Cottam, *Nationalism in Iran,* pp. 223-30. See also David Wise and Thomas B. Ross, *The Invisible Government* (New York: Random House, 1964), pp. 110-14. Between 1953 and 1963, United States military and economic grants to Iran totaled more than one billion dollars. Another two hundred million dollars in loans was also provided.

threatened. The staying power of the traditional patterns could also be seen in the personal rivalries that divided Muṣaddiq from other leaders such as Baghā'ī and Kāshānī.

The Muṣaddiq period marks an important turning point in the Shah's campaign to preserve his position within the traditional web-system. It was during this time that the Monarch was not only forced out of the national political network but nearly out of Iran as well. Much of this was due to the fact that the entire web-system was severely shaken and not simply because there were personal challengers. From this experience, it became evident that in order to preserve personal position and traditional power relationships, it was necessary to do more than outmaneuver particular personalities. A suitable policy had to be devised to deal with challenging social classes.

The 1963 Reform Program and the Evolution of Revolution[9]

With the fall of Muṣaddiq in August 1953, the Shah regrouped his forces and immediately began constructing a political cadre of unquestioned and unquestioning loyalty. An elaborate secret police network was established and military forces were expanded. These forces moved against all who had challenged the traditional web-system and discouraged any kind of opposition. By 1960, however, the new middle class that had first appeared and begun making scattered objections to the web-system in the 1940s and which had crystallized to support Muṣaddiq in the early 1950s broke a repressive period of silence and again began challenging the traditional system. Between January 1960 and January 1963, a dozen incidents of major proportions occurred in the streets of Tehran as the professional middle class led rallies, riots, and demonstrations. Students and teachers were the major participants. In January 1960, three students were killed and fifty injured in riots protesting tightened examination rules. In May 1961, one teacher was killed and two were injured during demonstrations demanding higher pay. The following January (1962), picketing students demanded free elections and the resignation of Premier Amīnī. One student was killed, two hundred injured, and some three hundred persons were arrested as Iranian commandos invaded Tehran University.[10]

9. Some of the analysis presented in this chapter appears in abbreviated form in James A. Bill, "Modernization and Reform from Above: The Case of Iran," *The Journal of Politics* 32 (February 1970): 19-40.

10. The Iranian commandos or paratroopers (*chatrbāzān*) are the Iranian equivalent of the United States Special Forces. Their ruthless attack with bayonets and rifle butts upon the Tehran University students (male and female) in 1962 shocked even the political elite. For partial accounts of this episode, see *Times* (London), January 22, 1962, p. 10 and *Economist* 202 (February 10, 1962): 538.

With the coming of the 1960s, the professional-bureaucratic intelligentsia had increased its size and demands to such a degree that it presented a serious threat to the traditional power patterns. Not only did the members of this class threaten the Shah's pattern of rule but also they confronted the class structure itself. Unlike the 1940s, a serious challenge now existed at the class level. In these circumstances, the Shah and political elite were pressed to develop a policy fundamentally different from the personal gestures made by the King in 1951. The following two-pronged program was adopted: (1) key members of the new class must be drawn into the traditional web-system; and (2) those classes that accept and support the traditional patterns must be reinforced. Although past Paḥlavi programs had always haphazardly pursued the former policy, they had never attempted the latter.

In attempting to persuade the members of the professional-bureaucratic intelligentsia to adopt the traditional relationships, the political elite had offered numerous incentives, particularly of an economic nature. These have been supplemented by occasional political offers centering around the Iran Novin Party and the various security organizations. As previous chapters indicate, this policy served to splinter the new class as many Maneuverers rushed to benefit from these concessions. In so doing, of course, they covertly or overtly joined the web-system by utilizing and fortifying the old processes.

Yet, with the violent upheavals of the early 1960s, it became eminently clear that growing sections of the professional middle class were refusing to relate. In such a situation, it was decided that those classes whose members supported traditional patterns had to be strengthened and brought in closer contact with the political elite. The peasant class was believed to be such a force. In January 1963, therefore, the Shah of Iran inaugurated his "White Revolution" or "Revolution of the Shah and the People." In this regard, the Monarch writes:

> The realization came to me that Iran needed a deep and fundamental revolution that could, at the same time, put an end to all the social inequalities and all the factors which caused injustice, tyranny and exploitation, and all aspects of reaction which impeded progress and kept our society backward.[11]

Such a revolution would not only gain the support of the peasant masses for the Shah and political elite but also it would represent ideological

11. *The White Revolution* (Tehran: Imperial Pahlavi Library, 1967), p. 15. This is a translation of the second edition of the book written by the Shah to explain and publicize the White Revolution.

concessions to the intelligentsia whose members had for years been voicing concern for the lower classes.

On January 9, 1963, the Shah of Iran outlined the principles of a six-point reform program. On January 26, this program was supported by a referendum and the White Revolution came into existence. The original six points plus six additional programs have come to form the heart of this *inqilāb* (revolution). The twelve points are:

1. Land reform
2. Nationalization of forests and pastures
3. Public sale of state-owned factories to finance land reform
4. Profit-sharing in industry
5. Reform of electoral law to include women
6. Literacy Corps
7. Health Corps
8. Reconstruction and Development Corps
9. Rural Courts of Justice
10. Nationalization of the waterways
11. National reconstruction
12. Educational and administrative revolution

Although these various programs have received wide publicity and have been described throughout the world, there has been little serious analysis of their implementation and effect. A fact of major significance, for example, is that the political elite has placed major emphasis upon the land reform and literacy corps while the other programs have done little more than exist.[12]

With the creation of this reform program, the Iranian political elite began speaking a revolutionary language that stressed the need for change. The Shah wrote that the era of rigid ideologies was over for "they cannot answer the needs of a society that is in a permanent state of revolution."[13] Prime Minister Huvaydā stated that "the old structure must be completely destroyed. Only then can a new system be built. You cannot build the new

12. The nationalization of forests, pastures, and waterways has received little attention and is clearly of peripheral importance. The inclusion of women in the electoral process is a vital concession on paper but means very little until the electoral process becomes meaningful. The profit-sharing plan represents a concession to the industrial working class, but it has been misunderstood and mismanaged. The factory owners have resisted the plan and the workers have failed to grasp its meaning. The educational and administrative point is of much greater significance since, if implemented, it would represent a fundamental effort to confront the demands of the new middle class. All indications are, however, that this revolution is to exist on paper only. The Tehran daily, *Āyandigān,* already refers to it as "The Forgotten Revolution."

13. *The White Revolution,* p. 19.

on the foundation of the old."[14] This language was picked up by the upper class and members of the various political organizations. By 1965 it came to prevail in the press, over the radio, and in public speeches. It became the language of the day for all who supported the web-system. The White Revolution, in effect, was intended to preserve rather than transform traditional interpersonal, intergroup, and interclass relationships. The indications are many.

All ideas relating to the "revolution" including its inception and implementation at all levels are credited to the Monarch. Stories were circulated and printed explaining how the idea for each of the various reforms came to the mind of the personality who stood at the center of the Iranian political system.[15] Many ambitious and creative individuals invented new points for reform and attempted to call them to the attention of the King in order that he might proclaim them part of his White Revolution.[16] Individuals vital to the implementation of certain reforms were not allowed to become too successful or well known for this tended to disrupt the central political web. The actual architect of the entire land reform program, Ḥasan Arsanjānī, became extremely popular in rural Iran where he continually traveled and campaigned for the peasants.[17] When Arsanjānī was forced to resign as Minister of Agriculture in March 1963, he was quickly removed from the scene by being appointed Iranian Ambassador in Rome. Since then, all official publications that treat the land reform program have erased and omitted Arsanjānī's name and picture. The crucial role that Arsanjānī played in the land reform program has been erased from official Iranian history and this challenge was thus overcome.

The administration of the White Revolution has been established according to traditional power relationships. The overall literacy program, for example, has been directly guided by the most powerful members of the political elite including the Shah's sister and his Minister of Court (see figure 6, points 2 and 14). The Ministry of Education has also been involved with the various undersecretaries in charge of competing programs. The land reform program operated in much the same way with the Ministries of Agriculture, Interior, and Finance competing for control on one level

14. Personal interview, May 27, 1967.

15. See, for example, the article entitled "Brilliant Idea Was Born on a Murky Day," *Kayhan International,* November 22, 1966, p. 4. This article explains how the idea of a Literacy Corps suddenly came to the Shah's mind.

16. Among the various ideas that individuals have sought to present to the Shah so that the latter could present them as part of the White Revolution are an Industrial Corps, a Student Corps, and a Religious Corps. Others have come up with regional development plans, elaborate crop and planting procedures, and new educational proposals. All such plans, however, are developed with the sole hope of getting them to the Shah. Such is the pattern of innovation in this kind of traditional system.

17. During the course of a 1966 field trip, a team of Tehran University social scientists found villagers who knew little about the Shah of Iran but were very familiar with the name Arsanjānī.

while a separate land reform department was established by the Monarch on another level.[18] The picture was further complicated by the existence of numerous other power points including agricultural and credit banks, cooperative organizations, the provincial bureaucracy, and the gendarmerie. All have interacted with one another in interlocking competition. The major event that forced the land reform program deep within the administrative web-system occurred in March 1963, when Ḥasan Arsanjānī resigned as Minister of Agriculture. Arsanjānī was an individual who spoke a revolutionary language and pursued revolutionary programs. He resented his position of subservience to the Shah and as such he represented a dangerous threat to the Pahlavi web-system.[19] He was replaced as Minister of Agriculture by a military general who represented the ideal guide for a program designed to preserve traditional relationships.

Similar to the events of 1951–53, the 1963 reform proposals were followed by a period of violent activity. These included the massive riots in the streets of Tehran in June 1963, the assassination of Prime Minister Manṣūr in January 1965, and the attempt on the life of the Shah in April of that same year. Violence in the wake of significant reform announcements has stemmed from many sources. There are those who feel that the change will truly uproot the traditional system and this they oppose. On the other hand, there are those who see the changes as an attempt to preserve relationships that need uprooting. The masses who rioted in June 1963, for example, represented such conservative forces as clerics, along with radical elements such as students and teachers. These post-reform reactions reveal the depth of the involvement that individuals feel toward the issue of change in the fundamental relationships that mark their lives. The nature of the establishment and administration of the 1963 reform program clearly indicates its aim to preserve these relationships. Further evidence, however, can be drawn from an analysis of the direction of the reform program itself. It has been especially designed to build and strengthen those classes that support the traditional web-system.

The Politics of Land Reform and the Peasantry

Muḥammad Riẓā Shāh has indicated many times his deep faith in the peasant class of Iran. In 1960, he wrote: "Our millions of rural folk possess

18. In 1967, the Department of Land Reform became an autonomous Ministry.

19. Between August 1966 and May 1967, the author had six long private discussions with Arsanjānī in Tehran. Arsanjānī was a brilliant man who combined shrewdness with a brutal directness. He was a tough crusader who, in his own words, pushed the land reform program "not as Minister of Agriculture but as a *rahbar* (leader)." He was one of a tiny number of Iranians who openly expressed his true feelings concerning the Shah. Ḥasan Arsanjānī died on May 31, 1969, at the age of 47.

wonderful qualities, not the least of which is their patriotism."[20] Despite this belief, there was no serious effort made to institute reforms that would benefit this lower class. Riẓā Shāh built his program of economic development upon the backs of the peasants and as Amin Banani points out, he "tipped the already uneven scale further to the advantage of the landlord and thereby added to social tension in rural Iran."[21] Riẓā Shāh's son made no serious effort to improve the living conditions of the Iranian peasant until the early 1960s. Over one-half of the points that constitute the program of the White Revolution are directly aimed at the peasant and the essence of the program is the land reform. The early threat of a new, educated middle class had produced a token attempt at distribution of the crown lands in the 1950s. By 1963, however, the threat had magnified to such an extent that the Shah and political elite sought a class ally.

European history is replete with examples of monarchs who have sought allies against the aristocracy.[22] At the same time they were threatened by the rise of the bourgeois middle class. In nineteenth-century Germany, for example, it was the bourgeoisie that blossomed and gained great economic power. Not only was this class a developing political threat, but it represented a force that was vital to the industrial growth and security of the nation. In Europe, the monarchs often allied themselves against their own nobility as well as curtailed the immediate threat of the middle class. The few successful examples of "revolution from above" occurred when the ruling monarch or elite formed an alliance with the middle class by making basic concessions to the expanding new class.[23]

The White Revolution in Iran represents a new attempt calculated to introduce reform from above that will in the end preserve traditional power patterns. Through land reform, the Shah has concentrated the aristocracy in the city by severing their connection with the countryside. He has then moved to ally himself with the peasantry against the professional middle class. The first step is designed to buttress the Monarch's position in the system by weakening the opportunity for upper-class challengers. Much of the Shah's time and energy has been expended in warding off challenges by individuals carrying the names of Qavām, Qashqā'ī, Bakhtiyār, and Amīnī.

---

20. *Mission for My Country,* p. 216.

21. *The Modernization of Iran,* p. 127. See also Joseph Upton, *The History of Modern Iran: An Interpretation* (Cambridge: Harvard University Press, 1965), pp. 64-72.

22. For a general analysis of the ruler-ruling class conflict and the various alliances this occasioned, see Lenski, *Power and Privilege,* pp. 231-42.

23. Imperial Germany under Bismarck in the latter half of the nineteenth century is a case in point. For an excellent analysis of the way Bismarck allied the rising bourgeois middle class with the old Prussian aristocracy, see Arthur Rosenberg, *The Birth of the German Republic, 1917–1918,* translated from the German by Ian F. D. Morrow (New York: Oxford University Press, 1931), especially pp. 1-32.

The greatest growing threat and one that is systemic and not merely personal, however, is posed by the professional-bureaucratic intelligentsia. The Shah has hoped to gain the support of the peasants against this class and it is in this spirit that the land reform program and the entire White Revolution has been proclaimed. The instructive example for this policy was set on January 24, 1963, when the Iranian government released the story that 15,000 peasants had marched on Tehran to support the Shah's reform program.[24]

The basic land reform law was signed on January 23, 1962. According to this law, each landlord was limited to one village. His remaining villages were to be purchased by the government in ten annual equal installments. The valuation of the lands purchased was to be based on the taxes that the landowners had paid on the land in the past. The government distributes the land to the peasants who are to pay for it in fifteen annual installments. The Ministry of Agriculture establishes cooperatives to which the new proprietors must belong and contribute. It is through the cooperatives that the seeds, fertilizers, and tools are acquired.[25] Since its appearance, this law has undergone various revisions. One of the principal alterations was to limit all landholders to between 30 and 150 hectares depending upon the fertility of the area. This greatly expanded the effect of the land reform law by forcing many medium-sized landowners either to divide the remaining lands according to the old basis of division, sell it to the farmers outright, or lease it to them.

Between 1963 and 1970, the Iranian government kept a continuous box score of the number of villages affected by the land reform program. By 1967, the first two phases of the program were declared completed and 52,818 villages were declared directly affected. Although the government statistics are of questionable accuracy, they are correct in implying that there have been very real steps taken to implement land distribution throughout the Iranian countryside. There have, however, been serious difficulties involved in the entire program and several of these relate directly to this study of class and change.

One of the first obstacles to land reform success has been the shortage of capital needed to finance the program. Financing such an undertaking involves astronomical sums of money. The landlords have to be compensated for their losses; cooperatives have to be established and staffed; special banks must be set up; and organizational and managerial personnel must be recruited, trained, and supported. In November 1963, for example, the government purchased 8,052 villages at a cost of 4,715,000,000 rials ($62,-

24. See *Washington Post,* January 25, 1963, p. B8.

25. For excellent coverage of this land reform law, see *Times* (London), January 24, 1962, p. 9; and *New York Times,* January 11, 1962, p. 8.

866,667). Of this sum, 496,000,000 rials ($6,613,333) had to be paid outright to the landlords as their first installment. At the same time, over 2,000 cooperatives were formed with a capital of 251,000,000 rials ($3,346,677) and the Agricultural Credits and Rural Development Bank was formed with capital of another 251,000,000 rials ($3,346,667).[26] Since that time, expenses continued to increase as the reform continually expanded and payments to former landowners kept coming due. The situation was complicated by the fact that the peasants were unable to pay their installments. Many have spent the credits given to them by the agricultural banks on new clothes, transistor radios, and gadgets. In spring 1967, some 240 peasants in the Qazvīn area were arrested and jailed because of their refusal to make the annual payments.[27] Despite gigantic oil revenues, the government has been having serious difficulties in financing the land reform. The other programs of system preservation require huge amounts of money also and these include the military-security organizations as well as the payments that go to personalities loyal to the web-system.

A serious unintended consequence of the Iranian land reform program is the growing intraclass gap that was referred to in chapter 1. This division has existed between those who have had the right (*nasaq*) to work a particular piece of land (*nasaqdār*s) and the *khushnishīn*s who had no such right. The latter are the agricultural laborers and village proletariat who in fact account for the majority of the rural population. The *khushnishīn*s have always been the poorest, most insecure, and dispossessed group in the peasant class and they have suffered severely from the lack of steady employment. The land reform law was formulated to assist the *nasaqdār*s who were the only peasants to receive land. The *khushnishīn*s were left outside of the entire plan and as a result their situation has steadily deteriorated while that of the new peasant proprietors has to some degree improved. The result has been a growing tension between the two rural peasant groups. This in itself carries significant implications for the Shah and the political elite in their attempt to preserve traditional patterns through alliance with the peasantry. A similar pattern developed in Tsarist Russia at the turn of the century and the result was instructive.

Between 1906 and 1911, Russian Minister of Interior Peter Stolypin engineered an extensive land reform program in Russia. In so doing, however, he created a class of wealthy peasants (kulaks) while the situation of the peasant masses remained unaltered. In the 1917 peasant uprisings, therefore, the great masses of peasantry arose not only against the landlords

26. This information has been drawn from Economist Intelligence Unit, *Three-Monthly Economic Review—Annual Supplement—Iran,* November 1963, p. 13.

27. This fact is based on personal interviews in Iran with several individuals involved. For a balanced and informed analysis of the Iranian land reform, see A. K. S. Lambton, *The Persian Land Reform, 1962–1966* (Oxford: Clarendon Press, 1969).

but against the well-to-do peasant landholders as well. In the Russian land reform program, which failed as an attempt at revolution from above, even those elements that had benefited from the reform showed no proclivity to support actively the old system and political elite. The Stolypin agrarian reforms, therefore, ultimately failed to reinforce a tottering system and a major reason was because the reform benefited only a minority of the Russian peasantry—those whom Stolypin called "the strong and the sober."[28] The intraclass tensions developing due to the Iranian land reform are strikingly similar to those that occurred in Russia and unless the situation is remedied it is always possible that the outcome will be the same. Unintended division in a force one chooses to ally oneself with can lead to destruction rather than preservation.

Another vital development in the implementation of the Iranian land reform program concerns the hesitancy the peasant shows in turning to government officials against the old landlord. After centuries of landlord protection against government agents, the peasant refuses to trust those who now say they have come to help him.[29] In the traditional pattern, the peasant realized he could relate to the landlord in a relationship of personal bargaining. The civil and military agents of government, however, constantly drove for the villager's subjection. The land reform, which has substituted government agent for landlord, has thrown the villager into the uncomfortable situation of not knowing how to relate with the new group. With the old landlord, the peasant always knew when he could push and how he could get what he needed. He had become an expert in dealing with the landlord and in living according to the traditional patterns.

Perhaps the greatest difficulty that the land reform program (as well as the entire White Revolution) has encountered is the serious shortage of technical, managerial, and organizational manpower. Large groups within the professional middle class refuse to dedicate themselves to programs which the political elite has planned and sponsored. In many cases it is not so much that these groups refuse to work as it is that they lack commitment. By mid-1967, 7,600 agricultural cooperatives had been established, yet there were only 1,200 managers and assistant managers to direct these cooperatives. These individuals were hastily trained in three- and six-month

---

28. Two other reasons were that the minority who did benefit from the reform failed to support the aristocracy and the war intervened and precipitated a series of agricultural crises which resulted in the termination of the land reform program. For fine studies of the Stolypin agrarian reforms as well as of the peasant uprisings in 1917, see Michael T. Florinsky, *Russia: A History and an Interpretation* (New York: The Macmillan Company, 1948), pp. 161-65, 178-85. See also Leon Trotsky's discussion of the peasantry in his *History of the Russian Revolution,* translated from the Russian by Max Eastman (New York: Simon and Schuster, 1932), 1:390-409.

29. In February 1966, the Director of Land Reform in Fārs Province named this as one of the biggest obstacles to implementation of land reform.

courses. The shortage of trained manpower to direct the land reform became so severe that the Reconstruction and Development Corps personnel were converted to land reform officials.

The political elite made an early and obvious attempt to buy the loyalty and commitment of the land reform officials. This occurred with the formation of the Twenty-first Majlis in 1963. A block of nearly fifty representatives were government officials involved in the land reform program. Many were graduates of Karaj Agricultural College and all were selected for the Majlis despite the fact that they were political unknowns. Although this policy may have persuaded a few individuals to pursue careers in land reform, it failed to produce dedication and commitment in many who were actually in charge of land reform at the provincial level. Between 1964 and 1970, the Iranian news channels carried numerous stories about on-the-job failure of land reform officials. Several dozen officials in the districts of Khumayn, Sanandaj, Kirmān, Gīlān, Kurdistān, Tavālish, Dārāb, Alīgūdarz, Ābādah, Miyānah, Qum, and Kirmānshāh were removed from their positions and charged with misconduct, corruption, and incompetence.[30] In a situation of great manpower shortage, it is doubly debilitating to have disinterest and a lack of project commitment among the existing personnel. Much of this, however, was built into the program when it was organized according to the old power patterns. It is evident that one of the fundamental difficulties in implementing the land reform has been this lack of technical and managerial support and commitment. This can only be supplied by the force most threatening to the traditional web-system—the professional-bureaucratic intelligentsia.

The Professional-Bureaucratic Intelligentsia: Participation without Representation

Article XIV of the Majlis Election Law of 1907 states that six classes (*ṭabaqāt*) will be represented in supervising national electoral procedures. These are the clerics, nobles, landlords, businessmen, tradesmen, and farmers. The absence of any professional class is not surprising since such a class hardly existed at the time. With the inauguration of the six-point reform program in 1963, however, the nobles and landlords were struck from the list and were replaced by the workers and peasants. No reference was made

30. There were, of course, many dedicated land reform officials. This was especially so at the beginning of the program when Arsanjānī surrounded himself with young men who worked in the provinces at great risk to themselves. In March 1971, a United Nations report stated that "although the land reform programme is virtually complete, and most villagers now own the land they till, they remain starved of knowledge of modern farming techniques, starved of credit and marketing facilities, and much dependent on the avaricious middlemen to whom they often have to pawn their crops. The Government's extension service is far too scanty to reach anywhere near most of the villages. . . ." UNDP in Iran, *Annual Report for 1970,* mimeo, p. 7

to include any professional middle class. The omission signified the stance taken by the political elite concerning the intelligentsia and indicated the direction that the White Revolution would take.[31]

In general, the members of the Iranian professional middle class feel that they have been deliberately bypassed in the reform program. They point to the list of reforms and argue that not one is directed to them and that their demands for fundamental change in the political system as well as in the areas of health, education, and justice have been obviously ignored. The situation was summed up by a series of articles that appeared in the Iranian press in December 1966. The key selection appeared in the magazine *Nigīn* and was reprinted in the biweekly digest *Khvāndanīhā.* It portrayed the attitude of the members of the new class concerning their place in contemporary Iran in general and in the White Revolution in particular.

> Nevertheless, there remains a vacuum—a vacuum which exists for the trained minds.[32] Well, what have you done for these minds?
>
> Yes, minds also have some rights and perhaps the exigencies of the time may be such that minds and ideas should be granted their rights. Otherwise, we will again experience the bitter taste of reality in the future.
>
> If you give the minds a chance, if you give them the right to express themselves, if you encourage them to think freely, then you will create a bright and shiny tomorrow for the country and an informed and alert generation will be gratefully at your service.
>
> In democratic systems, thinking individuals grow up with independence, will power, and self-confidence and their countries are never lacking in minds and character. In other systems, however, it is quite the opposite. All the minds will disappear and their country will lack real "human" beings. Then everyone will think of themselves as quiet

31. On January 9, 1963, as part of the Shah's six-point reform program, the Iranian Cabinet approved an amendment to the Election Law and this amendment was ratified by the National Referendum of January 26 of the same year. Article IV of this amendment changed the class representation outlined in Article XIV of the old election law. Information provided by the Iranian government concerning this change is both confusing and revealing. In the Shah's latest book, for example, it is incorrectly stated that the original election law "stipulated that the supervisory electoral bodies would consist exclusively of landlords and the wealthy." See *The White Revolution,* p. 89. For our purposes, however, the Ministry of Information's *Points for Progress* contains an especially relevant and meaningful inaccuracy. In the enumeration of the six classes represented on the supervisory election councils as provided by the original electoral law, it is stated that one of these classes was "the professional class (doctors, university professors, lawyers)." This is an interesting error. See *Points for Progress,* p. 28. For the accurate Persian text of Article XIV of the original election law, see Qāsimzādah, *Ḥuqūq-i Asāsī,* p. 48.

32. The Persian term is *maqz-hā-yi parvarash-yāftah.* The terms *"maqz-hā"* and *"maqz-hā-yi mutafakkir"* are also used and are translated as "minds" and "thinking minds." Perhaps the best English equivalent is "intelligentsia," however, the translation carries the more exact terminology.

and obedient sheep looking for a shepherd on whom to rely and who will hopefully rescue them from the man-eating wolves. It is for this reason that we ask: What have you done for the minds? Certainly the most basic national problem is the fact that the success of all reforms in industry, agriculture, economics, and finance depend on the firm foundation of the trained minds and nothing else. Have you sufficiently strengthened such foundations in our country?[33]

This article, which was written by a member of the professional middle class, concluded by stating that "when the air around a lamp gets less, the lamp will begin to smoke and then its flame will die out. The freedom of thought for the thinking minds is exactly like air for the lamp."[34] One week after this article was carried in *Khvāndanīhā,* the political elite replied in the same magazine through a letter to the editor signed by a Majlis deputy. The retort was intimidating and indicated that there would be no more such traitorous discussion in the Iranian press. It read in part as follows:

Really, whom do you address? This ruling elite who you ask to give the people the right of free expression . . ., are not they themselves among the thinking minds? Then you, Your Excellency, who are you? Who am I? Who are your colleagues?

If you consider depriving the feudals and reactionaries of their freedom and silencing the pens and mouths which are the loudspeakers of reaction. . . . a kind of limitation of social freedom, then how much better it would be if you let our young society continue on its way in this limited freedom. Let those persuasive pens, delightful expressions and brilliant minds which are used against the deprived masses rest for the time being. . . .

Mr. Editor! What kind of traitor to the homeland and what kind of foreign worshipper and opponent of the freedom-giving revolution do you think could launch more serious and cowardly attacks on the victories and goals of Iran's revolution than this article has done![35]

In 1970, the same explosive issue broke again into the pages of the Iranian press as an editorial in the Tehran daily *Āyandigān* of November 15 deplored the intelligentsia's failure to participate in the revolution. This was explained by the elite in terms of the intelligentsia's stupidity, conceit,

33. Dr. Yaḥyā Marvastī, "Maqz-hā-yi Mutafakkir-rā Dar Yābīd" [Rescue the Thinking Minds], as reprinted under the title "Bi-Mardum Ḥaqq-i Iẓhār-i Vujūd Bidahīd" [Give the People the Right to Show They Exist], in *Khvāndanīhā,* 12 Āẕar 1345/3 December 1966, p. 3.

34. *Ibid.,* p. 4.

35. Sa'īd Vazīrī, "Kudām Maqz-hā-yi Mutafakkir-rā Mifarmā'īd" [Which Thinking Minds Are You Speaking Of?], *Khvāndanīhā,* 19 Āẕar 1345/10 December 1966, pp. 3-4.

negativism, and individualism. These examples explain the nature of the gap that separates the professional middle class and the political elite. The latter labels those members of the intelligentsia who criticize publicly "traitors to the revolution." Yet the same political elite recognizes that the participation of the new class is essential to the success of the reform program. It is very difficult to carry out selective social reform without skilled managerial-technical talent. The policy of the political elite, therefore, has been to attempt to purchase the participation of the members of the intelligentsia and the concessions are primarily economic in nature.

The most dramatic successes of the contemporary Iranian elite have taken place in the area of economics. By 1970, Iran was the scene of an annual economic growth rate second only to Japan in Asia. The petroleum industry accounts for well over a billion dollars in revenue every year and this figure continues to increase sharply. Iran is now the world's third largest oil producer. Industrial development in the areas of agro-business, copper, natural gas, and petrochemicals indicates that the economic dynamism of the 1960s has carried over into the 1970s. This kind of wealth has provided the Iranian political elite with an enormous resource with which to attract the alienated intelligentsia.

Offers are usually made in terms of numerous projects, jobs, and advisory positions. These not only pay well but also keep the more critically inclined constantly occupied. Such inducements are offered to any member of the new middle class regardless of whether that individual is an Uprooter, Technocrat, or Maneuverer. Thus, economic concession is the most common and general policy for gaining the participation of the professional-bureaucratic intelligentsia.[36] It offers little threat to the ongoing system for jobs and wealth can be easily allocated within the old network. It is not essential that individuals accept the web-system before they are provided with financial-occupational priorities. The intended and common result is that once having accepted such inducements, the challenging individual ceases to threaten the traditional relationships.

Political offers are also common. Most important political prizes, however, are reserved for the Maneuverers. The political elite is especially careful to choose for key political posts only those members of the professional middle class who accept the prevailing methodology of power. Thus, there is the elaborate screening process described in chapter 5. It is during this process that the individual must repeatedly assure the hierarchy that he supports the system.

---

36. An excellent example of this occurred in April 1967 when some 5,000 secondary school teachers marched in the streets of Tehran in honor of the Shah's miraculous escape from the assassination attempt of April 1965. A few days later, the government announced that the secondary school teachers were to receive 210 million rials. This was to be supplied from the military budget and was actually to go toward paying back wages owed the teachers for years.

Large numbers of the intelligentsia view the reform program in terms of a measure initiated against them. They see none of the major programs directed to their own benefit and argue that the politicians nonetheless demand that the educated middle class participate and sacrifice. The sporadic and discriminate economic and political concession are viewed as temporary bribes to obtain their support for an antagonistic opponent's program. Certain circles of Iranian scholars describe the entire program as "bribery of the intellectuals (*rushvah dādan bi-rawshanfikrān).*"[37] The White Revolution is viewed in terms of an obvious attempt to turn the peasants against the professional middle class and in the long run to preserve the traditional web-system.

By attempting to buy the commitment of large numbers of the professional-bureaucratic intelligentsia in order to implement the White Revolution, the political elite has in fact intensified the intraclass conflict that marks the new class. Just as the intelligentsia has introduced a situation of fractured relationships at the class level, so it too is split internally. While Uprooters and Technocrats are constantly appearing in greater and greater numbers, the Maneuverers also are in great supply. The intraclass struggle revolves around those who wish to uproot the traditional patterns and those who wish to preserve them. By initiating the White Revolution, the political elite has stiffened the resistance of those members of the intelligentsia who lean toward system preservation. In the first place, the revolutionary language and the social need for land reform has led certain middle-class individuals to decide that the ongoing system is to be supported. Secondly, the political elite's need for professional participation has in turn caused them to redouble their efforts to convince the members of the intelligentsia to cooperate. Thus, the economic enticements, for example, have become more numerous and appealing.[38]

The Iranian political elite has recognized a severe challenge to the traditional system on both the intraclass and interclass levels. This challenge, which expresses itself in terms of great division at both levels, is being addressed by an attempt to present both an intraclass and an interclass solution. Old relationships are promoted and buttressed within the new class by offering rewards and encouraging Maneuverers. On the interclass level, a concerted attempt is made to fashion an alliance with a class that generally supports the traditional web-system. Such efforts are all bound together within the program of the White Revolution.

---

37. This term is often used by young Iranian teachers and professors to describe the policy of the political elite.

38. According to newspaper reports, the Prime Minister of Iran during a Spring 1967 visit to Germany promised Iranian students there that if they returned they would receive a minimum salary of 40,000 rials ($520) per month. The agreement was that they worked in the provinces. See *Kayhan International,* May 1, 1967, p. 2.

The Unintended Consequences of System Preservation

The beginning of the White Revolution in Iran represented a dramatic attempt to preserve the traditional power relationships that infused the web-system. This is especially true because it offers a class solution in a situation where class relationships have survived centuries of violent challenges. Despite the rise and fall of Shahs, tribes, Prophets, and dynasties, class relationships in Shī'ī Iran have resisted transformation. With the appearance of the professional-bureaucratic intelligentsia, characterized by large numbers of individuals who opposed and resented the ongoing patterns, the guardians of these patterns were forced to adopt fundamentally different tactics.[39] By instituting a land reform program as well as by introducing welfare corps into the countryside, it was hoped that the political elite who operated at the center of the old political system would be able to forge an alliance with the peasant masses. The latter had lived for centuries according to the old web-system and appeared to provide vital support for this system. Such a policy was intended to weaken the landed aristocracy who were a continual threat to whoever was monarch. More significantly, it was intended to strengthen and support the peasantry against the professional middle class who represented a fundamental threat to the traditional patterns through which the political elite gained its nourishment and preserved its existence.

The program of the White Revolution, however, also carries with it far-reaching unintended consequence. Many of these have already begun to appear while others are important possibilities that demand critical analysis. With the actual commencement of many of the reform programs, the Iranian political elite began traversing a path from which there is no retreat. Daily publicity has been accorded the reforms and Iran Radio has ceaselessly broadcast all the benefits that were to accrue to the peasant population. The landlords were violently criticized and castigated and the evils and sufferings of the past were credited to them. The government published articles and stories that stressed landlord atrocities and pictures commonly appeared showing the landlord whipping and torturing the peasant. This campaign that has accompanied the commencement of the reform program has gradually alerted the peasant to the possibilities that are his and he has come to expect a new life via land reform and literacy.[40] One of the last things that Minister of Agriculture Arsanjānī did before he left office was

39. It is important to remember, however, that these new tactics were preceded by numerous incidents of violence and upheaval. The Monarch himself survived many close calls.

40. This idea of rebirth has also been propagated by the government. See section entitled "Like Being Born Again" in the Ministry of Information's *Points for Progress.*

to call a national congress of peasants that met in Tehran in January 1963. This meeting stressed to the peasants their new rights and position and showed them the way to organize.[41] Since its inception, the rural reform program has been steadily gathering momentum and it has become very difficult to control and direct. Unforeseen divisions occurred within the peasant class, for example, as certain peasants benefited while others suffered from the changes. The administration of the reform has been weak and inadequate and the lack of managers, agronomists, agricultural engineers, and administrators has led the program to begin to veer out of control. The vital cooperative network has existed largely on paper and cooperative supervisors and managers have been too few and too inexperienced. In 1970, an alternative system of farm corporations was in operation on an experimental basis.

In the meantime, the villagers have been increasing their demands and voicing new expectations.[42] The literacy program has led the newly literate to demand further formal education and the right to attend secondary and vocational schools. The scattered but nationwide presence of the Health Corps has led many villagers to appeal for doctors, clinics, and hospitals. Thus, not only are many of the programs beginning to take unpredictable turns but also the very people who were intended to benefit from the reform are beginning to make increasing demands. In such a situation, the Iranian political elite needs the skilled manpower to direct and control the forces that have been recently unleashed. This can only be provided by a participating and committed professional-bureaucratic intelligentsia.

---

41. This Congress which was officially entitled the Rural Cooperatives Congress met between January 9-13, 1963. Some 50,000 peasant cooperative members reportedly participated. This Congress generated a great deal of excitement and did much to heighten rural expectations in Iran. It is important to realize that less than two weeks following this Congress the Shah announced his six-point reform program which became the heart of the White Revolution. It should also be noted that it was less than two months after this Congress that Minister of Agriculture Arsanjānī announced his resignation. Fascinating documentation of this Congress is provided by an illustrated volume prepared by the Ministry of Agriculture. This volume, which was published just before Arsanjānī's resignation, contains an illustrated history of land reform in Iran. It carries fifty pictures of Arsanjānī, more than anyone else including the Shah. See Ministry of Agriculture, *Avvalīn Kungrah-yi Millī-yi Shirkat-hā-yi Ta'āvunī-yi Rūstā'ī-yi Īrān* [The First National Congress of the Rural Cooperatives of Iran], Isfand 1341/March 1963.

42. In February 1966, this writer was the only foreigner to accompany the Governor-General and his staff on an extended inspection tour of the Mamassanī region of Fārs Province. The Governor-General at that time was an extremely active and dedicated individual and projects and programs were in progress throughout the area. During observation and discussion with villagers and local officials in such villages as Khānahzīnān, Dasht-i Arzhang, Pul-i Ābgīnah, Dihak, and Nūrābād and the city of Kāzirūn, the following pattern emerged. The villages with wells were demanding electricity; those with wells and electricity asked for grade schools; those with wells, electricity, and grade schools pleaded for high schools; those with wells, electricity, grade schools, and high schools requested girls' schools; and Kāzirūn, with all these facilities, was demanding a technical college. Such are the increasing demands that are rising from the countryside.

The new middle class, however, is not committed since many of its members refuse to participate to preserve relationships that work against them. The White Revolution which is itself implemented according to traditional patterns is a sharp reminder of the persistence of the past throughout the society. The Uprooters and Technocrats are certainly hesitant to join such a program. Even the Maneuverers who accept positions in the reform administration are not committed to the task at hand but are generally occupied in the personal and private conflict that marks the traditional web-system. One of the most serious implications of the White Revolution is that it is attempting to build successful reforms through the traditional patterns of personalism, pārtī, and pervasive tension. The lack of institutions and rationalization result in insecurity and inefficiency which are already evident in many instances in rural Iran. This has begun to alienate many of the villagers who are told that they are to begin new lives but who in fact see themselves the victims of government agents.[43]

But even where the reform programs have met with success, new problems are generated. The offspring of villagers through literacy and land reforms are beginning to acquire the tools that will enable them to penetrate the middle class in larger and larger numbers. One of the deepest unintended consequences of the White Revolution is the accelerating growth of the professional middle class. Yet this is the same class that threatens the ongoing patterns. And it is the same class that is needed to control and guide the explosive reform program. Thus, the dilemma that faces the Iranian political elite inheres in the very reform program that they dramatically chose to reinforce the traditional system. First, the elite requires the participation and commitment of the very class which threatens them, in order that the reforms be implemented and controlled. Second, many of those peasants who benefit from the reforms will move into the already expanding professional middle class and here they will join in a new level of criticism and demand. The forces of time reveal the inevitability of the ascendance of the professional middle class in the political system. Whether or not this class will forge new relations or whether it will construct its own version of the traditional web-system remains to be seen. One last unintended consequence of the reform policy of Muḥammad Riẓā Shāh and the Iranian political elite concerns the special effort that is being made to embed the new class into the old network of power patterns. The effect of the fissures that this has occasioned and intensified within the professional middle class may well be felt long after this class has come to political power. It certainly will

43. The peasants of one village dealt with each new government agent dispatched to their village in the same way. One of the *rīsh-sifīds* (graybeards) would crumble some dry leaves between his hands and then show the shreddings to the new official. With all the villagers crowding around, the old man would ask the new arrival what kind of seeds these were. Invariably, the official would recognize the type of seed. Personal interview with land reform official, May 30, 1967.

complicate the struggle that certain members of the new class will have to wage in order to fashion patterns and processes that will enable Iranian society to meet the continuing challenge of social transformation.

The Iranian experience has indicated that the class level is of crucial significance to the politics of social change and to system preservation and transformation. The fact that personalities, elites, and groups spring from social classes is also important and explains in part the connections that exist between individual, group, and class relationships. Classes represent a common collective experience in power relationships and the members of a class have used this power to come to grips with change in similar ways. Classes represent especially potent forces since a society requires broad commitment and participation in order to meet the immoderate challenges of change. Partly because they are composed of large collectivities of individuals, it is more difficult to transform class relationships. At the same time, however, it is also more difficult to reknit and reestablish such relationships once they have been transformed.

The challenge to a traditional system which is marked by ruptured class relationships demands a fundamentally different policy by those who would seek to preserve the traditional patterns. Just as the juggling of personalities will seldom introduce fundamental change in class patterns, neither will it serve to preserve class relations. The snapping of linkages at the class level represents a threat that must be dealt with at this level.

Yet, even if there is an effort made in class terms, it is highly unlikely that a breakdown in traditional relationships here can be remedied in a way that will preserve ongoing patterns. Much of the reason is that a policy of preservation in the face of a demand for transformation carries numerous unintended consequences. This is especially true in situations where policy is directed around and against those classes that refuse to relate according to the traditional relationships. The politics of system preservation in the midst of a rapidly transforming world is a risky and costly business. The most resilient and persistent of patterns inevitably crumble under the demands of new social forces. In Iran, new groups and classes are in the process of challenging the traditional patterns of politics.

Bibliography

Books and Monographs

Algar, Hamid. *Religion and State in Iran, 1785–1906.* Berkeley and Los Angeles: University of California Press, 1969.

Arasteh, A. Reza. *Education and Social Awakening in Iran.* Leiden: E. J. Brill, 1964.

———. *Final Integration in the Adult Personality.* Leiden: E. J. Brill, 1965.

———. *Man and Society in Iran.* Leiden: E. J. Brill, 1964.

Avery, Peter. *Modern Iran.* London: Ernest Benn, 1965.

Baldwin, George B. *Planning and Development in Iran.* Baltimore: Johns Hopkins Press, 1967.

Banani, Amin. *The Modernization of Iran, 1921–1941.* Stanford: Stanford University Press, 1961.

Barth, Fredrik. *Nomads of South Persia.* New York: Humanities Press, 1964.

———. *Political Leadership Among Swat Pathans.* London: Athlone Press, 1959.

Barthold, V. V. *Turkestan Down to the Mongol Invasion.* 2d ed. London: Oxford University Press, 1928.

Bartsch, William H. *Problems of Employment Creation in Iran.* Geneva: International Labour Office, 1970.

Bayne, E. A. *Persian Kingship in Transition.* New York: American Universities Field Staff, 1968.

Binder, Leonard. *Iran: Political Development in a Changing Society.* Berkeley and Los Angeles: University of California Press, 1962.

Bottomore, T. B. *Classes in Modern Society.* New York: Pantheon Books, 1966.

______. *Elites and Society.* New York: Basic Books, 1964.

Browne, Edward Granville. *A Literary History of Persia.* Reissue. 4 vols. Cambridge: University Press, 1928.

______. *The Persian Revolution of 1905–1909.* Cambridge: University Press, 1910.

______. *A Year Amongst the Persians.* 3d ed. London: Adam and Charles Black, 1950.

Chardin, J. *Voyages.* 10 vols. Paris: Le Normant, 1811.

Christensen, Arthur. *L'Iran Sous les Sassanides.* Copenhague: Ejnar Munksguard, 1944.

Cottam, Richard W. *Nationalism in Iran.* Pittsburgh: University of Pittsburgh Press, 1964.

Curzon, George N. *Persia and the Persian Question.* 2d printing. London: Frank Cass and Co., 1966.

Dahrendorf, Ralf. *Class and Class Conflict in Industrial Society.* Revised Eng. ed. Stanford: Stanford University Press, 1959.

Demorgny, G. *Essai sur l'Administration de la Perse.* Paris: Ernest LeRoux, 1913.

Development of a Middle Class in Tropical and Sub-Tropical Countries, Record of the XXIX Session Held in London from 13–16 September 1955. Brussels: International Institute of Differing Civilizations, 1956.

Djilas, Milovan. *The New Class: An Analysis of the Communist System.* New York: Frederick A. Praeger, 1957.

Elwell-Sutton, L. P. *Modern Iran.* London: George Routledge and Sons, 1941.

______. *Persian Oil: A Study in Power Politics.* London: Laurence and Wishart, 1955.

English, Paul Ward. *City and Village in Iran.* Madison: University of Wisconsin Press, 1966.

Esfandiary, F. M. *The Day of Sacrifice.* New York: McDowell, Obelensky, 1959.

______. *Identity Card.* New York: Grove Press, 1966.

Farmayan, Hafez F. *The Beginnings of Modernization in Iran: The Policies and Reforms of Shah Abbas I (1587–1629).* Research Monograph No. 1, Middle East Center, University of Utah, Salt Lake City, 1969.

Forbes-Leith, F. A. C. *Checkmate: Fighting Tradition in Central Persia.* New York: Robert M. McBride and Co., 1927.

Frye, Richard N. *The Heritage of Persia.* Cleveland and New York: World, 1963.

Gardet, Louis. *La Cite Musulmane: Vie Sociale et Politique.* Paris: Librairie Philosophique J. Vrin, 1961.

Gaudefroy-Demombynes, Maurice. *Muslim Institutions.* Translated by John P. MacGregor. London: George Allen and Unwin, 1950.

Gibb, H. A. R. and Harold Bowen. *Islamic Society and the West.* 2 vols. London: Oxford University Press, 1950.

Goitein, S. D. *Studies in Islamic History and Institutions.* Leiden: E. J. Brill, 1966.

Haas, William S. *Iran.* New York: Columbia University Press, 1946.

Hall, Melvin. *Journey to the End of an Era.* New York: Charles Scribner's Sons, 1947.

Halpern, Manfred. *The Politics of Social Change in the Middle East and North Africa.* Princeton: Princeton University Press, 1963.

Hedayat, Sadegh. *The Blind Owl.* Translated by D. P. Costello. London: John Calder, 1957.

Jacobs, Norman. *The Sociology of Development: Iran as an Asian Case Study.* New York: Frederick A. Praeger, 1966.

Kai Ka'us Ibn Iskandar. *The Qabus-nama.* Translated from the Persian by Reuben Levy. London: Cresset Press, 1951.

Kamshad, H. *Modern Persian Prose Literature.* Cambridge: University Press, 1966.

Kazemzadeh, Firuz. *Russia and Britain in Persia, 1864–1914.* New Haven and London: Yale University Press, 1968.

Keddie, Nikki R. *Historical Obstacles to Agrarian Change in Iran.* Claremont Asian Studies, Number 8, September 1960.

______. *Religion and Rebellion in Iran—The Iranian Tobacco Protest of 1891–1892.* London: Frank Cass and Co., 1966.

Lambton, Ann K. S. *Landlord and Peasant in Persia.* London: Oxford University Press, 1953.

______. *The Persian Land Reform, 1962–1966.* Oxford: Clarendon Press, 1969.

Laqueur, Walter Z., ed. *The Middle East in Transition: Studies in Contemporary History.* New York: Frederick A. Praeger, 1958.

Leiden, Carl, ed. *The Conflict of Traditionalism and Modernism in the Muslim Middle East.* Austin: University of Texas Press, 1966.

Lenczowski, George. *Russia and the West in Iran, 1918–1948.* Ithaca, N.Y.: Cornell University Press, 1949.

Lenski, Gerhard. *Power and Privilege: A Theory of Social Stratification.* New York: McGraw-Hill, 1966.

Lockhart, L. *Nader Shah: A Critical Study Based Mainly Upon Contemporary Sources.* London: Luzac and Co., 1938.

Malcolm, Sir John. *The History of Persia From the Early Period to the Present Time.* 2 vols., 2d ed. London: John Murray, 1829.

Marshall, T. H., ed. *Class Conflict and Social Stratification.* London: LePlay House Press, 1938.

Mills, C. Wright. *White Collar: The American Middle Classes.* New York: Oxford University Press, 1951.

Millspaugh, Arthur C. *Americans in Persia.* Washington: Brookings Institution, 1946.

______. *The American Task in Persia.* New York and London: Century Co., 1925.

______. *The Financial and Economic Situation of Persia—1926.* Tehran: Imperial Persian Government, 1926.

Minorsky, V. *La Domination Des Dailamites.* Paris: Librairie Ernest Leroux, 1932.

______. *Tadhkirat al-Mulūk.* E. J. W. Gibb New Series, XVI. London: Luzac and Co., 1943.

Moore, Barrington, Jr. *Social Origins of Dictatorship and Democracy.* Boston: Beacon Press, 1966.

Morier, James. *The Adventures of Hajji Baba of Ispahan.* 2d ed. London: John Murray, 1824.

Mosca, Gaetano. *The Ruling Class* [*Elementi di Scienza Politica*]. Translated by Hannah D. Kahn. New York: McGraw-Hill, 1939.

Mostofi, Khosrow. *Aspects of Nationalism.* Salt Lake City: University of Utah Research Monograph No. 3, 1964.

Nasr, Seyyed Hossein. *Ideals and Realities of Islam.* London: George Allen and Unwin, 1966.

Nieuwenhuijze, C. A. O. van. *Social Stratification and the Middle East: An Interpretation.* Leiden: E. J. Brill, 1965.

Nirumand, Bahman. *Iran: The New Imperialism in Action.* New York and London: Monthly Review Press, 1969.

Nizam ul-Molk. *Siyasat-nama or Siyar al-Muluk.* Translated from the Persian by Hubert Drake. London: Routledge and Kegan Paul, 1960.

Ossowski, Stanislaw. *Class Structure in the Social Consciousness.* Translated from the Polish by Sheila Patterson. London: Routledge and Kegan Paul, 1963.

Pahlavi, Mohammed Reza Shah. *Mission for My Country.* London: Hutchinson and Co., 1960.

______. *The White Revolution.* Tehran: Imperial Pahlavi Library, 1967.

Patai, Raphael. *Golden River to Golden Road: Society, Culture, and Change in the Middle East.* Philadelphia: University of Pennsylvania Press, 1962.

Ramazani, Rouhollah K. *The Foreign Policy of Iran, 1500–1941.* Charlottesville, Va.: University of Virginia Press, 1966.

Rawlinson, George. *The Seventh Great Oriental Monarchy or the Geography, History, and Antiquities of the Sassanian or New Persian Empire.* New York: Dodd, Mead and Co., 1882.

Riggs, F. W. *The Ecology of Public Administration.* London: Asia Publishing House, 1961.

Rūmlū, Ḥasan, *Aḥsan al-Tavārīkh.* Vol. II. Baroda: Oriental Institute, 1931.

Sadighi, Gholam Husayn. *Les Movements Religieux au IIe et au IIIe Siecle de l'Hegire.* Paris: Les Presses Modernes, 1938.

Sarwar, Ghulam. *History of Shāh Ismā'īl Ṣafawī.* Aligarh: Muslim University, 1939.

Schuon, Frithjof. *Understanding Islam.* Translated by D. M. Matheson. London: George Allen and Unwin, 1963.

Shuster, W. Morgan. *The Strangling of Persia.* New York: Century Co., 1912.

Soraya, Princess. *The Autobiography of H.I.H. Princess Soraya.* Translated from the German by Constantine Fitzgibbon. London: Arthur Barker, 1963.

Upton, Joseph. *The History of Modern Iran: An Interpretation.* Cambridge: Harvard University Press, 1965.

Vaughan, Leo. *The Jokeman.* London: Eyre and Spottiswoode, 1962.

Weiner, Myron. *The Politics of Scarcity: Public Pressures and Political Response in India.* Chicago: University of Chicago Press, 1962.

Wilber, Donald. *Contemporary Iran.* New York: Frederick A. Praeger, 1963.

______. *Iran Past and Present.* 6th ed. Princeton: Princeton University Press, 1967.

Wise, David and Thomas B. Ross. *The Invisible Government.* New York: Random House, 1964.

Wittfogel, Karl A. *Oriental Despotism: A Comparative Study of Total Power.* New Haven: Yale University Press, 1957.

Yar-Shater, Ehsan, ed. *Iran Faces the Seventies.* New York: Praeger, 1971.

Zabih, Sepehr. *The Communist Movement in Iran.* Berkeley and Los Angeles: University of California Press, 1966.

Zonis, Marvin. *The Political Elite of Iran.* Princeton: Princeton University Press, 1971.

Articles and Periodicals

Abrahamian, Ervand. "Communism and Communalism in Iran: The *Tudah* and the *Firqah-i Dimukrat.*" *International Journal of Middle East Studies* 1 (October 1970): 291-316.

______. "The Crowd in Iranian Politics 1905–53." *Past and Present* 41 (December 1968): 184-210.

Ashraf, Ahmad. "An Evaluation on Land Reform." In N. Afshar Naderi, ed., *Seminar on Evaluation of Directed Social Change.* Tehran: Institute for Social Studies and Research of University of Tehran, 1967, pp. 143-69.

______. "Historical Obstacles to the Development of a Bourgeoisie in Iran." *Iranian Studies* 2 (Spring-Summer 1969): 54-79.

Bachrach, Peter and Morton S. Baratz. "Two Faces of Power." *American Political Science Review* 56 (December 1962): 947-52.

Bakhash, Shaul. "The Evolution of Qajar Bureaucracy: 1779–1879." *Middle Eastern Studies* 7 (May 1971): 139-68.

Berger, Morroe. "The Middle Class in the Arab World." In Walter Z. Laqueur, ed. *The Middle East in Transition.* New York: Frederick A. Praeger, 1958, pp. 61-71.

Berque, Jacques. "L'Idee de Classes Dans L'Histoire Contemporaine Des Arabes." *Cahiers Internationaux de Sociologie* 38 (1965): 169-84.

Bill, James A. "Class Analysis and the Challenge of Change." *Comparative Political Studies* 2 (October 1969): 389-400.

______. "Class Analysis and the Dialectics of Modernization in the Middle East." *International Journal of Middle East Studies* 3 (1972).

______. "The Dynamics of Traditional Society and Strategies of Change." *Journal of International Affairs* 24 (1970): 309-16.

______. "Modernization and Reform from Above: The Case of Iran." *The Journal of Politics* 32 (February 1970): 19-40.

______. "The Plasticity of Informal Politics: The Case of Iran." In Amin Banani, ed., *State and Society in Islamic Iran,* forthcoming.

______. "The Politics of Legislative Monarchy: The Iranian Majlis." In Herbert Hirsch and M. Donald Hancock, eds., *Comparative Legislative Systems: A Reader in Theory and Research.* New York: Free Press, 1971, pp. 360-69.

______. "The Social and Economic Foundations of Power in Contemporary Iran." *Middle East Journal* 17 (Autumn 1963): 400-18.

Binder, Leonard. "The Cabinet of Iran: A Case Study in Institutional Adaptation." *Middle East Journal* 16 (Winter 1962): 29-47.

______. "The Proofs of Islam: Religion and Politics in Islam." In George Makdisi, ed., *Arab and Islamic Studies in Honor of Hamilton A. R. Gibb* (Cambridge: Harvard University Press, 1965), pp. 118-40.

Bolles, Blair. "Egypt, Iran and U.S. Diplomacy." *Foreign Policy Bulletin* 31 (August 15, 1952): 3.

Cottam, Richard. "Image and Reality in Iran." *Land Reborn* 12 (May 1961): 10-11.

______. "Political Party Development in Iran." *Iranian Studies* 1 (Summer 1968): 82-95.

______. "The United States, Iran and the Cold War." *Iranian Studies* 3 (Winter 1970): 2-22.

Courtois, V. "The Tudeh Party." *Indo-Iranica* 7 (June 1954): 14-22.

Dickson, Martin B. "The Fall of the Ṣafavī Dynasty." *Journal of the American Oriental Society* 82 (October–December 1962): 503-17.

Doerr, Arthur. "An Assessment of Educational Development: The Case Study of Pahlavi University, Iran." *Middle East Journal* 22 (Summer 1968): 317-23.

Elwell-Sutton, L. P. "Nationalism and Neutralism in Iran." *Middle East Journal* 12 (Winter 1958): 20-32.

______. "Political Parties in Iran, 1941–1948." *Middle East Journal* 3 (January 1949): 45-62.

English, Paul Ward. "The Preindustrial City of Herat, Afghanistan." In Carl Brown, ed., *Urban Planning and Prospects in the Middle East.* Princeton: Princeton University Press, forthcoming.

Farman Farmayan, Hafez. "The Forces of Modernization in Nineteenth Century Iran: A Historical Survey." In W. L. Polk and R. L. Chambers, eds., *Beginnings of Modernization in the Middle East: The Nineteenth Century.* Chicago: University of Chicago Press, 1970, pp. 119-51.

Firoozi, Ferydoon. "Demographic Review—Iranian Censuses 1956 and 1966: A Comparative Analysis." *Middle East Journal* 24 (Spring 1970): 220-28.

Gallagher, Charles F. "Contemporary Islam: The Plateau of Particularism." *American Universities Field Staff Reports Service.* Southwest Asia Series, Vol. XV, No. 2, 1966.

Garthwaite, Gene R. "The Bakhtiyari Khans, the Government of Iran, and the British, 1846–1915." *International Journal of Middle East Studies* 3 (1972).

______. "Pastoral Nomadism and Tribal Power." In Amin Banani, ed., *State and Society in Islamic Iran,* forthcoming.

Gastil, Raymond D. "Middle Class Impediments to Iranian Modernization." *Public Opinion Quarterly* 22 (Fall 1953): 325-29.

Halpern, Manfred. "The Rate and Costs of Political Development." *The Annals* 358 (March 1965): 20-28.

______. "A Redefinition of the Revolutionary Situation." *Journal of International Affairs* 22 (1969): 54-75.

Jazayery, Mohammad Ali. "Recent Persian Literature." *Review of National Literatures: Iran* 2 (Spring 1971): 11-28.

Keddie, Nikki R. "The Iranian Power Structure and Social Change 1800–1969: An Overview." *International Journal of Middle East Studies* 2 (January 1971): 3-20.

______. "The Iranian Village Before and After Land Reform." *Journal of Contemporary History* 3 (July 1968): 69-91.

______. "Religion and Irreligion in Early Iranian Nationalism." *Comparative Studies in Society and History* 4 (April 1962): 265-95.

______. "The Roots of the Ulama's Power in Modern Iran." *Studia Islamica,* 1969, pp. 31-53.

Lambton, Ann K. S. "The Impact of the West on Persia." *International Affairs* 33 (January 1957): 12-25.

______. "Persia: The Breakdown of Society." In P. M. Holt, *et al.,* eds., *The Cambridge History of Islam.* Cambridge: The University Press, 1970, 1: 430-67.

______. "Persian Society Under the Qajars." *Royal Central Asian Journal* 48 (April 1961): 123-39.

______. "Quis Custodiet Custodes." *Studia Islamica* 5-6 (1956): 125-46.

______. "Secret Societies and the Persian Revolution of 1905–6." *St. Antony's Papers,* 1958, pp. 43-60.

Mahdavy, Hossein. "The Coming Crisis in Iran." *Foreign Affairs* 44 (October 1965): 134-46.

McClelland, David C. "National Character and Economic Growth in Turkey and Iran." In Lucian W. Pye, ed., *Communication and Political Development.* Princeton: Princeton University Press, 1963, pp. 152-81.

McLachlan, K. S. "Land Reform in Iran." In W. B. Fisher, ed., *The Cambridge History of Iran.* Cambridge: The University Press, 1968, 1: 684-713.

Miller, William Green. "Political Organization in Iran: From Dowreh to Political Party." *Middle East Journal* 23 (Spring 1969; Summer 1969): 159-67, 343-50.

Millward, William G. "Traditional Values and Social Change in Iran." *Iranian Studies* 4 (Winter 1971): 2-35.

Naraghi, Ehsan. "Elite Ancienne et Elite Nouvelle Dans l'Iran Actuel." *Revue des Etudes Islamiques,* 1957, pp. 69-80.

Nieuwenhuijze, C. A. O. van. "Iranian Development in a Sociological Perspective." *Der Islam* 45 (1969): 64-80.

Pfaff, Richard H. "Disengagement from Traditionalism in Turkey and Iran." *Western Political Quarterly* 16 (March 1963): 79-98.

Ramazani, R. K. " 'Church' and State in Modernizing Society: The Case of Iran." *American Behavioral Scientist* 7 (January 1964): 26-28.

Razi, G. Hossein. "Genesis of Party in Iran: A Case Study of the Interaction Between the Political System and Political Parties." *Iranian Studies* 3 (Spring 1970): 58-90.

______. "The Press and Political Institutions of Iran: A Content Analysis of *Ettela'at* and *Keyhan.*" *Middle East Journal* 22 (Autumn 1968): 463-74.

Riggs, Fred W. "The Theory of Developing Polities." *World Politics* 16 (October 1963): 147-71.

Saidi, Farrokh. "The Return of the Native." *Harvard Medical Alumni Bulletin* 40 (Spring 1966): 6-12.

Savory, R. M. "Modern Persia." In P. M. Holt, *et al.,* eds., *The Cambridge History of Islam.* Cambridge: The University Press, 1970, 1: 595-626.

______. "The Principal Offices of the Safawid State During the Reign of Ṭahmāsp I (930–84/1524–76)." *Bulletin of the School of Oriental and African Studies* 24 (1961): 65-85.

Schulz, Ann T. "An Expanded Role for the Majlis Committee." *Iranian Studies* 3 (Winter 1970): 34-45.

Shils, Edward. "The Intellectuals in the Political Development of the New States." *World Politics* 12 (April 1960): 329-68.

Stauffer, Thomas R. "The Economics of Nomadism in Iran." *Middle East Journal* 19 (Summer 1965): 284-302.

Tapper, R. "Black Sheep, White Sheep and Red-Heads: A Historical Sketch of the S̲hāhsavan of Āzarbāijān." *Iran* 4 (1966): 61-84.

Vieille, Paul. "Un groupment feodal en Iran." *Revue Francaise de Sociologie* 6 (April–June 1965): 175-90.

Walden, Jerrold L. "The International Petroleum Cartel in Iran—Private Power and the Public Interest." *Journal of Public Law* 11 (Spring 1962): 3-60.

Westwood, Andrew F. "Elections and Politics in Iran." *Middle East Journal* 15 (Spring 1961): 153-64.

______. "Politics of Distrust in Iran." *The Annals* 358 (March 1965): 123-35.

Young, T. Cuyler. "Iran in Continuing Crisis." *Foreign Affairs* 40 (January 1962): 275-92.

______. "The Problem of Westernization in Modern Iran." *Middle East Journal* 2 (January 1948): 47-59.

______. "The Social Support of Current Iranian Policy." *Middle East Journal* 6 (Spring 1952): 128-43.

Zabih, Sepehr. "Change and Continuity in Iran's Foreign Policy in Modern Times." *World Politics* 23 (April 1971): 522-43.

Public Documents

Government of Iran, Plan Organization, National Statistical Center. *National Census of Population and Housing: November 1966—Demographic, Social and Economic Characteristics of the Population—Advance Sample Data for Total Country, Urban and Rural,* Bulletin No. 3, May 1967.

Government of Iran, Ministry of Interior. "Number and Distribution of the Inhabitants for Iran and the Census Provinces." *National and Province Statistics of the First Census of Iran: November 1956.* Tehran, August 1961, I.

______. "Social and Economic Characteristics of the Inhabitants for Iran and the Census Provinces." *National and Province Statistics of the First Census of Iran: November 1956.* Tehran, June 1962, II.

Government of Iran, Ministry of Information. *Points for Progress,* 1967.

Unpublished Material

Aspaturian, Vernon V. "The Challenge of Soviet Foreign Policy and the Defense of the Status Quo." Paper prepared for delivery at the 1961 Annual Meeting of the American Political Science Association, St. Louis, Missouri, September 6–9, 1961.

Barzegar, Ali. "Welfare State Ideologies in Iran." Unpublished M.A. thesis, University of South Dakota, 1966.

Bill, James A. "The Plasticity of Informal Politics: The Case of Iran." Paper delivered at the Conference on the Structure of Power in Islamic Iran, University of California, Los Angeles, June 26–28, 1969.

______. "Social Structure and Political Power in Iran." Unpublished M.A. thesis, Pennsylvania State University, 1963.

Borhanmanesh, Mohamad. "A Study of Iranian Students in Southern California." Unpublished Ph.D. dissertation, University of California, Los Angeles, 1965.

Dickson, Martin B. "Shāh Tahmāsb and the Ūzbeks" [The Duel for Khorāssān with 'Ubayd Khān], 930–946/1524–1540. Unpublished Ph.D. dissertation, Princeton University, 1958.

Gundersen, Kathryn Hubbs. "The Dynamics of Rural Relationships in Iran: Change and Modernization." Unpublished master's thesis, University of Texas at Austin, 1968.

Halpern, Manfred. "The Dialectics of Modernization in National and International Society—A Working Paper." Princeton University, Center of International Studies, unpublished manuscript, 1967.

Mazzaoui, Michel M. "Shī'īsm and the Rise of the Ṣafavids." Unpublished Ph.D. dissertation, Princeton University, 1965.

Nafisi, Habib. "The Brain-Drain: The Case of Iranian Non-Returnees." Paper presented at the Annual Conference of the Society for International Development, New York, March 17, 1966.

Nassefat, Morteza. "Les Situation des Étudiants Iraniens à l'Étranger et Leur Rôle dans l'Échange des Valeurs Culturelles entre l'Iran et Leurs Pays Hôtes." Tehran, unpublished manuscript, 1965.

Nasseri, Ali. "The Ecology of Staffing in the Government of Iran." Unpublished M.A. thesis, American University of Beirut, 1964.

Pašić, Najdan. "Elements and Outline of a Marxian Classification of Political Systems." Paper delivered at the International Political Science Association Meeting, Brussels, September 18–23, 1967.

Persian Sources

Ādamiyat, Firaydūn. *Fikr-i Āzādī Va Muqaddamah-yi Nihẕhat-i Mashrūṭiyat-i Īrān* [The Idea of Freedom and the Beginnings of the Constitutional Movement in Iran]. Tehran, 1340/1961.

Āl-i Aḥmad, Jalāl. *Gharbzadigī* [Western-Mania]. Tehran, 1341/1962.

———. *"Rawshanfikr Chīst? Rawshanfikr Kīst?"* [What Is an Intellectual? Who Is an Intellectual?] *Jahān-i Naw,* Nos. 4-5 (Shahrīvar-Mihr, 1345/1966): 15-32.

———. *"Rawshanfikr Khudī-ast yā Bīgānah?"* [Is the Intellectual One of Us or an Outsider?] *Jahān-i Naw* (Ābān-Bahman, 1345/1966): pp. 89-112.

Bahār, Dr. Mihdī. *Mirāṡ Khvar-i Isti'mār* [The Heir of Colonialism]. Tehran, 1344/1965.

Bahār, Muḥammad Taqī. *Tārīkh-i Mukhtaṣar-i Aḥzāb-i Sīyāsī-yi Īrān: Inqirāẓ-i Qājārīyah* [A Short History of Political Parties in Iran: The Fall of the Qājārs]. Tehran, 1321/1942.

Bihrangī, Ṣamad. *Kand-u-kāv Dar Masā'il-i Tarbiyatī-yi Īrān* [An Inquiry into the Educational Problems of Iran]. Tehran, n.d.

Bihrūz, Jahāngīr. "Parākandigī-yi Rawshanfikrān" [Dispersion of the Intellectuals]. *Āyandigān* (24 Ābān, 1349/15 November, 1970).

Dāryā. 1941–47.

Durūdiyān, Riẕā. *"Masā'il-i Rushd-i Ṭabaqah-yi Mutavassiṭ"* [Problems of Development of the Middle Class]. *Masā'il-l Īrān,* 4th yr., No. 2 (1345/1966): 28-33.

Fātiḥ, Muṣṭafā. *Panjāh Sāl Naft-i Īrān* [Fifty Years of Persian Oil]. Tehran, 1335/1956.

Fattāḥīpur, Aḥmad. *"Mushakhkhaṣāt-ī Ṭabaqāt-i Ijtimā'ī-yi Īrān"* [Characteristics of Social Classes in Iran]. *Masā'il-i Īrān* [Problems of Iran], 2nd yr., No. XI (Ābān, 1342–3/1963–4): 498-505.

Fāẕil, Javād, ed. *Sukhanān-i 'Alī* [The Sayings of 'Alī]. Tehran, 1345/1966.

Government of Iran, Ministry of Agriculture. *Avvalīn Kungrah-yi Millī-yi Shirkat-hā-yi Ta'āvunī-yi Rustā'ī-yi Īrān* [The First National Congress of the Rural Cooperatives of Iran]. Tehran, 1341/1962.

Government of Iran, Ministry of Interior, General Statistics Office. *Nashrīyah-yi Āmār-i Kārmandān-i Dawlat* [Publication of Government Employee Statistics], Tīr, 1335/1956.

Government of Iran, Ministry of Labor. *Barrasīhā-yi Masā'il-i Nīrū-yi Insānī* [Investigations of the Problems of Manpower]. 3 vols. Tehran, 1963–64.

Government of Iran, Plan Organization, Iranian Statistical Center. *Natāyij-i Āmārgīrī-yi Kārmandān-i Dawlat* [Results of the Census of Government Employees], Āẕar, 1342/1963.

Government of Iran, Plan Organization, Social Affairs Planning Group. *Barrasī-yi Muqaddamātī-yi Mushkilāt-i Ustānī Kardan-i Būdjah va Barnāmah dar Ustān-i Gīlān* [Preliminary Examination of the Difficulties of Ustān Budgeting and Planning in the Province of Gīlān]. Tehran, April 1966.

Ḥakīm-Ilāhī, Hidāyatullāh. *Az Shahr-i Naw tā Dādgustarī* [From the Red Light District to the Ministry of Justice]. Tehran, n.d.

Hidāyat, Ṣādiq. *Ḥājjī Āqā.* 2d ed. Tehran, 1330/1952.

Humāyūn, Dāriyūsh. *"Ṭabaqah-yi Mutavassiṭ Kāfī Nīst"* [The Middle Class Is Not Enough]. *Masā'il-i Īrān,* 1st yr., No. 10 (1342/1963): 488-90.

Hunarmand, Manūchihr. *Pahlavīsm: Falsafah-yi Sīyāsī, Iqtiṣādī, Ijtimā'ī* [Pahlavism: A Political, Economic, and Social Philosophy]. Tehran, 1345/1966.

I'timād al-Salṭanah. *Khayrāt-i Ḥisān* [The Deeds of Great Women]. N.p., 1304/1925.

______. *Rūznāmah-yi Khāṭirāt-i I'timād al-Salṭanah* [The Memoirs of I'timād al-Salṭanah]. Tehran, 1345/1966.

Jamālzādah, Sayyid Muḥammad 'Alī. *Khulqīyāt-i Mā Īrāniyān* [The Character of We Iranians]. Tehran, 1345/1966.

Jinābiyān, Shāhrukh. *"Rīshah-hā-yi Ravānī va Ijtimā'ī-yi Qumār dar Īrān"* [The Psychological and Social Roots of Gambling in Iran]. *Masā'il-i Īrān,* 3rd yr., Nos. 8-9 (1965–66): 237-42, 286-90.

Kasravī, Aḥmad. *Tārīkh-i Mashrūṭah-yi Īrān* [The History of the Iranian Constitutional Movement]. Tehran, 1316/1937.

Khusruvī, Khusraw. *"Muṭāli'ah-yi Dar Bārah-yi Qahvahkhānah-hā"* [A Study of the Coffeehouses]. *Kāvish,* 1st yr., No. 9 (Bahman, 1341/February, 1963): 84-92.

Maḥmūd, Maḥmūd. *Tārīkh-i Ravābiṭ-i Sīyāsī-yi Īrān va Inglīs dar Qarn-i Nūzdahum* [The History of Anglo-Iranian Diplomatic Relations in the Nineteenth Century]. 8 vols. Tehran, 1336–1341/1957–1962.

Malikzādah, Mihdī. *Tārīkh-i Inqilāb-i Mashrūṭīyat-i Īrān* [The History of the Iranian Constitutional Revolution]. 7 vols. Tehran, 1330/1951.

Marvastī, Dr. Yaḥyā. *"Maqz-hā-yi Mutafakkir-rā Dar Yābīd"* [Rescue the Thinking Minds], as reprinted under the title *"Bi-Mardum Ḥaqq-i Iẓhār-i Vujūd Bidahīd"* [Give the People the Right to Show They Exist]. *Khvāndanīhā* (Āẕar 12, 1345/1966): p. 3.

Military Governorship of Tehran. *Kitāb-i Siyāh* [The Black Book]. Tehran, 1333/1955.

Military Governorship of Tehran. *Sayr-i Kumūnīzm dar Īrān az Shahrīvar-i 1320 tā Farvardīn-i 1336* [The Evolution of Communism in Iran from September 1941 to March 1958]. Tehran, 1336/1958.

Mudarrisī, Taqī. *"Nākāmī-yi Khānivādah-yi Kārmandān"* [The Frustration of the Bureaucratic Family]. *Ṣadaf,* Nos. 9-10 (Murdād-Shahrīvar, 1337/1958): 692-94, 788-92, 899-903.

Mustawfī, 'Abdullāh. *Sharḥ-i Zindigānī-yi Man yā Tārīkh-i Ijtimā'ī va Idārī-yi Dawrah-yi Qājārīyah* [The Story of My Life or the Social and Administrative History of the Qājār Period]. 4 vols. Tehran, 1324–26/1945–47.

Muzākirāt-i Majlis [The Majlis Proceedings].

Nafīsī. 'Abd al-Ḥusayn, and Ṭabāṭabā'ī, Iftikhār. *Barrasī-yi Masā'il va Mushkilāt-i Javānān-i Dānishjū va Dānishāmūz-i Ṭihrān* [An Examination of the Problems and Difficulties of Tehran Secondary and University Students]. Tehran: Plan Organization Publication No. 4 of the Health and Social Welfare Planning Group, 1966.

Petrushevsky, I. P. *Kishāvarzī va Munāsibāt-i Arẓī dar Īrān: 'Aṣr-i Mughul: Qarn-hā-yi 13 va 14* [Agriculture and Land Relationships in Iran: Mongol Period: 13th and 14th Centuries]. Translated from the Russian by Karīm Kishāvarz. 2 vols. Tehran: Tehran University Press, 1344/1966.

Qāsimī, Abulfaẕl. *Tārīkh-i Siyāh yā Ḥukumat-i Khānivādah-hā dar Īrān* [The Black History or the Rule of Families in Iran]. Tehran, n.d.

Qāsimzādah, Dr. *Ḥuqūq-i Asāsī* [The Fundamental Laws]. Tehran, 1331/1952.

Rā'īn, Ismā'īl. *Farāmūshkhānah va Firāmāsūnirī dar Īrān* [Masonic Lodges and Freemasonry in Iran]. 3 vols. Tehran, 1347/1968.

Rāvandī, Murtiẕā. *Tārīkh-i Ijtimā'ī-yi Īrān* [The Social History of Iran]. 3 vols. Tehran, 1341/1962.

Rūmlū, Ḥasan. *Aḥsan al-Tavārīkh.* Vol. 1. Baroda: Oriental Institute, 1931.

Ṣāḥib al-Zamānī, Nāṣir al-Dīn. *Dībāchah'ī Bar Rahbarī* [An Introduction to Leadership]. Tehran, 1345/1966.

———. *Javānī-yi Purranj* [Suffering Youth]. Tehran, 1344/1965.

———. *Rāz-i Kirishmah-hā* (with the English title "The Play of the Mind"). Tehran, 1341/1962.

Shajī'ī, Zuhrah. *Nimāyandigān-i Majlis-i Shawrā-yi Millī dar Bīstuyik Dawrah-yi Qānūnguzārī* [The Representatives of the National Consultative Assembly During the Twenty-One Legislative Periods]. Tehran, 1344/1965.

Ṭabaqah-yi Ḥākimah-yi Īrān-rā Bishnāsīd [Know the Ruling Class of Iran]. Tehran, 1323/1944.

Ṭabāṭabā'ī, Muḥīt. *"Ṭabaqah-bandī-yi Ijtimā'ī"* [Social Stratification]. *Khvāndanīhā,* 26th yr., No. 99 (1 Shahrīvar, 1345/23 August, 1966): 14-15.

Turkumān, Iskandar Big. *Tārīkh-i 'Ālam-Ārā-yi 'Abbāsī.* 2 vols. Tehran, 1334/1955.

University of Tehran, Institute of Social Studies and Research. *Taḥqīq Dar Bārah-yi 'Ilal-i Tawfīq va 'Adam-i Tawfīq-i Sāzmān-hā-yi Idārī Dar Jalb-i Riẓāyat-i Mardum* [An Investigation into the Reasons for the Success and Lack of Success of the Administrative Organizations in Procuring the Satisfaction of the People]. Tehran, 1343/1964.

Vazīrī, Sa'īd. *"Kudām Maqz-hā-yi Mutafakkir-rā Mīfarmā'īd"* [Which Thinking Minds Are You Speaking of?] *Khvāndanīhā,* Āẕar 19, 1345/1966, pp. 3-4.

Zarrīnkūb, 'Abd al-Ḥusayn. *Du Qarn-i Sukūt* [Two Centuries of Silence]. Tehran, 1344/1965.

Zayn al-'Ābidīn, Ḥājj. *Siyāḥatnāmah-yi Ibrāhīm Big* [The Travel Diary of Ibrahim Big]. 3 vols. 1905–9.

Index